THE PELICAN GOSPEL COMMENTARIES

EDITED BY D. E. NINEHAM

*

THE GOSPEL OF ST LUKE

THE PELICAN GOSPEL COMMENTARIES

*

The Gospel of St Luke

G. B. CAIRD

SENIOR TUTOR OF MANSFIELD COLLEGE
OXFORD

Adam & Charles Black
London

FIRST PUBLISHED BY PENGUIN BOOKS LTD 1963
REPRINTED 1965

THIS EDITION 1968
A. AND C. BLACK LTD
4, 5 AND 6 SOHO SQUARE LONDON W. 1

© 1963 GEORGE BRADFORD CAIRD

SBN 7136 0899 4

PRINTED IN GREAT BRITAIN
BY JOHN DICKENS & CO LTD, NORTHAMPTON

CONIUGI DILECTISSIMAE ET AMANTISSIMAE

Contents

Editorial Foreword

Biblical commentaries are of various kinds. Some are intended solely for the specialist; others are devotional commentaries meant simply to help the Christian believer in his prayer and meditation. The commentaries in this series belong to neither class. Though they are based on full scholarly study and deal with technical points wherever necessary, the aim throughout has been to bring out the meaning the Evangelists intended to convey to their original readers. Since that meaning was religious, it is hoped that the commentaries, while being of interest to readers of any religious persuasion or none, and giving a fair indication of the current position in Gospel study, will help Christian readers to a deeper and more informed appreciation of the Gospels.

Technical terms have been avoided wherever possible; where used they have been fully explained in the Introductions, and readers are advised to read the Introduction to each volume before beginning on the commentary proper. The extended introduction to the volume on Mark is in some degree intended as an introduction to the series as a whole.

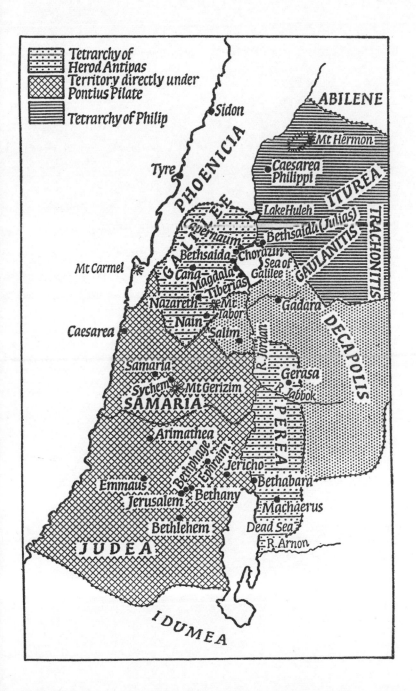

Tetrarchy of
Herod Antipas

Territory directly under
Pontius Pilate

Tetrarchy of Philip

ABILENE

Sidon

PHOENICIA

Tyre

Mt Hermon

Caesarea
Philippi

ITUREA

Lake Huleh

TRACHONITIS

Bethsaida (Julias)

GALILEE

Capernaum

Bethsaida

Chorazin

Sea of
Galilee

GAULANITIS

Mt Carmel

Cana

Magdala

Tiberias

Nazareth

Mt Tabor

Gadara

DECAPOLIS

Caesarea

Nain

Salim

R. Jordan

Samaria

Gerasa

Sychem

Mt Gerizim

R. Jabbok

SAMARIA

PEREA

Arimathea

Bethphage

Ephraim

Jericho

Emmaus

Bethany

Bethabara

Jerusalem

Machaerus

Bethlehem

Dead Sea

R. Arnon

JUDEA

IDUMEA

Introduction

On the night of 18 July A.D. 64, a fire broke out in Rome which burnt for a week and destroyed half the city. Rumour, spreading like the fire itself, laid the blame at the door of the Emperor Nero; and he, to divert suspicion from himself, looked for a scapegoat. His choice fell on the Christians, because, as Tacitus tells us in his account of the fire (*Annals*, xv, 44), they were already 'detested for their outrageous practices'. During the legal inquiries which followed, the Roman government learnt for the first time to distinguish Christianity from Judaism. Hitherto Christians had been officially regarded as a Jewish sect and therefore had benefited from the exceptional tolerance with which Rome had treated the Jews since the time of Julius Caesar. Christians had been harried by the Jews; they had incurred the resentment of their pagan neighbours on the grounds that their religion made them antisocial and different; like many another unpopular minority they had been suspected of nameless atrocities: but they had not been outlawed. The fire of Rome led not merely to a grim persecution of the Church in that city, but to a permanent change of legal status for all Christians throughout the empire.

Roman law recognized only national religion. Religion, to a Roman, was largely a matter of public ceremony, and it was part of a man's loyalty to his country that he should join in the worship of his country's gods. Officially non-conformity was treason or 'atheism', and the penalty was death. In practice this law could not be rigorously enforced. Every city of the empire had a cosmopolitan population, and where there were foreigners there would be foreign religions. The policy adopted by Rome was that foreign religions, though illegal, might be tolerated, provided that they did not cause a breach of the peace or interfere with the official cult. Any violations of this privilege were dealt with, not in the regular criminal courts, but by police procedure, in the administration of which the authorities had wide discretionary powers. As a general rule, however, a magistrate would take no action on a religious charge unless he felt that either public opinion or national safety compelled him to do so.

Once the initial persecution of the Church by Nero had come to an end, Christians found themselves in a precarious, though by no means a hopeless, situation. Their legal security had gone, for their faith was now regarded as a new, and therefore illegal, religion. Their one chance of survival lay in avoiding the unfavourable notice of the civil authorities, and this in turn depended on their ability to retain the goodwill of their neighbours, most of whom considered the Christian religion to be a barbarous superstition and associated it with all manner of depravities.

While the Church was adapting its life to this abiding menace, the first great apologia for the Christian faith was written – a two-volume work which we know as the Gospel according to St Luke and the Acts of the Apostles. That these two books belong together is proved by their common dedication to Theophilus and by a remarkable homogeneity of vocabulary and style. All the other books of the New Testament were written for use within the Christian community. The formal dedication of this work to Theophilus, whose title ('Your Excellency') shows that he held high office in the Roman government, strongly suggests that it was intended for publication and was therefore directed primarily to the outside world. The author's purpose was to supply Theophilus and others like him with the solid truth about this calumniated movement. Have Christians been condemned as the felonious followers of an executed felon? He will show that Christ and his disciples have justly been pronounced innocent by the representatives of Roman law. Is Christianity despised as an eccentric, foreign superstition? He will prove that it is the true fulfilment of the religious aspirations of the Old Testament, deserving all the tolerance that Rome has shown to the Jews, and that, unlike the nationalistic creed of the Jews, it is a world religion, adequate to meet the spiritual needs of a world empire. Have Christians been denounced as revolutionaries who are turning the Roman world upside down? His story will tell how Christ turned his back on political revolution in order to accomplish a profounder revolution in the realm of ideas and values. Are Christians suspected of antisocial behaviour? He will portray the author of their faith as a figure of nobility, grace, and charm, able to reproduce these same qualities in the lives of his followers and to raise to decency and dignity even the outcasts from the society of men.

THE AUTHOR

A study of the Gospel enables us to describe in some detail the man who wrote it. He was a second-generation Christian who had had ample opportunities of associating with those who had first-hand knowledge of the gospel story. He was an educated man who could adapt his Greek diction to different occasions, writing sometimes formal, classical prose, sometimes a racy narrative style in the vernacular of his own day, and sometimes the semitic 'Bible Greek' in which the Septuagint was written. His command of Greek, his constant interest in Gentiles, and his avoidance of matter of purely Jewish interest may be taken as indications that he himself was a Gentile, but he was one of those Gentiles who were deeply versed in the Greek Old Testament and in the ways of the synagogue. He had something of the poet in his make-up and an artist's ability to depict in vivid pen-portraits the men and women who inhabit his pages. He delighted in marvels and was a little inclined to emphasize the miraculous element in his story. He was more interested in people than in ideas. He had a lively social conscience and an inexhaustible sympathy for other people's troubles.

To the evidence of the Gospel must be added that of Acts. For in Acts there are certain passages where the narrator switches abruptly from the third person to the first person plural (16^{10-17}, $20^{5}-21^{18}$, $27^{1}-28^{16}$), and these 'we' sections can be plausibly explained only on the assumption that the author is using his own or somebody else's diary. But the 'we' sections are written in a style indistinguishable from the style of the rest of the book.* If, then, we suppose that the author was using as one of his sources a diary written by a companion of Paul, we must add that he rewrote it so thoroughly as to eliminate all traces of its original style and yet so carelessly that he did not always remember to make the change from first to third person. The simpler explanation is that the author was using his own diary, and allowed

* See Sir John Hawkins, *Horae Synopticae*, 2nd ed., pp. 182–9.

15

the first person to stand in order to indicate at what points he himself had been an eyewitness; and in that case it follows that the author was a companion of Paul. German and American scholars have on the whole favoured the theory that the author of the diary and the author of Luke–Acts were two different people, because Acts seemed to them to be at so many points in irreconcilable conflict with the evidence of the Pauline Epistles that they could not believe that it came from the hand of one who had personal acquaintance with Paul and his missionary work. British scholars, on the other hand, have on the whole been less impressed by the supposed inaccuracies of Acts than by the overwhelming linguistic evidence that the author of the book was also the author of the diary.*

What then was the author's name? The uniform belief of ancient writers is that he was Luke, the doctor whom Paul mentions as his companion and colleague (Col. 4^{14}, Philem. 24, 2 Tim. 4^{11}). Irenaeus, who became Bishop of Lyon about A.D. 178, argues in his treatise *Against Heresies* (III, 1) that the orthodox Churches are superior to the heretical ones because they know who were the authors of their Gospels, and names as the author of the third Gospel 'Luke the companion of Paul'. *The Muratorian Canon*, a doggerel description of those books which were regarded as authoritative at Rome in the latter half of the second century, declares Luke the physician to be the author of both the Gospel and Acts. The Anti-Marcionite Prologue, which is attached to the Gospel in a number of Latin manuscripts, records, along with more dubious information, that Luke was a native of Antioch, wrote the Gospel in Achaea, and died, unmarried and childless, in Boeotia at the age of eighty-four. Clement of Alexandria (*Stromateis*, v, 12), Tertullian (*Adversus Marcionem*, IV, 2), Origen (in Eusebius, *Historia Ecclesiastica*, VI, 25), Eusebius (*Historia Ecclesiastica*, III, 4, 24), and Jerome (*De viris illustribus*, VII) all hold Luke to be the author, and the last two add that he came from Antioch.

Not all the traditions of the early Church are to be accepted at their face value, but there are good reasons for accepting this one. A book which was written as a manual of instruction for use within the churches of a particular area might at first remain anonymous and later

* For the one side see *The Beginnings of Christianity*, ed. Foakes Jackson and Lake, Vol. II, pp. 207–359; and for the other side see B. H. Streeter, *The Four Gospels*, pp. 520–62.

INTRODUCTION

be supplied with an erroneous title on the basis of a garbled recollection; this is probably what happened in the case of the first Gospel.
But a book which was meant for publication must have borne its
author's name from the start.* In this respect the literary conventions
of the first century were stricter than ours, which allow an author to
hide behind a pen-name. Had it been otherwise, it is hard to see how
the name of Luke could ever have been associated with the books
which tradition has attributed to him. Luke can scarcely be described
as a prominent figure in the annals of first-century Christianity.
Granted that an ancient scholar might have deduced from the prologue to the Gospel that the author was not an apostle and from the
'we' sections of Acts that he was a companion of Paul, he still would
have had no means of putting a name to the author if there had not
been a valid tradition connecting the books with the name of Luke.

One other argument must be mentioned, because it has received a
great deal of notice, though it is doubtful whether much weight can
be placed on it. At one time it was claimed that the use of medical
terms in these books was striking enough to prove that their author
was a doctor.† It has since been shown that the same argument would
make doctors of almost all the writers of antiquity, and that the whole
thesis is in any case ill-founded, since Galen himself claimed not to
use a medical jargon but to write in the common parlance of ordinary
men.‡ The case is not entirely destroyed by this drastic criticism (see
Luke 4^{38}, 5^{12}, 8^{44}, and the Marcan parallels), but perhaps the most
that can properly be claimed is that the language used in Luke–Acts
to describe ailments and cures is compatible with the ancient tradition
that the author was a doctor.

THE SOURCES

The synoptic problem
The first three Gospels are called the Synoptic Gospels because it is
possible to set them out in parallel columns so as to provide a synopsis
or comprehensive view of their contents, and even a glance at such

* See M. Dibelius, *Studies in the Acts of the Apostles*, pp. 146ff.
† W. K. Hobart, *The Medical Language of St Luke*.
‡ H. J. Cadbury, *Harvard Theological Studies* VI, 'The Style and Literary
Method of Luke'; cf. *The Beginnings of Christianity*, II, pp. 349–55.

B   17

a synopsis reveals a complex pattern of relationships. There are passages of narrative or teaching which are common to all three, passages which occur in two Gospels but not in the remaining one, and passages which are peculiar to each. Sometimes the verbal parallels are slight, but at other times the similarity is so great that we are compelled to posit a documentary connexion between the Gospels. Somebody has copied from somebody else; and no conclusion in the field of New Testament study is more certain than that Mark was the earliest Gospel writer and that the other two Evangelists used his Gospel in compiling their own. Wherever the three Gospels overlap, Mark's version is always the longest, the roughest in style, and the best supplied with colourful, circumstantial detail: in short, always the most primitive. Matthew and Luke have abbreviated, polished, corrected; but even so, in the parallel passages, they still reproduce respectively 51 per cent and 53 per cent of Mark's actual words, and they follow his order so closely that there is only one small incident which is differently placed in all three Gospels. Matthew used about 600 out of the 661 verses of Mark, so that nowadays his book would be described as a second edition of Mark, revised and much enlarged. Luke used just over half of Mark, so that his method of compilation was clearly quite different.

When we have eliminated from Matthew and Luke all the material that they derived from Mark, there still remain about 200 verses, consisting mostly of teaching, which are common to these two Gospels. Where the verbal resemblance is slight (e.g. in the Beatitudes and the Lord's Prayer), the two writers may have been drawing on independent traditions. But there are enough passages where the resemblance is so close that we are bound once again to assume a documentary connexion. Either one has copied from the other, or both have copied from an earlier document. Nobody has ever suggested that Matthew copied from Luke. The theory that Luke used Matthew's Gospel is revived from time to time, but is never likely to command much support; for, after the temptation, not one of the passages of common material is found in the same context in both Gospels, and where the two versions show slight divergence, Luke's version is often manifestly the more original. There remains, therefore, the generally accepted theory that both writers were using a second common source, and this hypothetical document is known as

Q (an abbreviation of the German *Quelle*='source'). It was probably compiled in Antioch about A.D. 50.

Mark and Q together account for one half of Luke's Gospel. The other half consists of material peculiar to Luke, which we shall call L. It was once thought that this material comprised a third documentary source, so that the final author was little more than an editor. But Luke himself, according to the most natural interpretation of his prologue, claims to have made use of both written and oral sources. It is significant, too, that his most distinctive words and phrases occur more frequently in L passages than in passages where he is editing Mark or Q, and that all the interests and tendencies which characterize the Gospel as a whole belong in special measure to this material which is peculiar to it. This is what we should expect if Luke himself collected this material directly from oral tradition and himself reduced it to writing for the first time, perhaps during his two-year stay at Caesarea in A.D. 57-59, while Paul was in prison there (Acts 24^{27}).

This is not to say that some parts of Luke's special tradition may not have come to him in written form. The genealogy of Jesus is a case in point. The names from Adam to Abraham have been taken from the Septuagint. In particular, the name Cainan occurs three times in the Septuagint version (Gen. 10^{24}, 11^{12}, 1 Chron. 1^{18}), but not in the corresponding verses of the Hebrew text. The names from Abraham to Joseph have been taken from a source which was independent of the Septuagint, of the Masoretic (Hebrew) text, and of the genealogy in Matthew's Gospel. In the middle of this list occur the three names 'Joanan, the son of Rhesa, the son of Zerubbabel'. But Joanan is only another form of the name Hananiah, and Hananiah was the son of Zerubbabel; there never was such a person as Rhesa (1 Chron. 3^{19}). Rhesa is the Aramaic word for prince, and in the original list it must have been appended as a title to the name of Zerubbabel, the only man who could conceivably have been so designated after 586 B.C. The error which has crept into the Lucan list could have occurred only if the original list was compiled in the reverse order – 'Zerubbabel the prince begat Joanan'. All this leads to the conclusion that Luke was using a document, originally compiled in Aramaic, which traced the descent of Jesus back through David to Abraham, and that he himself completed the list by tracing the descent beyond Abraham to Adam.

The nativity stories may also have been derived from a documentary source, but among those who hold this view some think that it was written in Hebrew, others in Aramaic, and others again in Greek. The stories are thoroughly Jewish, not only in their diction but also in their presuppositions, and the most varied theories have been held about them. Some have held that the canticles were pre-Christian hymns representing the sentiments of first-century Judaism, others that the whole cycle of stories originated among the disciples of John the Baptist, before being adapted to Christian use. The prevalent theory is that the cycle had its origin in the traditions of the Jewish Christian churches of Judea, but that it was Luke himself who gave the stories their present literary form, deliberately adopting the language of the Septuagint to a more marked degree than in the rest of his work in order to reproduce the atmosphere of the Old Testament.

Luke's special material has one feature which is worthy of particular mention – its remarkable affinities with the fourth Gospel. Both agree that there was a second Judas among the twelve (Luke 6[16], John 14[22]); that the betrayal was due to Satan's entry into Judas Iscariot (Luke 22[3], John 13[27]); that the slave of the high priest lost his *right* ear in Gethsemane (Luke 22[50], John 18[10]); that Pilate three times declared Jesus innocent (Luke 23[4, 16, 23], John 18[38], 19[4, 6]); that Joseph's tomb had never been used (Luke 23[53], John 19[41]); that *two* angels appeared on Easter morning (Luke 24[4], John 20[12]); and that the risen Jesus appeared to the eleven in Jerusalem (whereas Mark implies and Matthew states that this happened in Galilee). All this could be explained by the assumption that John was using Luke's Gospel as a source, but this theory is totally inadequate to account for the rest of the evidence. For both Gospels contain a story of Peter and a miraculous catch of fish, but one places it early in the Galilean ministry, the other after the resurrection (Luke 5[1-11], John 21[1-14]). Both tell in remarkably similar language how Jesus was anointed by a woman, but in the one case it was by a prostitute in the house of a Pharisee and in the other it was by a close friend in her own home (Luke 7[36-38], John 12[1-8]). Both are aware of Jesus' friendship with Martha and Mary, though the illustrations they provide are quite different (Luke 10[38-42], John 11[1-44]). Luke records a parable about Lazarus which ends with a warning that even if he were to rise from the dead, men would not believe, and John describes as an actual event the raising of Lazarus and the incredulity that followed (Luke 16³¹, John 11⁴⁴⁻⁴⁷). Luke's account of the resurrection alludes in passing to a story which in John is told in full (Luke 24²⁴, John 20³⁻¹⁰). The unavoidable inference is that Luke and John were relying on two allied streams of oral tradition.

The oral tradition

Luke, as we have seen, used three main sources, two documents, and the oral traditions collected by himself. But Q cannot have been written before A.D. 50 nor Mark before A.D. 65, so that between the ministry of Jesus and the first written records of it there was a period of twenty to thirty-five years during which the contents of all these sources were handed on by word of mouth.

For the last forty years a great deal of scholarly attention has been focused on this period of oral transmission, largely because of the stimulus provided by the German exponents of *Formgeschichte* (Form Criticism).* The form critics started from the well-established principle that the contents of our Gospels, representing only a fraction of what Jesus did and said, were preserved by a process of natural selection, since the Church used, remembered, and recorded those incidents and sayings which were applicable to the current needs and interests of their community. They went on to claim that the community was not at first interested in biographical detail or connected narrative, and that such elements in the gospel story were editorial; that the teaching of Jesus and stories about him circulated, except for the Passion narrative, as detached units without context, because they were used either as sermon illustrations or as material for worship, education, or polemical debate; and that the needs of the community moulded these units or pericopae into a limited number of stereotyped forms (e.g. sayings, pronouncement stories, miracle stories, legends), amplified them with interpretation and comment, and even created new sayings and stories which were then attributed to Jesus. The object of Form Criticism was to discover rules governing the influence of oral transmission on the transmitted narratives and

---

* See Martin Dibelius, *From Tradition to Gospel*, tr. Bertram Lee Woolf; Rudolf Bultmann, *Die Geschichte der synoptischen Tradition*; and for a critique of Form Criticism, Vincent Taylor, *The Formation of the Gospel Tradition*.

sayings, so as to establish valid criteria of their historicity; and ultimately to recover the original form of the tradition.

It is now generally agreed that the form critics overstated their case and unduly disregarded the accepted results of earlier scholarship. They ignored the presence of eyewitnesses of the ministry of Jesus among the first generation of Christians. They drew questionable parallels between oral tradition in other cultures, where the period of transmission is reckoned in centuries, and oral tradition in the primitive Church, where the period is reckoned in decades. They attributed incredible powers to the community, not recognizing that creative work is rarely produced by committees. They forgot that Jesus cast much of his teaching into poetic form and, as a rabbi, expected his disciples to memorize it. They assumed that the early Church could not distinguish its own teaching from that of Jesus, when in fact we know that Paul was meticulously careful to do so (1 Cor. $7^{10, 25}$). They underestimated the historical value of the outline of Jesus' ministry preserved by Mark. And they failed to notice that many of the questions which, on the evidence of the Epistles, were hotly disputed in the apostolic age are not dealt with in the recorded teaching of Jesus, so that the Church cannot be accused of reading its own concerns back into the gospel tradition.

Having said all this, however, we must acknowledge that the form-critics have made an abiding contribution to synoptic studies. They have drawn our attention to a most important period in Christian history and have taught us to use the Gospels, not merely as sources for a knowledge of Jesus, but as mirrors to reflect the interests of the primitive Church. In other matters, too, they were partly justified. As we read Luke's Gospel we shall find that some sayings and stories have been handed down in more than one form, which is a clear indication of the modifying influence of tradition (e.g. Luke 19^{11-27}, cf. Matt. 25^{14-30}). We shall find groups of isolated sayings strung together by a catchword, like pearls on a string (e.g. Luke 11^{33-36}), sometimes standing by themselves and sometimes attached to a parable in such a way as to form a commentary on it (e.g. Luke 16^{1-13}). And constantly we shall find Luke attempting to supply an editorial framework for material which he had received without any indication of the historical context to which it belonged.

THE METHOD OF COMPOSITION

There have been two schools of thought about the manner in which Luke compiled his Gospel, one holding the Marcan Hypothesis,* the other the Proto-Luke Hypothesis.† The proponents of the Marcan Hypothesis tell us that Luke, like Matthew, used Mark's outline as the framework of his Gospel, into which he inserted the material from his other sources. They claim that after the first two chapters the non-Marcan material comprises four passages of very unequal length (5^{1-11}, 6^{20-83}, $9^{51}-18^{14}$, 19^{1-27}), together with some editorial insertions in $3^{1}-4^{30}$ and $22^{14}-24^{53}$ these passages being essentially Marcan; and that this material owes such semblance of continuity as it displays wholly to the Marcan framework in which it has been set. The advocates of the Proto-Luke Hypothesis assert that, up to the Passion narrative, the Gospel consists of alternate strips of Mark (4^{31-44}, $5^{12}-6^{19}$, $8^{4}-9^{50}$, 18^{15-43}, $19^{28}-22^{13}$) and of Q and L combined ($1^{1}-4^{30}$, 5^{1-11}, 6^{20-83}, $9^{51}-18^{14}$, 19^{1-27}), that in the Passion narrative there is a non-Marcan framework with Marcan insertions, and that the only reasonable explanation of this pattern is that Luke had already woven his Q and L material into a first draft of a Gospel before he became acquainted with Mark, so that this Proto-Luke provided the outline into which the blocks of Mark were incorporated.

It will be observed that the crux of the problem lies in two passages ($3^{1}-4^{30}$ and $22^{14}-24^{53}$), since there is little difference of opinion about the rest of the Gospel. If in these two passages we hold that Mark has been used as the primary source, we shall agree with the first school that the framework of the Gospel is Marcan. Otherwise we shall be inclined to give our vote to the Proto-Luke school. This controversy might appear at first sight to be of merely academic interest, but the verdict we give here will make a considerable difference to our estimate of the historical value of the Gospel. For the Marcan Hypothesis involves the corollary that Luke used wide editorial freedom in rewriting his sources. It is therefore well worth while to study the evidence in some detail.

* See J. M. Creed, *The Gospel according to St Luke*; S. M. Gilmour, *The Interpreter's Bible*, VIII, pp. 16–18.

† See B. H. Streeter, *The Four Gospels*, pp. 201–22; Vincent Taylor, *Behind the Third Gospel*.

1. The first point to notice is that Luke's Gospel contains eleven doublets – sayings which occur twice in different contexts. The facts can be tabulated as follows:

Mark		Luke A	Luke B		Matthew	
4^{21}	=	$\cdot 8^{16}$	11^{33}	=	5^{15}	Q
4^{22}	=	8^{17}	12^{2}	=	10^{26}	Q
4^{25}	=	8^{18}	19^{26}	cf.	25^{29}	Q ?
6^{6-11}	=	9^{3-5}	10^{3-12}	cf.	10^{7-15}	Q partly
8^{34}	=	9^{23}	14^{27}	=	10^{38}	Q
8^{35}	=	9^{24}	17^{33}	=	10^{39}	Q
8^{38}	=	9^{26}	12^{9}	=	10^{33}	Q
9^{34}	=	9^{46}	22^{24}			
12^{38-39}	=	20^{46}	11^{43}	cf.	$23^{6f.}$	Q probably
13^{11}	=	21^{14-15}	12^{11-12}	cf.	10^{19}	Q probably
		14^{11}	18^{14}	cf.	23^{12}	Q ?

In ten out of the eleven cases the reason for the doublet is that Luke has included one version of a saying from Mark and another version from one of his other sources. It follows from this that Luke's three sources occasionally overlapped, so that, if a passage in Luke has a Marcan parallel, this does not necessarily mean that he derived it from Mark. This inference has an immediate bearing on our study of Luke $3^{1}-4^{13}$. Like Mark 1^{1-13}, this passage contains an account of the Baptist's preaching and of the baptism and temptations of Jesus. But a comparison of these two passages with Matt. $3^{1}-4^{11}$ shows that Q also began with a similar and fuller version of the same stories, and that, while Matthew after his usual fashion has conflated the two sources, Luke is mainly dependent on Q and has used Mark, if at all, only in a supplementary way.

2. Where Luke is demonstrably using Mark, he normally follows Mark's order (see, for example, the first two columns of the list above). But there are seventeen places where he diverges from the order of Mark $1^{1}-14^{11}$:

Mark	Luke		Matthew	
1^{16-20}	$*5^{1-11}$			
3^{20-27}	11^{14-23}	=	12^{22-27}	Q
3^{28-30}	12^{10}	=	12^{32}	Q
4^{30-32}	13^{18-19}	=	13^{31-32}	Q
6^{1-6}	4^{16-30}			
8^{15}	12^{1}			

Mark	Luke		Matthew	
9^{42}	17^2	=	18^6	Q
9^{50}	14^{34}	=	5^{13}	Q
10^{11-12}	16^{18}	=	5^{32}	Q
10^{31}	13^{30}	cf.	8^{11-12}	Q ?
10^{42-45}	22^{25-27}			
11^{23}	17^6	=	17^{20}	Q
11^{25}	11^4	cf.	6^{9-13}	
12^{28-34}	*10^{25-37}			
13^{15-16}	17^{31}			Q ?
13^{21-23}	17^{23}	=	24^{26}	Q
14^{3-9}	*7^{36-50}			

This table confirms our conclusion about the overlapping of sources, but it enables us to carry the discussion a step further. It shows that, in a number of cases where Mark and Q overlapped, Luke has used the Q version to the exclusion of the Marcan one. Thus in at least half of the places where Luke diverges from Mark's order there is no question of his having deliberately altered Mark. He has simply omitted a passage from Mark because he has included elsewhere a parallel passage from Q. In the three cases marked with an asterisk it is equally clear that he has omitted a Marcan story because he had an equivalent and more picturesque story from L. From here it is but a step to the formulation of a general principle that where Luke appears to diverge from Mark's order he is actually following another source. There is, therefore, a high degree of probability that the story of Jesus' visit to Nazareth in Luke 4^{16-30} is not a free rewriting of Mark 6^{1-6} but an independent tradition drawn from L.

3. In Luke $22^{14}-24^{53}$, out of a total of 163 verses, there are 87 verses which have some counterpart in Mark, but only 20 in which there is the sort of verbal similarity which is normally regarded as evidence of dependence. When Luke is indisputably following Mark, he uses 53 per cent of Mark's words, but here he uses only 27 per cent, and many of the words which he shares with Mark are words without which the Passion story could not have been told at all. Moreover, this part of the Gospel contains no less than twelve transpositions of Mark's order. In view of the evidence that we have adduced from the earlier part of the Gospel concerning Luke's use of his sources we are bound to conclude either that Luke has here drastically departed

25

from his ordinary methods of composition or that he was relying principally on a non-Marcan source to which he made occasional additions from Mark. The idea that Luke had at his disposal, besides Mark, an independent tradition, whether oral or written, of events from the Last Supper to the resurrection is a thoroughly reasonable one when we remember that the Passion narrative, being the very core of the Church's preaching, must have been repeated in continuous form from the earliest days in all the various centres of Christian activity. It is, moreover, quite certain that L contained a resurrection narrative, which is unlikely to have circulated without a Passion narrative to precede it.

4. In 4^{31}–22^{13} Luke has regularly combined Q and L material in a composite narrative and has left the Marcan material in separate blocks. There are two possible explanations of this phenomenon. Either Luke valued Mark so highly above his other sources that he determined to keep it distinct from them, or he had already combined Q and L before he knew anything about Mark. It is not hard to make a choice between these alternatives. Our investigations have not led us to suppose that Luke set so much store by Mark as the first theory implies. Two-thirds of his Gospel is drawn from other sources; he omitted nearly half the contents of Mark, including the so-called 'Great Omission' (Mark 6^{45}–8^{26}); and, where his sources overlapped, we have seen that he frequently preferred Q and L to Mark.

5. Matthew and Mark never refer to Jesus as 'the Lord' in narrative. Luke does so fourteen times. The usage is clearly editorial, for it occurs in both Q and L passages; but, as it never occurs when Luke is editing Mark, it cannot be regarded as characteristic of the final redaction of the Gospel. Similarly, Luke uses two names for the experts in the Jewish law, who are regularly called lawyers (*nomikoi*) in Q and L passages and scribes (*grammateis*) in passages derived from Mark. This is intelligible if Luke composed his Gospel in two stages.

6. Luke's Gospel contains two mission charges, one addressed to the twelve and drawn from Mark, the other addressed to the seventy and drawn from Q and L (9^{3-9}, 10^{2-12}). But when Jesus later reminds the twelve that they had gone out *with no purse or bag or sandals* (22^{35}), he is echoing the charge given to the seventy. This editorial lapse is readily understandable if, when Luke first wrote the account of the Last Supper, he had only one mission charge to refer to.

7. There are several indications that 3$^{1-2}$ was originally intended to be the opening of the Gospel. The portentous, six-fold date has a ring about it that is reminiscent of the beginning of the prophetic books; John is introduced as though for the first time; and the attachment of the genealogy of Jesus to the story of his baptism instead of to the story of his birth, as in Matthew's Gospel, is perfectly natural if originally it followed the first mention of his name. But if the birth stories were not included in the earliest plan of the Gospel, this is further evidence that the book went through two stages of composition.

These seven considerations together may not constitute a proof of the soundness of the Proto-Luke theory, but they do reveal the total inadequacy of its rival. As a working hypothesis for our present study, then, we shall assume that Luke began his literary undertaking by collecting information about Jesus from eyewitnesses and others, probably during the years when Paul was imprisoned at Caesarea. At the same time, or shortly afterwards, he combined the material he had accumulated with the teaching tradition of Q, so as to form the first draft of a gospel. Subsequently, when a copy of Mark came into his hands, he augmented his original document with Marcan insertions. He then added the infancy stories and the prologue to bring his work into its final form. And perhaps it is not out of place to add that in every stage of composition he left the imprint of his own peculiar artistry and charm.

HISTORICAL ACCURACY

The account we have given of Luke's literary procedure consists entirely of deductions drawn from a careful study of his Gospel, but it coincides almost exactly with what he himself has to tell us in his prologue. There he claims that the story he is about to recount in his two-volume work is solid truth based on eyewitness evidence, that some of this evidence has come to him through the writings of others and some directly, and that he himself has been conducting his researches for some time past (or he may mean that he has been personally involved in the events he has recorded, i.e. since A.D. 49 when he joined Paul at Troas). As far as the Gospel is concerned – and we cannot here undertake to discuss the historicity of Acts – Luke has made good his claim to be a trustworthy historian, provided that we do not make the blunder of judging him by the canons of modern, scientific historiography. His three sources, Mark, Q, and L, represent, in all probability, the traditions guaranteed by the three influential centres of Rome, Antioch, and Caesarea. The picture of Jesus which he gives is thus established 'at the mouth of two or three witnesses', and this is particularly significant in the Passion narrative, where his independent account confirms and supplements that of Mark. From his use of Mark we can see that he has followed his sources faithfully with regard to substance and order and has altered the wording only in the interests of style and brevity. Moreover, he alone has attempted to set the Christian story against the background of world history, so as to provide us with data without which any chronology of the New Testament would be out of the question.

Luke's accuracy as a historian has been impugned on three grounds: his editorial freedom in rewriting his sources, his chronological inexactitude, and his fondness for the miraculous. The first charge is inseparably bound up with the Marcan theory which we have discussed and discarded. Whether or not we accept the Proto-Luke theory as a whole, this much is certain, that passages such as Luke 4^{16-30} can no longer be regarded as drastically edited versions of Mark.

It is not so easy to estimate the weight of the second criticism. Luke's sixfold dating of the Baptist's ministry shows that he had access to reliable sources of information, even if we find some of his information less lucid than we could have wished. On the other hand, he has almost certainly been guilty of an anachronism in making Gamaliel refer in his address in the Sanhedrin to the revolt of Theudas, which took place over ten years later (Acts 5^{36}). What, then, are we to say about the census by which Luke seeks to fix the date of the nativity? Is this another instance of Luke's access to precise information or another case of anachronism? Quirinius is known to have conducted a census in Palestine in A.D. 6–7; but Jesus was born in the lifetime of Herod the Great, who died in 4 B.C., and the governors of Syria during the closing years of Herod's reign were C. Sentius Saturninus (9–6 B.C.) and P. Quintilius Varus (6–4 B.C.). Josephus, who might be expected to know about a census in Judea, is silent about this one. On the other hand, we know that Augustus held a census of Roman citizens as sole censor in 8 B.C. It is quite likely that on the same occasion he inaugurated the Egyptian system of census-taking at fourteen-year intervals, of which there are records from A.D. 20 to A.D. 258. Tertullian (*Adversus Marcionem*, IV, 19) mentions the nativity census, but gives the name of the governor as Saturninus, and he could hardly have corrected Luke in this way unless he had access to some sort of official record. It is possible, therefore, that Luke was right about the census, but that either he or his source made an error over the name of the governor who conducted it.

Luke's interest in miraculous occurrences is undeniable, for both volumes of his work are full of them. But this was an interest which he shared with all other members of the early Church, and one which grew out of the very nature of the story he was telling. We have to allow for the possibility that the stories about Jesus have undergone some legendary accretion in the process of transmission, but sober criticism cannot get behind the gospel record to a plain, commonplace tale, devoid of the miraculous and the supernatural. The early Christians believed that, in Christ, God had been at work in new and astonishing ways and they had the evidence of their own eyes to support their faith. Luke cannot justly be accused of exaggerating the miraculous element in his narrative. He omits Mark's most difficult miracle, the story of the barren fig tree. It is true that he also goes one step beyond Mark in recording a cure performed at a distance by a word of command, but this story, the healing of the centurion's servant, was taken from Q, his most trustworthy source. He has sometimes been taken to task for emphasizing the physical nature of the resurrection, since it is in his Gospel alone that the risen Jesus eats and drinks with his disciples. But here too he is simply reproducing with fidelity the sources on which he was relying. For in Acts 10$^{37-42}$ he puts into the mouth of Peter an almost credal utterance which is clearly derived from an Aramaic source and which presents the same picture of the resurrection as we find in the Gospel.

We thus arrive at the interesting and important conclusion that, where Luke's modern detractors have thought him a careless historian, the sum of his fault has usually been that he was meticulously following his sources.

A more intricate problem is presented to us by Chapters 1 and 2. These tales of angelic visitants, inspired utterances, and heavenly choirs are obviously not to be placed in the same category as the

INTRODUCTION

accounts of the Galilean ministry which constituted the apostolic tradition. That they contain a basis of historic fact we need not doubt, but it is fact which has been lifted out of the realm of prose and precise reporting into the realm of poetry and worship. Some light can be thrown on the nature of these stories by the Jewish distinction between two types of scriptural exposition. The *Halakah* (from the verb walk) was the commentary on scripture which adduced from it rules for daily life; the *Haggadah* (from the verb tell) was the recital of scriptural stories to bring out their religious import. Because Jewish orthodoxy consisted more in rightness of practice than in rightness of belief, the traditions of the *Halakah* were preserved with scrupulous exactitude, but the *Haggadah* was regarded as a legitimate field for the godly exercise of creative imagination. The nativity stories are *Haggadah*. Luke wanted to tell the story of the ministry of Jesus with a minimum of editorial comment and interpretation, and he used these introductory stories to express his own theological beliefs that the ministry was God's great act of deliverance accomplished in accordance with his ancient promises.

But are we to say that the virgin birth of Jesus belonged to the original substratum of fact or to the subsequent elaboration? Certainly it formed no part of the earliest apostolic preaching. Mark and John could tell the gospel story without reference to it, though John has an echo of a hostile Jewish report that Jesus was born out of wedlock (John 8⁴¹). For Paul, who undoubtedly believed in the divinity of Christ, the important fact was that, in entering life by the normal gateway of birth (Gal. 4⁴), he had taken upon himself manhood with all its entail of inherited evil (Rom. 8³, 2 Cor. 5²¹, Gal. 3¹³, Phil. 2⁷). Matthew believed in a virgin birth, and Luke apparently did, though it is hardly too much to say that it is as peripheral to his story as to the New Testament in general. There are in fact only two verses in Luke's Gospel that imply a virgin birth (1³⁴ and 3²³), and in both places the belief is hinted at rather than stated. Apart from these two verses the story reads like an account of a normal human birth, miraculous only because through it God has chosen to act for the deliverance of his people. Joseph is consistently referred to as Jesus' father, and it is through Joseph that Jesus is descended from David.

Davidic descent through Joseph is not entirely incompatible with the virgin birth. The Jews were well accustomed to the notion of legal parentage, since in the curious institution of levirate marriage (Deut. 25⁵⁻⁶) a child's legal descent was reckoned through his mother's first husband instead of through his actual father. But there can be little doubt that the Lucan genealogy was compiled by someone who believed that Jesus was the son of Joseph and was accommodated to the belief in a virgin birth by the editorial parenthesis – *being the son (as was supposed) of Joseph* (3²³). This being so, it is clearly in order to ask whether the nativity story has at some time undergone a similar revision.

There are two reasons for believing that in the original Judean tradition Joseph was regarded as the father of Jesus, and some will find them more convincing than others. In the first place, it would never have occurred to a Jew to consider the overshadowing of Mary by the Holy Spirit as a substitute for normal parenthood (see *Niddah*, 31a: 'There are three partners in the production of man: the Holy One, blessed be He, the father, and the mother.' Cf. *Sotah*, 17a; *Genesis R.* 8⁹). But this manner of speech could very readily be misunderstood by a Gentile. Secondly, both Matthew and Luke make use of the prophecy of Isa. 7¹⁴, the one by direct quotation, the other by allusion. In the early Palestinian Church this verse must have been applied to Jesus because of the name Immanuel. For in its original Hebrew form this prophecy said nothing of a virgin birth: 'a young woman shall conceive and bear a son, and shall call his name Immanuel'. In the Septuagint version, however, the Greek word *parthenos* (virgin) was used (the translator responsible for the book of Isaiah was not a very competent linguist). As long as the story circulated in its original Judean setting, the Immanuel prophecy could have carried only its Hebrew connotation. But when the gospel was disseminated throughout the Greek world, and the Immanuel prophecy was cited in its Greek form as an authoritative word of scripture about the birth of Jesus, it would naturally give the impression that Jesus was born of a virgin.*

* For a parallel, though less important, example of the influence of prophecy on tradition see Matt. 21⁷, where the evangelist has added an extra donkey to the story in Mark in order to make it conform to what he erroneously believed to be the meaning of Zechariah's prophecy; and for the conversion of poetry into miracle see Joshua 10¹²⁻¹³, where Joshua's highly dramatic prayer that darkness should not overtake his army before full victory had been achieved, was turned by a prosaic editor into a most improbable miracle.

THE TEXT

The first printed text of the Greek New Testament was that of Erasmus, published in 1516. Prior to that date the text was preserved only in manuscripts, laboriously copied by the pens of many scribes. Of these manuscripts about 4,700 survive today, ranging from small fragments of papyrus to complete vellum codices. The texts of all of them vary considerably, and none of them can be regarded as free from error. The work of the copyist was exacting, and he might well suffer from inattention, weariness, or astigmatism. However conscientious he was, he made mistakes, and these mistakes were perpetuated in any copies that were later made from his copy. Most existing manuscripts of any size have undergone further alteration at the hands of correctors, who did not always manage to restore the true reading. It follows from this that all copies and copies of copies which were derived from a single parent manuscript will exhibit family resemblances. It is the aim of the science of textual criticism to arrange all known manuscripts in family groups, so as to get behind them all to their common progenitor, the long-lost original manuscript or autograph.

The vast majority of manuscripts of the New Testament follow the official, ecclesiastical text, produced in Byzantium on the basis of an edition prepared by Lucian. This text was adopted with only minor changes by Erasmus and subsequently by the translators of the English version of 1611. Modern critical texts, however, are based almost entirely on older manuscripts, more recently discovered, which were unaffected by the Byzantine revision. These manuscripts belong to three main families: the Alexandrian text, represented especially by the great codices, Vaticanus (B) and Sinaiticus (א); the Western text, represented by Codex Bezae (D) and the Old Latin translation; and the Eastern text, represented on the one hand by the early Syriac translations and on the other hand by the Koridethi manuscript (Θ).

The text of Luke's Gospel has been subject to the same vicissitudes as that of the other books of the New Testament, but there are three points in its history which require special mention.

1. The third of the Synoptic Gospels was more liable than the others

to receive attention from harmonizers. A scribe who had already
worked his way through Matthew and Mark was likely either to
reproduce a familiar passage from memory, not noticing that the
text before him was different, or deliberately to alter the text before
him to bring it into harmony with what he had already written in
another Gospel, on the assumption that a previous scribe had blundered. For example, Luke's shorter version of the Lord's Prayer has
been made in many manuscripts to conform to Matthew's longer
version.

2. In A.D. 144 Marcion of Sinope, a brilliant and erratic theologian
who had recently taken up residence in Rome, broke with the Church
there and proceeded to found a vigorous heretical movement of his
own. He taught that the true God, a God of love and mercy, had sent
Jesus to deliver men from bondage to an inferior god of law and
justice, the creator-god of the Old Testament. To rival the Old
Testament scriptures, which he repudiated, he produced the first
'New Testament', consisting of 'Gospel and Apostle'. His 'Apostle'
was Paul's letters; his 'Gospel' was Luke, so edited as to eliminate all
Old Testament references. The exact limits of his Gospel have yet to
be determined; he is known to have retained sixty per cent of Luke
and to have excised sixteen per cent, but for his treatment of the rest
there is no evidence. In view of the immense and prolonged influence
of Marcion, we have to allow for the possibility that his version of
Luke affected the orthodox text, particularly in the West.

3. The Western text of Luke and Acts exhibits some striking
divergences, by way of addition and subtraction, from the Alexandrian and Byzantine texts. In the Gospel the additions are few and
unimportant. But, inasmuch as the normal tendency of the Codex
Bezae is to embellish and expand, the great English textual scholars,
Westcott and Hort, were disposed to take seriously the eight omis-
sions (Luke 22^{19b-20}, 24$^{3, 6, 12, 36, 40, 51, 52}$), to which they gave the
name 'Western non-interpolations' – meaning that the Western text
was the only one which at these points had escaped interpolation.
Their verdict used to be generally accepted, but in recent times the
question has been reopened, and many modern scholars prefer to
settle each case separately on its own merits.

CHRISTIANITY ACCORDING TO ST LUKE

The Divine Plan

This Jesus, delivered up according to the definite plan and foreknowledge of God, you crucified and killed by the hands of lawless men (Acts 2²³). These words, which Luke has put into the mouth of Peter, are the core of his own theology. He sees the ministry of Jesus from baptism to ascension as the working out of a drama of world redemption in which, though the human characters are free to act on their own volition, the plot has been determined by God. Men may reject the purpose of God, as the Pharisees and lawyers did when they ignored John's baptism (7³⁰), but the Cross is the proof that God can turn even the ultimate rejection into victory.

The divine plan was both foretold and prefigured in the scriptures of the Old Testament. It was an integral part of the apostolic tradition which Luke inherited that the life, death, and resurrection of Jesus had happened 'according to the scriptures' (1 Cor. 15³⁻⁴), and this same theme has been developed in various ways by other New Testament writers. Luke's special interest in this subject is displayed in three ways. He introduces the idea of fulfilment into contexts where it was not present in his source (18³¹; cf. Mark 10³³). He repeatedly affirms that this method of scriptural interpretation had its origin in Jesus himself, who found in the Old Testament the blueprint of his own ministry (4²¹), and taught his disciples how to use the Old Testament as Christian scripture (24²⁷, ⁴⁴). But these last two passages further assert that Jesus fulfilled not just a few isolated promises made by the prophets, but the whole tenor, purport, and pattern of Old Testament teaching and history. In particular he fulfilled the Exodus and the Passover. The Exodus, in which God had brought his people through slavery to freedom, had made them a nation, had bound them to himself by a gracious covenant, and had provided the basic pattern for the interpretation of Israel's subsequent history. The Lord their God who had brought them out of Egypt would redeem them from every other humiliation, deserved or undeserved, and bring them in the end through the cleansing fires of affliction to their destined glory. This faith was kept alive by the annual memorial service of the Passover, which looked back to the historic emancipation and forward to God's future reign of righteousness and peace. Thus when Luke calls Christ's death 'his exodus which he was to fulfil in Jerusalem' (9^{31}) and later links that death with the fulfilling of the Passover in the Kingdom of God (22^{16}), he means us to understand that in Christ God has brought to completion the great plan of redemption of which the whole story of the Old Testament was a prophetic forecast.

Because Luke believed that Jesus was the servant of a divine purpose, which he had found to be delineated in the scriptures, he constantly portrays him as acting under the authority of a divine necessity. In Mark's Gospel, Jesus had once spoken of the necessity of his death (Mark 8^{31}), but Luke uses this same Greek verb (*dei*) no less than ten times in connexion with Jesus' ministry (2^{49}, 4^{43}, 9^{22}, $13^{16, 33}$, 17^{25}, 22^{37}, $24^{7, 26, 44}$). We are not meant to think that Jesus was a fatalist, but that at every period in his life he responded with willing obedience to the necessity that was laid upon him by his vocation. God could not be held responsible for the perfidy of Judas or for any of the other sins which contributed to bring about the crucifixion, yet not even this happened outside the control of his determined plan. *For the Son of man goes as it has been determined; but woe to that man by whom he is betrayed* (22^{22}).

Four times Luke describes the ministry of Jesus as a divine visit. *God . . . has visited and redeemed his people* (1^{68}; cf. 1^{78}, 7^{16}, 19^{44}). God is not merely the playwright who has devised the plot for the drama of redemption; he is an actor who makes a personal appearance on the stage and whose presence brings the whole action to its denouement. The same idea is conveyed by Luke's frequent use of the verb *euangelizesthai* (to 'bring good news'), which he uses in preference to the noun *euangelion*, because in his mind it carried definite associations from its use in the Old Testament. *O thou that tellest good tidings to Zion . . . say to the cities of Judah, 'Behold your God'. Behold, the Lord God comes . . .* (Isa. 40^{9-10}). *How beautiful upon the mountains are the feet of him who brings good tidings . . . who says to Zion, 'Your God reigns'* (Isa. 52^{7}). As to the prophet, so to Luke, 'the gospel of the kingdom' meant the news that God had arrived among his people to assume his sovereign power. The coming of the Saviour was the coming of God.

35

God's activity in the working out of his purpose is also expressed by Luke through his numerous references to the Spirit. The Spirit was operative in the birth of Jesus (1^{35}), descended bodily upon him at his baptism (3^{22}), led him to his temptations to do battle with the devil (4^1), inspired and directed the whole conduct of his mission ($4^{14,\ 18}$). But Luke never allows us to forget that this divine presence and energy manifested itself through human obedience, and at every crisis in his career – at the baptism, in the midst of the Galilean ministry, before the appointment of the twelve, at Caesarea Philippi, on the mountain of transfiguration, in Gethsemane – we are shown Jesus on his knees, putting himself under the authority of his Father's will.

The rescue of the outcast

Luke believed that only Jesus and those with whom he chose to share his secret really understood what the gracious purpose of God was (10^{21-22}), but that, for those who had eyes to see it, that purpose was revealed in every episode of the ministry. It was nothing less than the restoration of men and women to their proper dignity as children of God. *For the Son of man came to seek and to save the lost* (19^{10}). The programme of the ministry was set forth in its opening scene in the synagogue at Nazareth, when Jesus declared that he had come in the power of the Spirit to proclaim the promised Jubilee, the year of God that was to see the end of all oppression and bondage. Those who took this to mean liberation from Rome were to be disappointed, for Jesus had in mind a campaign against more virulent and closer enemies. He was concerned with the demonic powers which held the whole of human life in thrall, exercising their authority through physical, mental, and moral illness (13^{16}, 8^2, 22^3), through inadequate ideals and misguided enthusiasm (4^{1-13}, 22^{31-34}), through injustice and the vain glory of riches, through privilege, discrimination, and self-righteousness. Satan, like a strong man fully armed, could keep his fortress intact until a stronger one should arrive to bind him and spoil him of his goods. Jesus' ministry, in which Satan's grip was loosened from one life after another, was proof that the stronger one had come, that the reign of God was already breaking in upon the reign of Satan (11^{20-22}).

The reign or kingdom of God still has for Luke a future aspect for which men must continue to pray (11^2, 22^{18}). But the fact that matters, the fact that constitutes the good news of the gospel, is that the kingdom has arrived (11²⁰, 16¹⁶, 7²⁸). The only evidence required to support this conviction is that which Jesus offered to John: *the blind receive their sight, the lame walk, lepers are cleansed, and the deaf hear, the dead are raised up, the poor have good news preached to them* (7²²). This to Luke is no prelude to a future kingdom: it is the kingdom already exerting its power. Indeed, his entire Gospel is a commentary on this theme. All his tenderness of heart and mastery of description are called into play as he presents to us the cavalcade of witnesses who can testify to the presence of the kingdom because they have discovered in Jesus the friend and champion of the sick, the poor, the penitent, the outcast, of women, Samaritans, and Gentiles. 'Blessed are you poor'; 'bring quickly the best robe'; 'this man went down to his house justified'; 'her sins, which are many, are forgiven'; 'salvation has come to this house'; 'he gave him to his mother'; 'ought not this woman . . . to be loosed from this bond'; 'he had compassion . . . and bound up his wounds'; 'now he was a Samaritan'; 'not even in Israel have I found such faith.'

God's servant and Son

Who, then, was this Jesus? Luke calls him Son of man, Saviour, Lord, Messiah, and Son of God; but only the last two of these titles were of real importance to his theology. Son of man was a traditional title which he took over from his sources without attempting to explore the reasons why Jesus had chosen this self-designation. As it appears in Mark's Gospel this title is clearly connected with the prophetic vision of Dan. 7¹³, but either Luke or his source has obliterated the connexion by omitting the key quotation (Luke 22⁶⁹; cf. Mark 14⁶²). The titles Saviour and Lord also had their roots in the apostolic tradition, but had grown in popularity as the Church expanded its Hellenistic mission, because these terms were also in common use in the religions of the Graeco-Roman world. Luke knew they would make a ready appeal to his Gentile readers, but he could not rely on them alone to convey any specifically Christian meaning.

The word Messiah meant simply 'anointed', and in the time of Saul and David was used as a title for the king, who had been anointed to his office and was therefore 'the Lord's Anointed' (1 Sam. 12³, 16⁶; etc). God had promised to David that one of his descendants would always sit upon his throne and that *I will be his father and he shall be my son* (2 Sam. 7^{14}). When the dynasty of David came to an end in 586 B.C., this promise gave rise to the hope that God would one day raise up from the royal house a king to sit upon the throne of David and to institute an endless reign of peace and justice. This Messiah would be in a special sense the Son of God. When at his baptism Jesus was addressed as 'my Son', this meant that he was being designated and anointed to his office as Messiah (cf. Luke 4^{18}, Acts 4^{27}, 10^{38}). In his temptations he repudiated the various popular conceptions of Messiahship, and thereafter avoided using the title for fear of being misunderstood. According to Luke, it was only after the resurrection that he was able to explain to his disciples what it meant to be Messiah and why it was necessary for the Messiah to suffer (24^{26}).

Luke believed that the Cross was part of the divine plan for the Messiah, which Jesus had found in the scriptures, and particularly in the prophecies of Isa. 40–66, to which there are at least eight references in the Gospel (2$^{25, 30-32}$, 3$^{4-6, 22}$, 4$^{18-19}$, 6$^{20-22}$, 7^{22}, 22^{37}). These prophecies contain a series of descriptions of a Servant of the Lord, who is called to carry God's salvation to the nations of the world with the promise that, in spite of scorn, injury, and death, he will see the triumph of his mission and usher in the reign of God. The Servant is Israel; but the prophet seems to have been in some doubt whether his vision would be fulfilled by the whole nation, by a small remnant, or by one man. Luke's contention is that Jesus identified the Servant of the Lord with the Messiah, and so interpreted his kingly office and authority in terms not of political grandeur and world conquest but of humble service and vicarious suffering.

As Messiah Jesus was also Son of God. But this meant something far more to him than an official appellation. At least from the age of twelve, as Luke informs us, he had a vivid awareness of God's paternal care and authority, which made it natural for him to speak of God as 'my Father' (2^{49}). To be Son of God meant to live in God's love, by his power, and for his purpose. Later Jesus was to discover that nobody else knew the Father with the same intimacy and certitude as himself and that the task for which he had been sent out with all the Father's authority was to lead others into the sonship which he himself enjoyed (10$^{21-22}$, 11^{2}). In his genealogy Luke traces the lineage of Jesus back through David to *Adam, the son of God* (3^{38}), and he clearly

means this to be a comment on the story of the baptism which immediately precedes it. Jesus, as Son of God, was the fulfilment not only of
Israel's destiny but of the destiny of mankind as well. Man was created
for the kind of relationship to God that Jesus realized in his own life
and so made possible for others also.

Because Luke omits the two Marcan sayings which give atoning
significance to the death of Christ (Mark 10^{45}, 14^{24}), it has often been
quite unjustly said of him that he has no theology of the Cross. We
have already seen that he regarded the Cross as the New Exodus, as
a necessity imposed on Jesus by the divine plan of redemption, as the
ultimate vocation of the Servant of the Lord. It is also the hour when
the powers of darkness exhaust their strength in a final effort to over-
come him (22^{53}). More than this Luke does not need to say, because
to him the death of Christ was only the inevitable outcome of the life
he had lived. If at the end *he was reckoned with transgressors* (22^{37}), it was
because he had always chosen to be numbered with them. This was
the price of friendship with tax gatherers and sinners.

In two of his parables Jesus warned the crowds not to join the
company of his disciples without first counting the cost (14^{25-32}). He
himself had done precisely that. He had made common cause with
the despised and rejected, knowing full well where this identification
would lead him. This is why Luke represents the latter part of the
ministry as a constant facing towards Jerusalem, the city that had first
claim on the lives of God's messengers (13^{33}). But at the very point
where he first announces this theme, Luke, with an almost Johannine
turn of phrase, calls Jesus' death his *analempsis* or assumption. *When
the days drew near for him to be received up, he set his face to go to Jerusalem*
(9^{51}). The road to the Cross is also the road to victory.

Luke 1¹⁻⁴

Prologue

I *Inasmuch as many have undertaken to compile a narrative of the things which have been accomplished among us,* ²*just as they were delivered to us by those who from the beginning were eyewitnesses and ministers of the word,* ³*it seemed good to me also, having followed all things closely*ᵃ *for some time past, to write an orderly account for you, most excellent Theophilus,* ⁴*that you may know the truth concerning the things of which you have been informed.*

a Or *accurately*

Luke opens his Gospel with a single resounding sentence in the delicately balanced style of classical rhetoric. Artistic judgement and fidelity to tradition have prompted him to tell his story in the vernacular Greek with a strong semitic accent, as it had been told and retold from the beginning; but by this one initial gesture he seeks to forestall the fastidiousness of educated men and to establish his claim upon their serious attention.

The ultimate authority for all that he has written is the group of eyewitnesses who had first-hand knowledge of the life of Jesus, including, of course, the twelve, for whose apostolic office such knowledge was an indispensable qualification (Acts 1²¹). But the traditions which these men had handed on to the Christian community were more than personal reminiscences. For they had also been ministers of the word – preachers, teachers, and pastors – who had discovered among their memories of Jesus that which met the deepest needs of men. Their testimony was therefore not merely historic fact; it was also religious truth which had proved its efficacy in satisfying the searching mind and in calling forth an answer from the heart. They bore witness to what they had seen and heard, but the facts were from the start presented in a framework of theological interpretation. Luke had certainly met at least one of these original disciples, for he stayed with Philip the Evangelist at Caesarea (Acts 21⁸), but he does not claim that all his information came to him direct. Much of it came to him through the works of his literary predecessors – the many whom,

43

incidentally, he is careful to distinguish from the eyewitnesses – and much again from Christian communities with a vivid sense of living contact with the apostolic tradition. He has for some time past been actively interested in the accumulation of material and has now been emboldened by the example of others to put his work into orderly form.

The practice of literary dedication was closely linked with the correlative practice of patronage, and this in itself makes it probable that Luke was dedicating his two-volume work to a Roman of high rank. The title *most excellent* ('Your Excellency' – cf. Acts 23^{26}, 24^{3}, 26^{25}) is a pointer in the same direction. But did Luke address his patron because he was a convert whose faith he wished to confirm or because he was an influential pagan whose support and sympathy he thought he could solicit? The name Theophilus ('beloved of God'), though a common enough name, may plausibly be regarded as a discreet pseudonym; but in that case is the incognito designed to protect a confessing Christian from the perils of persecution or a sympathetic official from the embarrassment of having his name associated with a suspect movement? Theophilus, we are told, had been informed about Christianity, and the word Luke uses can refer either to Christian instruction (Acts 18^{25}) or to the receipt of a hostile and inaccurate report (Acts 21$^{21, 24}$). The A.V. adopted the first of these interpretations, and the common assumption has been that Theophilus was a Christian. Scholarly speculation has identified him with Titus Flavius Clemens, cousin of the Emperor Domitian and father of Domitian's adopted heir, whose wife Domitilla was certainly a Christian, and who himself, having forfeited the Emperor's favour during the year of his consulship, was executed on a charge of 'atheism'. There are, however, at least as good reasons for holding the contrary view that Theophilus was a well-disposed non-Christian who had heard the slanderous and incriminating rumours which were circulating concerning the Christians, and that Luke determined to correct these false impressions by presenting the facts as he knew them. This view is in keeping with the formality of the dedication (so different from the normal greeting of Christian to Christian), and more particularly with the unquestionably apologetic character of the Lucan writings.

Luke 1⁵-2⁵²

The Promise of Deliverance

Luke is a Gentile writing history for Gentiles, but he has learned to see history through Hebrew eyes. To the Greeks history was, in the words of Aristotle, 'what Alcibiades did and had done to him' – a mere concatenation of events which could not be expected to lead anyone to ultimate truth. To the Hebrews history was 'the mighty acts of God', and God was Lord of history, whose character and purpose could be known only through his acts. 'I am the Lord your God, who brought you out of the land of Egypt' (Exod. 20²). Historical events were always seen against a background of faith, and history and theology tended to become inseparably intertwined. If the Hebrews had been given to dramatic production, they would have needed a stage with two levels, on which human events could be transacted in the foreground below, while their heavenly counterpart was represented above and behind. Something of this sort happens in the book of Job, where the prologue gives a heavenly setting to the intensely human wrestling with the mystery of iniquity which is the main concern of the book. Just so Luke opens his history with a series of stories which belong more to the poetry of worship than to the prose of the annalist, because the reader would miss the whole point of the events that follow, unless he saw them as the inbreaking of spiritual purpose and power upon the mundane affairs of men.

This method of writing history does not allow any easy answer to the modern historian's question: What actually happened? Luke certainly believed that he was dealing with real events, and it would be hypercriticism to doubt that behind these two chapters there is a substratum of the same sort of historical fact as we find described in a more down-to-earth manner in the remainder of the Gospel. Equally clearly Luke does not content himself with that which the television camera and microphone could have recorded. He would not have been a better historian had he done so. All history is an attempt to find pattern and meaning in a section of human experience, and every historian worthy of the name raises questions about man's ultimate destiny and the meaning of all history to which, as a historian, he can provide no answers. The answers belong to the realm of theology; and into this realm of metahistory Luke and the other evangelists are concerned to lead us. Whether we like it or not, we must be content to live with a measure of uncertainty as to where fact ends and interpretation begins. Of one thing, however, we may be sure – Luke was no simpleton. We do him a grave injustice if we suppose that, when he wrote in an elevated and imaginative style, he was naïve enough to take his own poetry with pedantic literalness.

In the earliest preaching of the primitive Church one of the most prominent themes was that the ministry, death, and resurrection of Christ had happened 'according to the scriptures' (1 Cor. 15$^{3-4}$), and that by his coming he had fulfilled all the promises and aspirations of the Old Testament. This theme is emphatically stated at the end of Luke's Gospel, where we find the risen Christ interpreting to his disciples *in all the scriptures the things concerning himself* (24$^{27, 44}$). It is also the dominant note of the first two chapters. These chapters are prophetic not merely because they contain predictions of the births of John and Jesus and of the divine act of deliverance of which John was to be the herald and Jesus the mediator, but also because they epitomize the spirit of expectancy which pervades the whole of the Old Testament. Here in a few picturesque episodes we are reminded of the prophet's faith in the divine control of history, of the priest's daily yearning for the nearer presence of God, of the Nazarite's dedication to utter purity, of the hopes for a kingdom of justice and peace that had collected around the name of David, and of the patient loyalty of humble folk who were waiting for the redemption of Israel. By an allusive use of Old Testament language Luke makes us aware, behind Zechariah and Elizabeth, Joseph and Mary, Simeon and Anna, of a host of Old Testament figures who lived by faith in God's promises and died without seeing the fulfilment of them.

How much of the Jewish character of these stories is due to Luke's Judean source, and how much to his own intimate knowledge of the Greek Old Testament, it is hard to estimate. But, one way or another, he has exquisitely recaptured the atmosphere of Jewish religion at its best, with all the richness of its piety, but with the limitations of its outlook as well. The messianic hope, so beautifully expressed in the Magnificat and the Benedictus, is still the hope of the old Israel, not yet illuminated and transfigured by the new light of the gospel. It involves a confusion of Israel's political destiny with her religious vocation, and a national self-concern from which Jesus had to dissociate himself before he could accept the role of Messiah.

48

⁵*In the days of Herod, king of Judea, there was a priest named Zechariah,ᵃ of the division of Abijah; and he had a wife of the daughters of Aaron, and her name was Elizabeth. ⁶And they were both righteous before God, walking in all the commandments and ordinances of the Lord blameless. ⁷But they had no child, because Elizabeth was barren, and both were advanced in years.*

⁸*Now while he was serving as priest before God when his division was on duty, ⁹according to the custom of the priesthood, it fell to him by lot to enter the temple of the Lord and burn incense. ¹⁰And the whole multitude of the people were praying outside at the hour of incense. ¹¹And there appeared to him an angel of the Lord standing on the right side of the altar of incense. ¹²And Zechariah was troubled when he saw him, and fear fell upon him. ¹³But the angel said to him, 'Do not be afraid, Zechariah, for your prayer is heard, and your wife Elizabeth will bear you a son, and you shall call his name John.*

¹⁴*'And you will have joy and gladness,*
and many will rejoice at his birth;
¹⁵*for he will be great before the Lord,*
and he shall drink no wine nor strong drink,
and he will be filled with the Holy Spirit,
even from his mother's womb.
¹⁶*And he will turn many of the Sons of Israel to the Lord their God,*
¹⁷*and he will go before him in the spirit and power of Elijah,*
to turn the hearts of the fathers to the children,
and the disobedient to the wisdom of the just,
to make ready for the Lord a people prepared.'

¹⁸*And Zechariah said to the angel, 'How shall I know this? For I am an old man, and my wife is advanced in years.' ¹⁹And the angel answered him, 'I am Gabriel, who stand in the presence of God; and I was sent to speak to you, and to bring you this good news. ²⁰And behold, you will be silent and unable to speak until the day that these things come to pass, because you did not believe my words, which will be fulfilled in their time.' ²¹And the people were waiting for Zechariah, and they wondered at his delay in the temple.*

²²And when he came out, he could not speak to them, and they perceived that he had seen a vision in the temple; and he made signs to them and remained dumb. ²³And when his time of service was ended, he went to his home.

²⁴After these days his wife Elizabeth conceived, and for five months she hid herself, saying, ²⁵'Thus the Lord has done to me in the days when he looked on me, to take away my reproach among men.'

a Greek *Zacharias*

The Old Testament contains many promises of the blessings that God purposes one day to pour upon Israel, but the sovereign blessing, which comprehends all the others, is that God himself will come among his people in all his chastening, cleansing, redeeming, and sanctifying power. In one sense, of course, Israel believed that God was always in their midst, but this faith was constantly assailed by the unpalatable fact that evil seemed more active and effective than the power of God. Just as Israel believed that God was eternally King and yet still prayed for the coming of his kingdom, so they believed in his presence and yet looked forward to his coming; and the temple had become the symbol both of the presence they enjoyed and of the fuller presence they expected. One of the latest prophecies to be added to the canon of scripture promised that *the Lord whom you seek will suddenly come to his temple* and that before his coming Elijah would return to inaugurate a great repentance (Mal. 3¹, 4⁵⁻⁶). It was appropriate, then, that the temple worship should provide the setting for the opening of the gospel story, as it does also for its close.

All male descendants of Aaron were priests, entitled to officiate at the temple sacrifices. They were divided into twenty-four groups, each of which served twice a year for a week at a time. There were so many priests in each division that the duties for each morning and evening sacrifice were assigned by lot. Any sincere priest would look forward to his term of service as a great privilege, and would await the drawing of lots with a thrill of anticipation. The most coveted task was *to enter the temple . . . and burn incense,* for the rising smoke was the symbol of the congregation's prayers rising to God; and, having represented the worshippers in their approach to God, the priest was expected to emerge from the sanctuary and pronounce God's blessing upon them. No priest was allowed to perform this function more than once, and many a priest never had the opportunity. It was therefore the greatest day in Zechariah's life when, his mind filled with the traditions and aspirations of his people, he entered the temple. Yet even over this day a shadow was cast by his personal tragedy; for among the Jews to have no child was regarded not merely as a sorrow but as a reproach. The prayers which he offered on behalf of the congregation were mingled with a prayer about his own private grief and, with his faculty of perception thus sharpened both by excitement and by sorrow, he received a religious experience which gave an answer at once to his individual and to his national longings. He and Elizabeth were to have a son, and a son who would be a joy to others besides themselves. Without taking upon himself the full Nazarite vow (Num. 6$^{1-8}$), he was to be utterly dedicated to God's service, for he would be the promised herald and would play the part of Elijah in preparing a people for the coming of God.

The message came to him through the angel Gabriel. It is inevitable that our religious experiences clothe themselves in garments provided by our habitual cast of thought. All those who have had any vivid sense of God's presence have wanted to speak of it in terms of seeing and hearing, though well aware that God himself can be neither heard nor seen. In early times the Israelites overcame this difficulty by speaking of God's presence as his 'angel' (Gen. 22^{11}; Exod. 23^{20}; cf. Isa. 63^9), and this reverential manner of speech later developed into a belief that God communicates with men through a host of messengers, among whom Gabriel was especially the angel of revelation.

Like many others after him, Zechariah found the good news too good for his credence, and he showed his unbelief by asking for proof. It was a Jewish failing to be always asking for signs (11^{29}; cf. 1 Cor. 1^{22}), i.e. for certainty which leaves no room for doubt and incidentally no room for faith. The quest for infallibility is always an illegitimate one, for, as Gabriel here implies, any word that comes to us from God carries its own credentials, and true religion consists in being able to recognize and respond to the authentic and authoritative note. Zechariah's request is, however, answered by a punitive sign. Luke seems to have had a special interest in the physical repercussions of an uneasy conscience (cf. Acts 5^5, 13^{11}).

THE SON OF GOD

²⁶*In the sixth month the angel Gabriel was sent from God to a city of Galilee named Nazareth,* ²⁷*to a virgin betrothed to a man whose name was Joseph, of the house of David; and the virgin's name was Mary.* ²⁸*And he came to her and said, 'Hail, O favoured one, the Lord is with you!'*ᵃ ²⁹*But she was greatly troubled at the saying, and considered in her mind what sort of greeting this might be.* ³⁰*And the angel said to her, 'Do not be afraid, Mary, for you have found favour with God.* ³¹*And behold, you will conceive in your womb and bear a son, and you shall call his name Jesus.*

³²*'He will be great, and will be called the Son of the Most High; and the Lord God will give to him the throne of his father David,*

³³*and he will reign over the house of Jacob for ever; and of his kingdom there will be no end.'*

³⁴*And Mary said to the angel, 'How can this be, since I have no husband?'* ³⁵*And the angel said to her,*

*'The Holy Spirit will come upon you, and the power of the Most High will overshadow you; therefore the child to be born*ᵇ *will be called holy, the Son of God.*

³⁶*And behold, your kinswoman Elizabeth in her old age has also conceived a son; and this is the sixth month with her who was called barren.* ³⁷*For with God nothing will be impossible.'*

³⁸*And Mary said, 'Behold I am the handmaid of the Lord; let it be to me according to your word.' And the angel departed from her.*

a Other ancient authorities add *Blessed are you among women!*
b Other ancient authorities add *of you*

The child of Zechariah and Elizabeth was sent to prepare the way for the coming of God. But how was God to come? Luke's answer is that he came in the coming of his Son, that the whole life and ministry of Jesus was the promised coming or visitation of God (cf. 1⁶⁸, 7¹⁶, 19⁴⁴). But what does it mean to call Jesus the Son of God?

The Old Testament was familiar with the concept of the divine fatherhood. Israel had been declared to be God's first-born son (Exod. 4²², Hos. 11¹, Jer. 31²⁰), and, because the nation's life, character, and

destiny were summed up in its ruler, the Davidic king was the particular embodiment of this sonship (2 Sam. 7¹⁴, Ps. 2⁷). Since the
monarchy came to an end, Israel had been waiting for its restoration
under the Lord's Anointed, the Messiah, 'great David's greater Son',
who would in a special sense be called the Son of the Most High. But
this for Luke was only the starting point. As the Gospel proceeds, we
shall see Jesus taking this inherited notion and remodelling it in the
crucible of his own experience. He spoke of God as 'my Father' and
of himself as 'the Son', not to expound a doctrine or to claim a rank
but to express his own personal relationship to God, whom he knew
intimately as only a son can know a father. What Luke is here concerned to tell us is that Jesus entered upon this status of sonship at his
birth by a new creative act of that same Holy Spirit which at the
beginning had brooded over the waters of chaos. It is this new creation
which is the real miracle of Jesus' birth and the real theme of Gabriel's
annunciation and Mary's wondering awe; and the miraculous character of the event is not at all affected by the question whether Jesus
had one human parent or two.

Those who believe that the virgin birth was simple history must
hold that the story came ultimately from Mary herself. For those who
find this belief an unnecessary impediment to faith an alternative
theory of its origin has been put forward in the Introduction – that
the doctrine arose out of a misunderstanding when the story was
taken from its original Judean environment into the Greek world.
Whatever be the truth in this instance, there can be no doubt that
mistranslation has in another respect affected the history of this passage. The Latin Vulgate version of Gabriel's salutation to Mary –
'Hail Mary, full of grace' – has contributed to the veneration paid to
Mary by her devotees, on the ground that she is able to dispense to
others from the plenitude of grace which she in her own right pos-
sesses. The Greek, however, does not admit of any such interpretation.
Mary is addressed simply as the favoured one, the recipient of a
privilege, the beneficiary of God's sovereign and unconditioned
choice; and her answer – 'let it be to me according to your word' – is the
only response that anyone can properly make to the free and gracious
bestowal of God's favour, the response of humility, faith, and
obedience.

53

39*In those days Mary arose and went with haste into the hill country, to a city of Judah,* 40*and she entered the house of Zechariah and greeted Elizabeth.* 41*And when Elizabeth heard the greeting of Mary, the babe leaped in her womb; and Elizabeth was filled with the Holy Spirit* 42*and she exclaimed with a loud cry, 'Blessed are you among women, and blessed is the fruit of your womb!* 43*And why is this granted me, that the mother of my Lord should come to me?* 44*For behold, when the voice of your greeting came to my ears, the babe in my womb leaped for joy.* 45*And blessed is she who believed that there would be^a a fulfilment of what was spoken to her from the Lord.'* 46*And Mary said,*

> *'My soul magnifies the Lord,*
> 47*and my spirit rejoices in God my Saviour,*
> 48*for he has regarded the low estate of his handmaiden.*
>   *For behold, henceforth all generations will call me blessed;*
> 49*for he who is mighty has done great things for me,*
>   *and holy is his name.*
> 50*And his mercy is on those who fear him*
>   *from generation to generation.*
> 51*He has shown strength with his arm,*
>   *he has scattered the proud in the imagination of their hearts,*
> 52*he has put down the mighty from their thrones,*
>   *and exalted those of low degree;*
> 53*he has filled the hungry with good things,*
>   *and the rich he has sent empty away.*
> 54*He has helped his servant Israel,*
>   *in remembrance of his mercy,*
> 55*as he spoke to our fathers,*
>   *to Abraham and to his posterity for ever.'*

56*And Mary remained with her about three months, and returned to her home.*

a Or believed, for there will be

When Elizabeth and Mary met, the unborn herald leaped for joy to greet his unborn Lord. We cannot but remember that in later life

John was by no means certain that Jesus was 'the Coming One' whose way he had been sent to prepare (7^{18}). This is idealized history, in which Luke is describing not the actual historical relationship between the two men but the prenatal relationship which existed in the predestining purpose of God. We must exercise a similar caution with regard to the Beatitude of Mary. Our inclination is to agree with Elizabeth and call Mary the most blessed among women. But another woman who called Mary blessed met with a rebuke from Jesus (11^{27-28}), which is also a rebuke to all sentimentality. Mary was not blessed because of any special understanding that she had for the mission of her son; for she and the rest of her family understood him as little as John did (2^{50}; cf. Mark $3^{21, \ 31-35}$). Her blessedness consisted simply in this, that, having been chosen for special service and having received an amazing promise, she believed that there would be a fulfilment of what was spoken to her from the Lord.

Mary's song is called the Magnificat, and like the Benedictus and the Nunc Dimittis which follow gets its name from the first word of the Vulgate version. All three are a mosaic of Old Testament texts, and the Magnificat is based largely on the Song of Hannah in 1 Sam 2^{1-10}. As in many of the Old Testament psalms the psalmist passes quite naturally from his individual concerns to those of the nation for which he is spokesman, so here Mary sings of her own exaltation from lowliness to greatness as typical of the new order which is to open out for the whole people of God through the coming of her son. She uses the past tense (vv. 51-55; cf. v. 68), not to describe God's past care for the down-trodden, but because God has already taken decisive action in the promised sending of his Son, and she foresees as an accomplished fact the results that will follow in his mission. If the Magnificat had been preserved as a separate psalm outside of its present context, we might have taken it to be the manifesto of a political and economic revolution. For centuries the Jews had lived under foreign occupation and tyranny, which allowed nobody to grow rich and powerful except the collaborators. 'The poor' had become almost a technical term for the faithful adherents of the Law, who trusted to God alone for their ultimate deliverance and vindication. Jesus was to take up this hope for the reversal of human fortunes and rid it of its limitations of nationalism and self-righteousness, so that it could become the basis of a more profound revolution than

the Jews had ever bargained for; and Luke's Gospel more than any of
the others does justice to this aspect of his ministry.

៙

46

In one or two Old Latin manuscripts and in quotations of this passage
by Irenaeus (c. A.D. 180) the name of Elizabeth is found here in the place
of that of Mary. Some scholars have argued that the Magnificat would
sound more natural on the lips of Elizabeth, since she is the one who,
like Hannah, had been raised from the humiliation of childlessness; and
that v. 56 implies a change of subject. This reading has been particularly popular among those who have held the view that the whole
nativity cycle originated among the followers of John the Baptist and
was later adapted to Christian purposes. On the other hand, the proper
place in the story for a psalm of thanksgiving from Elizabeth would
have been after v. 25. In any case the manuscript evidence is over-
whelmingly in favour of the generally accepted reading.

I 57–80   THE BIRTH OF JOHN

*57Now the time came for Elizabeth to be delivered, and she gave birth to a
son. 58And her neighbours and kinsfolk heard that the Lord had shown great
mercy to her, and they rejoiced with her.*

*59And on the eighth day they came to circumcise the child; and they
would have named him Zechariah after his father, 60but his mother said,
'Not so; he shall be called John.' 61And they said to her, 'None of your
kindred is called by this name.' 62And they made signs to his father, in-
quiring what he would have him called.*

*63And he asked for a writing tablet, and wrote, 'His name is John.' And
they all marvelled. 64And immediately his mouth was opened and his
tongue loosed, and he spoke, blessing God. 65And fear came on all their
neighbours. And all these things were talked about through all the hill
country of Judea; 66and all who heard them laid them up in their hearts,
saying, 'What then will this child be?' For the hand of the Lord was with
him.*

*67And his father Zechariah was filled with the Holy Spirit, and prophe-
sied, saying,*

⁶⁸'*Blessed be the Lord God of Israel,*
for he has visited and redeemed his people,
⁶⁹*and has raised up a horn of salvation for us*
in the house of his servant David,
⁷⁰*as he spoke by the mouth of his holy prophets from of old,*
⁷¹*that we should be saved from our enemies,*
and from the hand of all who hate us;
⁷²*to perform the mercy promised to our fathers,*
and to remember his holy covenant,
⁷³*the oath which he swore to our father Abraham,* ⁷⁴*to grant us that we,*
being delivered from the hand of our enemies, might serve him without
fear,
⁷⁵*in holiness and righteousness before him all the days of our life.*
⁷⁶*And you, child, will be called the prophet of the Most High;*
for you will go before the Lord to prepare his ways,
⁷⁷*to give knowledge of salvation to his people*
in the forgiveness of their sins,
⁷⁸*through the tender mercy of our God,*
when the day shall dawn upon^a us from on high
⁷⁹*to give light to those who sit in darkness and in the shadow of death,*
to guide our feet into the way of peace.'
⁸⁰*And the child grew and became strong in spirit, and he was in the*
wilderness till the day of his manifestation to Israel.

a Or *whereby the dayspring will visit.* Other ancient authorities read
since the dayspring has visited

To the Jews a name was more than a label: it was closely related to
the character and nature of the bearer. So pious parents would choose
a name expressive of their own faith or of their hopes for their child.
John is a shortened form of Jehohanan, which means 'God's gracious
gift',* and the choice of this name could be understood as a grateful
acknowledgement of the unexpected goodness of God in the gift of
a son to ageing parents. But the neighbours rightly suspect that more
lies behind the name than this. Elizabeth's obstinate departure from
family tradition, followed by Zechariah's dramatic recovery from his
loss of speech and his confirmation of his wife's decision, indicates
that both are acting, without collusion, under divine guidance. But

* cf. John 1⁶: *There was a man sent from God, whose name was John.*

when God names a man he determines his character and destiny also (Gen. 17⁵, 32²⁸). This is why we are told that fear came on all, not the fear men feel in the presence of danger but the awe they experience at the approach of the supernatural.

Like Mary, Zechariah speaks of the coming redemption of Israel as an accomplished fact. *God ... has visited ... his people.* This word is used in the Old Testament of Samson visiting his wife (Jud. 15¹), of David going to see how his brothers are faring in the camp of Saul (1 Sam. 17¹⁸), and frequently of a captain inspecting his troops. When it is used of God, it connotes a personal intervention for the purpose of punishment or redemption. Its use here implies that God himself has come upon the scene, and the following verse shows that his visit consists in the sending of Jesus.

The second theme in Zechariah's hymn is fulfilment. God's new act has happened in accordance with the words of his holy prophets, the promises made to the fathers, the covenant concluded with Israel at Sinai, and the oath sworn to Abraham. Each clause in this fourfold proclamation carries us one step farther back into antiquity, to remind us that behind the continuity of Israel's history, now reaching its climax in the arrival of the Messiah, there lies the divine plan, to which God is everlastingly faithful in spite of the faithlessness and recalcitrance of his human agents. This plan is still conceived in political terms: Israel must attain independence from pagan rule in order to render to God a pure worship, free from pagan defilement. The coming reign of peace is to be a deliverance from all who hate us, without any suggestion that hatred might be swallowed up in reconciliation. The hymn closes, however, on a more definitely religious note, for the national salvation is to take the form of the forgiveness of their sins.

ᔰᔰ

65

This verse is usually taken as evidence that the nativity cycle was preserved in the tradition of the Judean churches.

69

The horn is a common Old Testament metaphor for strength, so that a horn of salvation really means 'a mighty Saviour'. God is so described in Psalm 18², and it is quite in keeping with Luke's theology to transfer the description to Jesus.

78

The text followed by the A.V. had a past tense in the second line of this verse, but the future tense has better manuscript support. The salvation which in v. 68 was described as a present fact is now represented as a promise still to be fulfilled. Literally translated the Greek runs: 'the sunrise from on high shall visit us' – apparently a rather uneasy metaphor to depict the dawning of the messianic age. The difficulty would be in part relieved if the psalm was originally compiled in Greek and the author had in mind those passages in the Septuagint where the Greek word here used for sunrise (*anatolê*) is employed as a rendering of the Hebrew word for 'Branch' and so as an almost technical term for the Messiah (Jer. 23⁵; Zec. 3⁸, 6¹²). But if this reference is intended, there is certainly also a play on the common meaning of the word.

80

The wilderness, where John is said to have spent his youth, was the traditional home of prophetic inspiration and the place where John was ultimately to make his prophetic début. In the light of recent discoveries at Qumran it is interesting to speculate whether John's period of sojourn in the wilderness may not have been spent in one of the ascetic communities in the neighbourhood of the Dead Sea.

2^{1-20} THE BIRTH OF JESUS

2 *In those days a decree went out from Caesar Augustus that all the world should be enrolled.* ²*This was the first enrolment, when Quirinius was governor of Syria.* ³*And all went to be enrolled, each to his own city.* ⁴*And Joseph also went up from Galilee, from the city of Nazareth, to Judea, to the city of David, which is called Bethlehem, because he was of the house and lineage of David,* ⁵*to be enrolled with Mary, his betrothed, who was with child.* ⁶*And while they were there, the time came for her to be delivered.* ⁷*And she gave birth to her first-born son and wrapped him in swaddling cloths, and laid him in a manger, because there was no place for them in the inn.*

⁸*And in that region there were shepherds out in the field, keeping watch over their flock by night.* ⁹*And an angel of the Lord appeared to them, and the glory of the Lord shone around them, and they were filled with fear.* ¹⁰*And*

*the angel said to them, 'Be not afraid; for behold, I bring you good news of a
great joy which will come to all the people;* ¹¹*for to you is born this day in
the city of David a Saviour, who is Christ the Lord.* ¹²*And this will be a
sign for you: you will find a babe wrapped in swaddling cloths and lying in
a manger.'* ¹³*And suddenly there was with the angel a multitude of the
heavenly host praising God and saying,*

¹⁴*'Glory to God in the highest,
    and on earth peace among men with whom he is pleased!*ᵃ

¹⁵*When the angels went away from them into heaven, the shepherds said
to one another, 'Let us go over to Bethlehem and see this thing that has
happened, which the Lord has made known to us.'*

¹⁶*And they went with haste, and found Mary and Joseph, and the babe
lying in a manger.* ¹⁷*And when they saw it they made known the saying
which had been told them concerning this child;* ¹⁸*and all who heard it
wondered at what the shepherds told them.* ¹⁹*But Mary kept all these things,
pondering them in her heart.* ²⁰*And the shepherds returned, glorifying and
praising God for all they had heard and seen, as it had been told them.*

a Other ancient authorities read *peace, goodwill among men*

Luke's exquisite nativity story is compounded of three ingredients,
prophecy, history, and symbolism, which are so thoroughly inter-
mingled that it is hardly possible to separate them. He does not claim
in so many words that any prophecy was fulfilled; but, just as the
prophecies of Mal. 3¹–4⁶ and Isa. 7¹⁴ underlie the messages of Gabriel
to Zechariah and Mary, so here many strands from Mic. 5²–⁵ are
woven into the fabric of the narrative. This prophecy tells how in the
town of Bethlehem a mother in travail is to give birth to a prince of
ancient lineage, who will be shepherd of the scattered flock of Israel,
standing in the glory of the Lord and extending his authority to the
ends of the earth, with a proclamation of peace.

The point in the story that especially captured Luke's fancy was not
just that Jesus was born in Bethlehem according to the old prediction,
but that this promise of God came true because of an enactment of the
Roman government. God was working his purpose out not only
through the hesitancy of Zechariah, the exuberance of Elizabeth, and
the quiet faith of Mary; Caesar Augustus too, like Cyrus in earlier
days (Isa. 45¹), had become the unwitting coadjutor of a salvation
which would one day encompass his whole empire. For the modern

historian the account of the census presents difficulties which are discussed in the Introduction, but there can be no question about its symbolic value for Luke.

Nor is this the only symbolism in the story. There was no room for the Saviour in the common guest-room of the inn, just as later the Son of man had no place to lay his head, the King of the Jews no throne but a cross. His first worshippers, the shepherds, despised by the orthodox because their occupation made them neglectful of religious observance (*Shek.*, VII, 4; *Baba K.*, VII, 7, 80a), are the forerunners of the multitude of humble folk who were to throng him in his public ministry. The angelic chorus anticipates the jubilation which rings throughout the gospel and especially the joy in heaven which Jesus declared to ensue upon the rescue of the lost sheep. And the wonder with which the shepherds' story was greeted prepares us for the deeper and more abiding wonder to come.

ישע

11

The new-born baby is proclaimed to be Saviour, Christ (Messiah), and Lord. Saviour was a title with a universal appeal. The Jews, with centuries of foreign rule behind them, including persecution and other subtle interferences with their ancestral faith, were looking for a king to save them from oppression, but also from the national sins for which God had delivered them into the hands of their enemies. But Gentile religion, too, was a quest for salvation. Some found their saviour in Isis, who undertook to emancipate them from the fatalistic dominion of the stars, others in Asclepius, the divine healer, others in the deified Emperor, who had freed the whole world from the menace of war and want and had established the *Pax Romana*. But these cults left the real hunger of men unsatisfied, and Luke knew that the promise of a Saviour would always command a hearing. As Messiah, Jesus would bring the hopes of Israel to fulfilment, as Lord he would summon the Gentile world to obedience and faith.

13–14

The heavenly host is an expression which in the Old Testament sometimes denotes the stars, sometimes the angelic courtiers around the throne of the heavenly King. Frequently the two meanings converge, for the Jews, like all other ancient peoples, believed that the stars were spiritual beings. According to the Book of Job (38[7]), when God laid the cornerstone of the earth,

> *. . . the morning stars sang together*
> *And all the sons of God shouted for joy. . . .*

So now the same chorus gathers to celebrate the new creation, in which God's full glory will be displayed by the accomplishment of his eternal purpose, and man's true peace realized by the establishment of God's kingdom. The promise of peace or welfare is to men with whom God is pleased – a phrase which remains obscure until it is caught up by the words which Jesus heard at his baptism (*Thou art my beloved Son; with thee I am well pleased* – 3^{22}) and by his prayer of thanksgiving ('*Yea, Father, for such was thy gracious pleasure*' – 10^{21}).

'Peace, goodwill toward men' (A.V.) is the reading of nearly all the Greek manuscripts – except the really important ones.

2^{21-39} THE LIGHT AND THE SHADOW

²¹*And at the end of eight days, when he was circumcised, he was called Jesus, the name given by the angel before he was conceived in the womb.*
²²*And when the time came for their purification according to the law of Moses, they brought him up to Jerusalem to present him to the Lord* ²³(*as it is written in the law of the Lord, 'Every male that opens the womb shall be called holy to the Lord'*) ²⁴*and to offer a sacrifice according to what is said in the law of the Lord, 'a pair of turtledoves, or two young pigeons'.*
²⁵*Now there was a man in Jerusalem, whose name was Simeon, and this man was righteous and devout, looking for the consolation of Israel, and the Holy Spirit was upon him.* ²⁶*And it had been revealed to him by the Holy Spirit that he should not see death before he had seen the Lord's Christ.*
²⁷*And inspired by the Spirit*ᵃ *he came into the temple; and when the parents brought in the child Jesus, to do for him according to the custom of the law,* ²⁸*he took him up in his arms and blessed God and said,*
²⁹'*Lord, now lettest thou thy servant depart in peace,*
according to thy word;
³⁰*for mine eyes have seen thy salvation*
³¹*which thou hast prepared in the presence of all peoples,*
³²*a light for revelation to the Gentiles,*
and for glory to thy people Israel.'
³³*And his father and his mother marvelled at what was said about him;*

³⁴*and Simeon blessed them and said to Mary his mother,*
  'Behold, this child is set for the fall and rising of many in Israel,
  and for a sign that is spoken against
  ³⁵*(and a sword will pierce through your own soul also),*
  that thoughts out of many hearts may be revealed.'
  ³⁶*And there was a prophetess Anna, the daughter of Phanuel, of the tribe of Asher; she was of a great age, having lived with her husband seven years from her virginity,* ³⁷*and as a widow till she was eighty-four. She did not depart from the temple, worshipping with fasting and prayer night and day.* ³⁸*And coming up at that very hour she gave thanks to God, and spoke of him to all that were looking for the redemption of Jerusalem.*
  ³⁹*And when they had performed everything according to the law of the Lord, they returned into Galilee, to their own city, Nazareth.*

  a Or in the Spirit

Luke can hardly have had a deep personal interest in the details of Jewish ceremonial, and it is therefore remarkable that he should mention no less than five times (vv. 22, 23, 24, 27, 39) that the observances were carried out according to the Law. Jesus, we are to understand, was brought up in the strictest traditions of Jewish devotion. But at once we are introduced to two people of like devotion, whose loyalty to the Law, so far from making them satisfied with its provisions, had kindled in them a flame of expectancy. Simeon was looking for the consolation of Israel; Anna and others like her were looking for the redemption of Jerusalem. The piety of the Old Testament, properly understood, produced men and women agog for the coming of the Gospel.

The consolation of Israel is a standard rabbinic description of the messianic age, which has its origin in the opening words of the prophecies of the Second Isaiah (Isa. 40-55), and it is from these prophecies that a large part of Simeon's song, the Nunc Dimittis, is drawn. Simeon has been assured that he will live to see this prophecy come true, and, with the arrival of the infant Jesus, he can die in peace. For here is the bringer of the promised salvation which is to open the eyes of the Gentiles to the truth of God and to lead Israel into the glory of her national destiny.

Up to this moment Simeon, like Mary and Zechariah, may well have imagined the future glory of Israel as liberation from her enemies and restoration to the grandeurs of David's reign. But now, with the Messiah before him, and with the prophetic afflatus upon him, he paints a darker picture. This Messiah will lead his people to no easy or superficial triumph. He will be the centre of storm and controversy, which will reveal the secret disposition of many hearts, and will incidentally bring piercing grief to his mother. *The fall and rising of many in Israel* has usually been interpreted as the fall of some and the rising of others, i.e. a process of self-judgement in which men determine the verdict to be passed on their lives by the response they make to the coming of the Messiah. But the natural interpretation of Simeon's words, and the one which is better in accord with the facts of Luke's story, is that through the ministry of this one man Jesus the *many in Israel* will fall before they can rise to the promised glory, will pass through the valley of humiliation before they can ascend into the hill of the Lord. For in the actual event it was not true that the coming of Jesus meant the fall of some and the rising of others. Even his best friends had to be humbled by failure, and then it was only because he had chosen to share their humiliation that they were able to rise at all. We have here a first intimation of the great theme that will unfold throughout the Gospel and finally be expounded by the risen Jesus: that the Messiah, because he comes to lead Israel to her glory, must tread with her the path of suffering.

ဢ

21–24
The Mosaic Law provided three ceremonies to follow on the birth of a male child (Lev. 12, Exod. 13¹², Num. 18¹⁶). The first was circumcision, which took place on the eighth day from birth and was usually the occasion for the giving of the child's name (Jesus is the Greek equivalent of the Hebrew Joshua which means 'the Lord is salvation'). Then, in the case of the firstborn, there was the rite of redemption by the payment of a five-shekel offering; this could be done any time after the first month. Finally, after forty days, there was the purification of the mother, who up till then was regarded as unclean and therefore disqualified from any form of public worship. The purification involved the sacrifice of a lamb and a turtledove or young pigeon, but the poor were allowed to substitute a second dove or pigeon for the lamb; and Joseph and Mary made the poor man's offering. Luke appears to have confused the second and third ceremonies.

37

It is not clear from the Greek whether we are to take eighty-four years as the length of Anna's life or of her widowhood.

⁴⁰*And the child grew and became strong, filled with wisdom; and the favour of God was upon him.*

⁴¹*Now his parents went to Jerusalem every year at the feast of the Passover.* ⁴²*And when he was twelve years old, they went up according to custom;* ⁴³*and when the feast was ended, as they were returning, the boy Jesus stayed behind in Jerusalem. His parents did not know it,*

⁴⁴*but supposing him to be in the company they went a day's journey, and they sought him among their kinsfolk and acquaintances;* ⁴⁵*and when they did not find him, they returned to Jerusalem, seeking him.*

⁴⁶*After three days they found him in the temple, sitting among the teachers, listening to them and asking them questions;* ⁴⁷*and all who heard him were amazed at his understanding and his answers.* ⁴⁸*And when they saw him they were astonished; and his mother said to him, 'Son, why have you treated us so? Behold, your father and I have been looking for you anxiously.'* ⁴⁹*And he said to them, 'How is it that you sought me? Did you not know that I must be in my Father's house?'* ⁵⁰*And they did not understand the saying which he spoke to them.* ⁵¹*And he went down with them and came to Nazareth, and was obedient to them; and his mother kept all these things in her heart.*

⁵²*And Jesus increased in wisdom and in stature,ᵃ and in favour with God and man.*

a Or *years*

Prophetic voices have spoken over the infant Jesus their messages of hope and foreboding, but he himself has yet to grow into awareness of that which God has in store for him. In the days of his maturity he was to display remarkable capacities of mind and spirit, but they came to him gradually, by the normal process of development, under the influence of home, school, and synagogue. His teaching reveals to us

E　　　　65

a mind deeply appreciative of nature, scripture, and the common life of ordinary folk; and all three must have made their impact on him during his formative years. Wherever he looked he saw that which spoke to him of God, and his growing understanding of God showed itself in a gracious and attractive personality.

To illustrate the thirty years of growth which led to the climax of his baptism, Luke records but one incident. At the age of twelve a Jewish boy became *bar mitzvah*, a son of the Law, able to accept for himself the responsibilities and obligations to which his parents had committed him by the rite of circumcision. For Jesus this occasion was celebrated by a family visit to Jerusalem for the Passover. When the seven-day festival was over, his parents started for home along with a caravan of other Galilean pilgrims, not realizing that Jesus was left behind. The great city had laid its charm upon him, and he was taking advantage of his opportunities to learn from the rabbis in the temple courts, so utterly engrossed in the exciting new world of intellectual adventure as to be oblivious to the consternation he was causing. To Mary's mild rebuke he replied in words of profound significance for our understanding of his later career. His parents should have known where to look for him – in his Father's house. This description of the temple betokens that the doctrine of the divine fatherhood, long a tenet of Israel's faith, had become for him an intimate personal experience. Besides becoming a *bar mitzvah* he had become intensely aware of being Son of God, and henceforth he was to live his life not merely under the Law but under the higher authority of his filial consciousness. Luke's Gospel is more than the story of what Jesus did and taught: it is also the story of what Jesus experienced. He was, as the Epistle to the Hebrews has it, 'the pioneer of our salvation', blazing a new trail for others to follow. It was his calling to explore to the uttermost what it means to call God 'Father'.

מצ

48
Throughout the birth and infancy narrative Joseph is consistently referred to as the father of Jesus. The reply of Jesus to his mother picks up the word, but should not be regarded as a repudiation of his earthly father.

Luke 3^1-4^{13}

Preparation for Service

A NEW CHAPTER IN WORLD HISTORY

3 *In the fifteenth year of the reign of Tiberius Caesar, Pontius Pilate being governor of Judea, and Herod being tetrarch of Galilee, and his brother Philip tetrarch of the region of Iturea and Trachonitis, and Lysanias tetrarch of Abilene, ²in the high-priesthood of Annas and Caiaphas, the word of God came to John the son of Zechariah in the wilderness; ³and he went into all the region about the Jordan, preaching a baptism of repentance for the forgiveness of sins. ⁴As it is written in the book of the words of Isaiah the prophet,*

'The voice of one crying in the wilderness:
Prepare the way of the Lord,
make his paths straight.
⁵Every valley shall be filled,
and every mountain and hill shall be brought low,
and the crooked shall be made straight,
and the rough ways shall be made smooth;
⁶and all flesh shall see the salvation of God.'

The Gospel which Luke has to proclaim is a gospel of world salvation. But he is writing for educated Romans, and he is well aware how hard it must be for them to believe that the ultimate truth about human destiny is to be sought in a member of a despised race, who was executed on a criminal charge at the order of a Roman governor in an outlying province of the empire. Somehow he must find the means of overcoming this initial handicap, and he starts his main narrative boldly by claiming that the events he is about to relate are a part of world history. Like Paul before Festus, he wishes to say to his readers, *'this was not done in a corner'* (Acts 26²⁶). Incidentally he has given us one of the few pieces of chronological information in the New Testament (see below).

In making John the beginning of his Gospel Luke is in line with the early preaching of the apostles (Acts 10³⁷), with Q, and with Mark.

John occupies this position partly because we need to know about him to understand the baptism of Jesus, but more particularly because the Gospel is not a biography of Jesus but the story of an act of God in which John has his own part to play. The word of God came to him, as it had come to other prophets, and this word is to be understood as more than a message from heaven; it is God's active power going out from him to achieve results in the world – 'He spoke and it was done' (Ps. 33⁹; cf. Isa. 55¹¹). The prophets believed that when God's word came to them it meant that God was about to act and was taking them into his confidence (Amos 3⁷). He was King and they were heralds, so that, when he spoke through them, his purpose was being let loose into the world. This was especially true of the symbolic acts in which they embodied God's message. When Jeremiah smashed his pitcher in the valley of Hinnom (Jer. 19), he could say, 'There goes Jerusalem!', because through him God had spoken his sentence of doom and the city was as good as in ruins. God always keeps his word. John's baptism was a symbolic act of this prophetic kind, the purpose of which was to convey to men not merely what God was saying to them but what he was already beginning to do with and for them.

There is good reason to believe that baptism was already in use among the Jews as a part of the ceremony by which a proselyte was incorporated into Israel, and that it symbolized the cleansing away of his Gentile defilement. But John gave to baptism a new meaning and a new urgency. When it is said that he preached baptism, we are not to understand that he delivered sermons on this theme; rather he proclaimed a baptism, much as a king at his accession might proclaim an amnesty. For God was about to establish his kingdom and had sent John to prepare for its coming. He required even Jews to submit to his baptism as an admission that by the defilement of sin they had forfeited their right to be called the people of God; for his baptism was the prophetic sign which carried with it the assurance of God's forgiveness to the penitent and of their incorporation into the new Israel. The baptism was, in fact, the first scene in the divine drama of redemption.

Characteristically Luke also gives us, in an Old Testament quotation, a hint of what the final scene is to be. All the evangelists identify John with the voice crying in the wilderness, but Luke alone completes the quotation with words which to him were a forecast of the world mission of the Church: all flesh shall see the salvation of God.

※

1

Luke's date has been interpreted in three different ways. (1) The Romans counted an emperor's reign from the day of his accession. Augustus died on 19 August A.D. 14, so that by the normal Roman reckoning the fifteenth year of Tiberius would run from 19 August A.D. 28 to 18 August A.D. 29. But this leaves too little time between the baptism of Jesus and the probable date of the crucifixion (7 April A.D. 30). (2) Augustus made Tiberius co-emperor in A.D. 11, and, if we count his reign from there, the fifteenth year would be A.D. 25–26. But there is no evidence from coinage that Tiberius ever dated his reign in this way. (3) There remains the Jewish system of reckoning, employed certainly by the historian Josephus (who was also writing for Romans) and probably here by Luke. A series of calendar reforms had left the Jews with two New Years (just as in England the calendar year and the financial year begin at different times). The ecclesiastical year, used for festivals and the reigns of Jewish kings, began on 1 Nisan (which fell in March or April); and the civil year, used for secular affairs, including the reigns of foreign kings, began six months later on 1 Tishri (see *Rosh Hashanah* 1, 1). Reigns were reckoned from the New Year preceding accession, so that by this system Tiberius began his fifteenth year on 1 Tishri A.D. 27.

1–2

When Herod the Great died in 4 B.C., his kingdom was divided among his three sons, Archelaus, Antipas, and Philip. In A.D. 6 Archelaus was deposed for misrule, and from that time on Judea was administered by Roman procurators, one of whom was Pontius Pilate (A.D. 26–36). Antipas, the Herod of the Gospels, ruled Galilee and Perea until A.D. 39, when he was deposed by Caligula. Philip ruled the territory to the north and east of the Sea of Galilee until his death in A.D. 34. Nothing is known of Lysanias, except that his name occurs in an inscription of this period. Strictly speaking, there was only one high-priest, but the Romans had frequently deposed one and appointed another. Annas (A.D. 6–15) had been succeeded by several members of his family, including his son-in-law, Caiaphas (A.D. 18–36), but still exercised unofficially much of his former authority.

^{7}*He said therefore to the multitudes that came out to be baptized by him,*
'You brood of vipers! Who warned you to flee from the wrath to come?
^{8}*Bear fruits that befit repentance, and do not begin to say to yourselves, "We*
have Abraham as our father"; for I tell you, God is able from these stones to
raise up children to Abraham. ^{9}*Even now the axe is laid to the root of the*
trees; every tree therefore that does not bear good fruit is cut down and thrown
into the fire.'

$^{10-11}$*And the multitudes asked him, 'What then shall we do?' And he*
answered them, 'He who has two coats, let him share with him who has
none; and he who has food, let him do likewise.' ^{12}*Tax collectors also came*
to be baptized, and said to him, 'Teacher, what shall we do?' ^{13}*And he said*
to them, 'Collect no more than is appointed you.'

^{14}*Soldiers also asked him, 'And we, what shall we do?' And he said to*
them, 'Rob no one by violence or by false accusation, and be content with
your wages.'

^{15}*As the people were in expectation, and all men questioned in their*
hearts concerning John, whether perhaps he were the Christ,

^{16}*John answered them all, 'I baptize you with water; but he who is*
mightier than I is coming, the thong of whose sandals I am not worthy to
untie; he will baptize you with the Holy Spirit and with fire. ^{17}*His*
winnowing fork is in his hand, to clear his threshing floor, and to gather the
wheat into his granary, but the chaff he will burn with unquenchable fire.'

^{18}*So, with many other exhortations, he preached good news to the people.*
^{19}*But Herod the tetrarch, who had been reproved by him for Herodias, his*
brother's wife, and for all the evil things that Herod had done, ^{20}*added this*
to them all, that he shut up John in prison.

Luke, in retrospect, might see in John the harbinger of a world-wide
salvation, but John's own vision of the future was one of world-wide
and imminent judgement. He saw the woodsman ready to raise his
axe for the first stroke, the farmer with winnowing shovel in hand
striding towards the threshing floor. A mightier than he was coming,
in whose service the most menial of household duties would be for
him a privilege. John was an austere man with a religion of high

moral earnestness, and he could not conceive of greatness except in terms of a severity excelling his own. The coming crisis would see the mighty overthrow of ancient wrong, the settling of accounts on the basis of strict justice. Before such a prospect the Jews must not claim preferential treatment on the grounds of their ancestry. Trees are judged not by their roots but by their fruits. With a play on words, which seems to have been a normal concomitant of prophetic inspiration (Amos 8^{1-2}, Jer. 1^{11-12}), John declared that God is able from the stones (*abnayya*) of the wilderness to raise up children (*benayya*) to Abraham. Behind their racial and religious arrogance, their smug confidence in the historic continuity of tradition, lay the fallacious assumption that a man could satisfy God by offering him the obedience of his fathers. The one escape from the coming wrath was John's baptism, and even this was effective only for those who proved the sincerity of their repentance by a genuine reform. All others were but snakes, hurrying in panic from a grass fire.

The religious leaders ignored John (7^{30}), but for others, including the most unlikely people, his preaching had an irresistible fascination. To each class he spelled out in simple terms the meaning of repentance. To ordinary, selfish folk, blind to the needs of others because of their preoccupation with security, to tax collectors whose trade was a form of licensed extortion, to soldiers accustomed to line their pockets by intimidation and blackmail, he gave the same injunction: renounce your besetting sin. When we compare such teaching with the profundity of the teaching of Jesus, we can see that John's passionate urgency was not matched by any penetrating analysis of man's moral problem.

> 'Here on this lowly ground,
> Teach me how to repent; for that's as good
> As if thou hadst seal'd my pardon, with thy blood.'

There were depths which John, for all his heroic stature, was unqualified to explore.

At least John was aware of his own limitations. His task was to create an immense tide of messianic expectation, and then to make way for the Messiah. His baptism with water was but a prelude to another baptism. It is, however, open to question whether John regarded this other baptism as a promise or a threat. According to

Mark, the coming baptism was to be *with the Holy Spirit* (Mark 1⁸); and, if this is what John had in mind, he was echoing the ancient prophecy that on his restored people God would bestow the gift of the Spirit (Ezek. 36²⁷, Isa. 44³, Joel 2²⁸). According to Q, the source Luke is here following, the baptism was to be with the Holy Spirit and with fire; and this may be taken either as a hendiadys – 'with the sacred flame of the Spirit' – or as a description of a dual baptism, the gracious gift for the penitent and the rigours of retribution for the obdurate. A third possibility is that what John really predicted was a baptism of fire (i.e. judgement), and that the versions given by Mark and Q are the result of reinterpretation by the Christian Church in the light of the experience of the apostles at Pentecost, when the Spirit was seen to descend in tongues of flame. The theory fits well with John's repeated emphasis on a fiery judgement, and with the fact that twelve of his disciples professed never to have heard of the Holy Spirit (Acts 19²); and a prediction of this kind seems to be reflected in a saying of Jesus in which his death is described as a fire that he has been sent to kindle and a baptism that he must undergo (12⁴⁹⁻⁵⁰).

Even if this third view is adopted, however, it must not be thought that John was a prophet of unrelieved gloom. This would be to do less than justice to his winnowing metaphor. The ancient method of winnowing was to toss shovelfuls of mixed grain and chaff into the air, so that the wind might blow away the chaff, while the grain fell back on the threshing floor. The primary purpose of the winnower was not to dispose of the chaff, but to gather the wheat into his granary. In the same way, the Messiah would come to gather to himself the new Israel over which he was to reign as King, and it is for this reason that Luke can describe even the fulminations of John as a preaching of good news.

The outspoken censor of public morals must expect to make powerful enemies. Herod Antipas, on a visit to Rome, had met Herodias, the wife of his half-brother Herod, who was being held there as hostage, and had persuaded her complaisant husband to divorce her so that she might be free to marry him. He himself was already married to the daughter of the king of Nabatea, and his divorce of her was later to involve him in a war with her father. On this subject, as on all others, John spoke his mind, and so found himself incarcerated in the fortress of Machaerus to the east of the Dead Sea. Josephus tells us that Herod was also alarmed at John's growing influence with the people (*Antiquities*, XVIII, 5, 1).

ᴁ

Luke tells here the story of John's imprisonment, not because it happened at this time (cf. Mark 6¹⁴⁻²⁹), but because he liked to round off one story before going on to the next. In exactly the same way, having mentioned Agabus' prophecy of famine, he goes on at once to tell how, some years later, in the reign of Claudius, the prophecy was fulfilled (Acts 11²⁷⁻³⁰). There is no question of Luke here deliberately altering Mark's order of events.

3²¹⁻³⁸   THE ANOINTING OF THE MESSIAH

²¹*Now when all the people were baptized, and when Jesus also had been baptized and was praying, the heaven was opened,* ²²*and the Holy Spirit descended upon him in bodily form, as a dove, and a voice came from heaven, 'Thou art my beloved Son;ᵃ with thee I am well pleased.'ᵇ*

²³*Jesus, when he began his ministry, was about thirty years of age, being the son (as was supposed) of Joseph, the son of Heli,* ²⁴*the son of Matthat, the son of Levi, the son of Melchi, the son of Jannai, the son of Joseph,* ²⁵*the son of Mattathias, the son of Amos, the son of Nahum, the son of Esli, the son of Naggai,* ²⁶*the son of Maath, the son of Mattathias, the son of Semein, the son of Josech, the son of Joda,*

²⁷*the son of Joanan, the son of Rhesa, the son of Zerubbabel, the son of Shealtiel,ᶜ the son of Neri,* ²⁸*the son of Melchi, the son of Addi, the son of Cosam, the son of Elmadam, the son of Er,* ²⁹*the son of Jesus, the son of Eliezer, the son of Jorim, the son of Matthat, the son of Levi,* ³⁰*the son of Symeon, the son of Judas, the son of Joseph, the son of Jonam, the son of Eliakim,* ³¹*the son of Melea, the son of Menna, the son of Mattatha, the son of Nathan, the son of David,*

³²*the son of Jesse, the son of Obed, the son of Boaz, the son of Sala, the son of Nahshon,* ³³*the son of Amminadab, the son of Admin, the son of Arni, the son of Hezron, the son of Perez, the son of Judah,*

³⁴*the son of Jacob, the son of Isaac, the son of Abraham, the son of Terah,*

the son of Nahor, ³⁵the son of Serug, the son of Reu, the son of Peleg, the son of Eber, the son of Shelah, ³⁶the son of Cainan, the son of Arphaxad, the son of Shem, the son of Noah, the son of Lamech, ³⁷the son of Methuselah, the son of Enoch, the son of Jared, the son of Mahalaleel, the son of Cainan, ³⁸the son of Enos, the son of Seth, the son of Adam, the son of God.

    a Or *my Son, my* (or *the*) *Beloved*
    b Other ancient authorities read *today I have begotten thee*
    c Greek *Salathiel*

John was a great man. But his greatest contribution to the kingdom of God was one of which he himself was quite unconscious: he excited to open flame the hidden fires in the soul of Jesus of Nazareth. The stories of the baptism and temptations must have been told to the disciples by Jesus himself. The pious ingenuity of the early Church could no more have created these stories than the parables of the Good Samaritan and the Prodigal Son. On this subject Luke has two pertinent editorial comments. Jesus was praying: the rending heaven, the descent of the dove, the voice, are all part of a religious experience which belonged to Jesus' life of private converse with God. But the Spirit descended in bodily form, i.e. not in hallucination or phantasy, but in real event, spiritual and private, but none the less objective.

Jesus also was baptized. Why? To be baptized was to ask God's forgiveness, and it is the uniform witness of the New Testament that Jesus had no sins of his own to confess (Acts 3¹⁴, 2 Cor. 5²¹, 1 Pet. 1¹⁹, Heb. 7²⁶, John 8⁴⁶). In his own teaching there is no suggestion that he ever experienced the alienation from God which is the most baleful consequence of sin. Yet his scathing attacks on empty formalism forbid us to believe that he would have undergone baptism unless the ceremony had held for him, as for others, a profound significance. The story of his baptism, brief as it is, gives us Jesus' own answer to this question.

The voice from heaven addressed Jesus in a composite quotation from scripture (Ps. 2⁷, Isa. 42¹). Psalm 2 proclaims the accession of the anointed king, who is to rule the nations with a rod of iron. Isa. 42¹⁻⁶ is the first of a series of prophecies about the Servant of the Lord, who has been chosen to carry true religion to the Gentiles and who, in achieving this mission, must suffer indignity, rejection, and death.

Thus the words which he heard must have meant to Jesus that he was being designated to both these offices, *anointed ... with the Holy Spirit and with power* (Acts 10³⁷; cf. Luke 4¹⁸), sent out to establish the reign of God, not with the iron sceptre but with patient and self-forgetful service. Remembering Luke's story of the boy Jesus, we cannot suppose that all this now flashed upon him as a new and startling revelation, that up to this moment it had never occurred to him that God had singled him out for a special vocation. The baptismal experience represented the end of a long development, of deepening appreciation of the divine fatherhood and his own filial responsibility, of growing insight into his mission and the world's need, of meditation on the meaning of the scriptures and their application to himself.

Jesus went to be baptized, then, not for private reasons, but as a man with a public calling. John had summoned all Israel to repentance, and with Israel Jesus too must go. He dwelt in the midst of a people with unclean lips and could not separate himself from them. Rather he must be fully identified with them in their movement towards God. If he was to lead them into God's kingdom, he himself must enter it by the only door open to them. He must be their representative before he could be their king. He must be *numbered with the transgressors* before he could see the fruit of the travail of his soul (Isa. 53¹¹⁻¹²). The words from heaven were more than a divine appointment: they were the divine approval of the course to which Jesus had committed himself in accepting baptism. To him who had chosen to identify himself with his people in their need and their expectation the ratifying voice declared, 'Yes! That is what it means to be my Son, to be my Anointed One, to be my Servant.'

At this point Luke appends a genealogy of Jesus, by which he provides a fourfold commentary on the story of the baptism. He shows that Jesus, declared to be Son of God, is no demigod from pagan mythology but a real man with a family tree. He substantiates Jesus' messianic claims by adducing evidence of his Davidic descent (cf. Rom. 1³, Mark 10⁴⁸, Acts 2³⁰). By tracing his ancestry back to Adam, he reminds his readers that Jesus was bound by ties of kinship not only to Israel but to humanity, and that his mission was ultimately to all mankind. By calling Adam son of God he makes a link between the baptism and God's purpose in creation. Man was designed for that close filial relationship to God which was exemplified in Jesus, and which Jesus was to share with those who became his disciples.

ΙΩΙ

22

In Codex Bezae and some Old Latin manuscripts the words of the heavenly voice have been assimilated to the text of Ps. 2⁷ (*today I have begotten thee*). This reading has the support of a number of the Church fathers, but the main weight of manuscript evidence is in favour of the commonly accepted text.

4^{I-I3}   THE TEMPTATION OF THE MESSIAH

4 *And Jesus, full of the Holy Spirit, returned from the Jordan, and was led by the Spirit ²for forty days in the wilderness, tempted by the devil. And he ate nothing in those days; and when they were ended, he was hungry. ³The devil said to him, 'If you are the Son of God, command this stone to become bread.' ⁴And Jesus answered him, 'It is written, "Man shall not live by bread alone."' ⁵And the devil took him up, and showed him all the kingdoms of the world in a moment of time, ⁶and said to him, 'To you I will give all this authority and their glory; for it has been delivered to me, and I give it to whom I will. ⁷If you, then, will worship me, it shall all be yours.' ⁸And Jesus answered him, 'It is written,*

"*You shall worship the Lord your God,*
   and him only shall you serve."'

⁹*And he took him to Jerusalem, and set him on the pinnacle of the temple, and said to him, 'If you are the Son of God, throw yourself down from here; ¹⁰for it is written,*

"*He will give his angels charge of you, to guard you,*"
¹¹*and*

"*On their hands they will bear you up,*
   lest you strike your foot against a stone."'

¹²*And Jesus answered him, 'It is said, "You shall not tempt the Lord your God."' ¹³And when the devil had ended every temptation, he departed from him until an opportune time.*

The temptations of Jesus are the sequel to his baptism. Conscious of a unique vocation and endowed with exceptional powers, he must set aside all unworthy interpretations of his recent experience. He has heard a voice saying, 'Thou art my Son'; now he hears another voice, 'If you are the Son of God . . .', and he must decide whether or not it comes from the same source. Three times he makes up his mind that the voice which prompts him to action is that of the devil.

For many modern readers the mention of the devil invests the story with an air of unreality and even of superstition. Let us grant that the devil is a mythological figure. But myth is not to be confused with legend or fairy-tale. Myth is a pictorial way of expressing truths which cannot be expressed so readily or so forcefully in any other way; and there are at least five such truths which are safeguarded by belief in a devil. (1) Evil is real and potent. It is not just the sum total of individual bad deeds, but a power which gets a grip on human life and society. (2) Evil is personal. The very distinction between good and evil can arise only where there is free choice to obey God or to rebel against him. (3) Evil is distorted good. In a world which God has created good, evil exists only by perverting the good gifts of God. The devil himself is a fallen angel. (4) Evil masquerades as good. The devil is the 'slanderer' who misleads men by telling them lies about God. (5) Evil is the enemy. The armchair sociologist may tell us that certain deplorable types of human behaviour are 'normal', because they occur regularly in his statistical surveys; but those who love the people concerned know better.

But can a good man really be exposed to temptation like the rest of us? The man who turns back at his garden gate knows nothing of the strength of the gale in comparison with the man who battles his way through to his destination; and he whose destination is on the mountain tops knows more than others. Even so, the good man who resists temptation knows more about its power than the weakling who submits to its first onset; and the saint knows most of all. It is unlikely that Jesus ever felt any temptation to do the things which are commonly regarded as immoral or antisocial. But that does not mean that his temptations were the less real or the less powerful. All temptation is to do what is attractive, and the subtlest and strongest temptation is to do what appears to be good. The strength of a temptation is in proportion to the attractiveness of the goal. A man of fervent and dedicated spirit, feeling himself called to liberate the oppressed and to establish the reign of justice and peace, would be open to three types of temptation: to allow the good to usurp the place of the best, to seek God's ends by means alien to God's character, and to force God's hand by taking short cuts to success. And these are the three temptations of Jesus.

Jesus was hungry: by experience he discovered what hunger can do to a man, forcing his attention ever to the immediate and material need and dulling his senses to all the higher claims of life; and he learned sympathy with the multitudes who lived on intimate terms with hunger. Yet did not God provide for his children? Was it not his will that they should be fed? Would it not be proper for the Messiah to give full rein to his compassion and devote himself to meeting this most clamant of all human needs? The Messiah was indeed expected to give bread from heaven, as Moses had done long ago (John 6^{30}); and to a nation accustomed to privation the most popular picture of the messianic age was a great Banquet (Isa. 25^{6-8}). It is good to feed the hungry, but for the Messiah, as for others, the good can be the enemy of the best. To give priority to man's physical needs is to strip him of his dignity and make him one with the beasts that perish.

Next, in ecstatic and imaginative vision, Jesus is caught up into the air (the matter-of-fact Matthew has him ascend a mountain) to see stretched out beneath him the kingdoms of the world which God has given him as his inheritance (Ps. 2^8). They are his by right, but how are they to become his in fact? Over all this territory imperial Caesar reigns. What could Jesus not achieve were he on Caesar's throne? How simple then would be his task of world-wide mission! Among the Jews there was a party known as the Zealots who expected the Messiah to be a conqueror who would lead them in a war of liberation, and there were scriptures which endorsed their view (Ps. 2^9, Zech. 12^{7-9}). Were they perhaps the practical men, the realists who would get results while the visionary was still dreaming his dreams? It is good to be realistic, but the greatest reality is God, and true realism is to believe that only God's purpose is worth striving for and only God's methods can achieve it. The devil claims that all worldly power has been delivered to him, and Jesus does not dispute his claim to be able to give it to whom he will; but he cannot receive this power at the devil's hands. He has come in the name of God to wrest it out of the devil's keeping (see 11^{14-23}). The paths of this world do not lead to the kingdom of God, and to pin one's faith to worldly wisdom or authority is to worship that which is not God. To worship God is to trust him and leave the results in his hands.

But how can men be made to recognize the efficacy of such faith? Still in the same spiritual exaltation Jesus imagines himself on the pinnacle of the Royal Porch of the Jerusalem temple, overlooking the sheer drop of 450 feet to the Kidron valley below. All things are possible to him who believes. If he were to cast himself from the pinnacle, could he not trust God to bring him safe to the ground and so to provide spectacular proof of the power of faith, which would compel men's assent? But to test God is the opposite of trusting him. He who asks for proof has not learnt the meaning of faith.

Each of these three temptations attacked Jesus not at a point of weakness but at his greatest strength – his compassion, his commitment, his faith. In each case he recognized that he was dealing not with God's will but with the wiles of the devil. Each of the devil's proposals he rebutted by a quotation from Deuteronomy, finding a parallel to his own experience in the trials of Israel in the wilderness (Deut. 8^3, 6^{13}, 6^{16}). Reminded of the divine authority with which he has been endowed, he replies by asserting his humanity: 'If you are the Son of God . . .'; 'It is written, "Man shall not live by bread alone."' He puts himself under the authority of scripture and so under the authority of God. His role is to worship and to serve – to be, in fact, the Servant of the Lord.

Luke tells us that the devil departed from Jesus for the time being. Jesus had won an initial victory, but these same temptations were to recur throughout his ministry. The insistent demands upon his compassion, the enthusiasm that would make him a national hero, the suspicion that required a sign from heaven – all this was to end only with the mocking cry, '*If you are the King of the Jews, save yourself!*' (23^{37}).

Luke 4^{14}-9^{50}

The Ministry in Galilee

¹⁴*And Jesus returned in the power of the Spirit into Galilee, and a report concerning him went out through all the surrounding country.*

¹⁵*And he taught in their synagogues, being glorified by all.*

¹⁶*And he came to Nazareth, where he had been brought up; and he went to the synagogue, as his custom was, on the sabbath day. And he stood up to read;* ¹⁷*and there was given to him the book of the prophet Isaiah. He opened the book and found the place where it was written,*

¹⁸*'The Spirit of the Lord is upon me,*

because he has anointed me to preach good news to the poor.

He has sent me to proclaim release to the captives

and recovering of sight to the blind,

to set at liberty those who are oppressed,

¹⁹*to proclaim the acceptable year of the Lord.'*

²⁰*And he closed the book, and gave it back to the attendant, and sat down; and the eyes of all in the synagogue were fixed on him.* ²¹*And he began to say to them, 'Today this scripture has been fulfilled in your hearing.'* ²²*And all spoke well of him, and wondered at the gracious words which proceeded out of his mouth; and they said, 'Is not this Joseph's son?'* ²³*And he said to them, 'Doubtless you will quote to me this proverb, "Physician, heal yourself; what we have heard you did at Capernaum, do here also in your own country."'*

²⁴*And he said, 'Truly, I say to you, no prophet is acceptable in his own country.* ²⁵*But in truth, I tell you, there were many widows in Israel in the days of Elijah, when the heaven was shut up three years and six months, when there came a great famine over all the land;*

²⁶*and Elijah was sent to none of them but only to Zarephath, in the land of Sidon, to a woman who was a widow.* ²⁷*And there were many lepers in Israel in the time of the prophet Elisha; and none of them was cleansed, but only Naaman the Syrian.'* ²⁸*When they heard this, all in the synagogue were filled with wrath.* ²⁹*And they rose up and put him out of the city, and led him to the brow of the hill on which their city was built, that they might throw him down headlong.*

³⁰*But passing through the midst of them he went away.*

Mark records the rejection of Jesus by the people of Nazareth almost
at the end of the first year of his ministry (Mark 6$^{1-6}$). Luke's account is
probably an independent version of the same incident (vv. 22b and 24
may have been added from Mark), and implies a previous ministry of
some duration in Capernaum. Nevertheless he places the incident at
the beginning of his story of the Galilean ministry, because it announces the pattern which the ministry is to follow, and for this
reason he has condensed into a brief compass events which may have
taken longer to develop. Having repudiated in his temptations the
various false conceptions of Messiahship current among the Jews,
Jesus publishes his commission to bring in God's year of Jubilee, is
greeted first with enthusiasm and then with doubt, and finally is
threatened with mob violence when he hints at the inclusion of the
Gentiles within God's purpose of grace. The rest of the Gospel is
simply the working out of this programme.

Jesus claims that the scripture has been fulfilled in their hearing.
They are listening to the promised preaching, the good news of which
the prophet spoke. He has not merely read the scripture: as King's
messenger he has turned it into a royal proclamation of amnesty and
release. He is the Servant of the Lord, sent to announce to Israel that
'Your God reigns' (Isa. 52^7); and that this kingly power of God is to
be exercised in pardon, healing, and liberation. Beyond all this the
reader of the Gospel is expected to recognize echoes of Jesus' baptismal
experience, which would be missed by the Nazareth congregation.

Jesus' announcement that the messianic age had dawned was
received at first with rapt attention and excited comment, but, when
the people began to realize that he had incidentally laid claim to a
central position for himself in the inauguration of God's reign,
admiration turned first to doubt, then to hostility. Their earthbound
eyes saw in him only the son of Joseph, and it did not occur to them
that he might also be Son of God. Jesus saw that behind their scepti-
cism lay injured pride. 'Physician, heal yourself' was a popular
proverb, akin to 'Charity begins at home'; but it had an apt reference to the present situation. The people of Nazareth felt that, if the
son of Joseph had anything to offer, his own home town should have
had the first benefit of it. But those who stand upon their rights and
insist on preferential treatment are not likely to appreciate one who
offers the chance to spend and be spent in the service of others and a

Gospel which leaves no room for privilege. The stories of Elijah and Elisha should, indeed, have taught them that with God charity begins wherever there is found human need to call it forth and faith to receive it, irrespective of class or race. In fact, however, the suggestion that Gentiles could be admitted to God's kingdom produced an outburst of nationalist fervour which would have ended in the death of Jesus had the crowd not been overawed by the sheer majesty of his commanding presence.

ഇരു

16

The synagogue was a place of worship and education and the centre of the Jewish religious life. It was controlled by a board of elders and had an attendant (*hazzan*), who combined the functions of janitor, beadle, and school-teacher. There was no ordained minister, and anyone of sufficient learning might be invited to take part in the services. The sabbath service began with the *Shema* (Deut. 6¹⁻⁹), and included prayers, *parashah* (a fixed reading from the law) and *haphtarah* (a free reading from the prophets), both read in Hebrew with a running translation into the vernacular, a sermon, delivered sitting, and the blessing. Thus when Jesus was invited to preach at Nazareth, he was able to choose for the *haphtarah* the passage of Isaiah that was to be the text of his sermon (Isa. 61¹⁻², 58⁶).

4³¹⁻⁴⁴ POPULARITY: (I) A DAY AT CAPERNAUM

³¹*And he went down to Capernaum, a city of Galilee. And he was teaching them on the sabbath;* ³²*and they were astonished at his teaching, for his word was with authority.* ³³*And in the synagogue there was a man who had the spirit of an unclean demon; and he cried out with a loud voice,* ³⁴'*Ah!ᵃ What have you to do with us, Jesus of Nazareth? Have you come to destroy us? I know who you are, the Holy One of God.'* ³⁵*But Jesus rebuked him, saying, 'Be silent, and come out of him!' And when the demon had thrown him down in the midst, he came out of him, having done him no harm.* ³⁶*And they were all amazed and said to one another, 'What is this word? For with authority and power he commands the unclean spirits, and they come out.'* ³⁷*And reports of him went out into every place in the surrounding region.*

38And he arose and left the synagogue, and entered Simon's house. Now Simon's mother-in-law was ill with a high fever, and they besought him for her. 39And he stood over her and rebuked the fever, and it left her; and immediately she rose and served them.

40Now when the sun was setting, all those who had any that were sick with various diseases brought them to him; and he laid his hands on every one of them and healed them. 41And demons also came out of many, crying, 'You are the Son of God!' But he rebuked them, and would not allow them to speak, because they knew that he was the Christ.

42And when it was day he departed and went into a lonely place. And the people sought him and came to him, and would have kept him from leaving them; 43but he said to them, 'I must preach the good news of the kingdom of God to the other cities also; for I was sent for this purpose.' 44And he was preaching in the synagogues of Judea.b

a Or *Let us alone*
b Other ancient authorities read *Galilee*

Nazareth was in the hills, 1,300 feet above the sea. From there Jesus went down to Capernaum (Tell Hûm), a trading city on the northwest shore of the Sea of Galilee, 682 feet below sea level. This was to be his headquarters for his Galilean ministry. At first the synagogues welcomed him as a preacher and the congregations were astonished at the authoritative way in which he taught. Other rabbis, trained in the regular schools, could cite long lists of learned authorities on the meaning of the sacred text, but here was one whose sole authority was his own intimate knowledge of the God in whose name he spoke. The same authority was seen in his treatment of the possessed.

Ancient opinion ascribed to demon possession any disease which involved loss of control – epilepsy, delirium, convulsions, nervous disorders, mental derangement – and which therefore suggested the presence of an invading power. As may be seen in the cases here described, the demons were popularly supposed to have preternatural knowledge. Modern medicine can provide other explanations for most of the symptoms, but this does not mean that demon possession can be dismissed as outmoded science. It was primarily not a medical but a religious diagnosis. To call a man possessed was to assert that his illness was an evil thing, a manifestation of the kingdom of evil which extended the tentacles of its power into every phase of human life, and from which men could be rescued only by the superior power of God. The exorcisms of Jesus were thus the preliminary skirmishes in the campaign to be waged by him on behalf of the kingdom of God against the kingdom of Satan. To Jesus all diseases were caused by Satan (cf. 13¹⁶), though not all by possession, so that with each of his cures he was driving further back the frontiers of Satan's dominion. There was always a danger, however, that the enthusiasm of the crowds would turn him into a mere miracle-worker and that they would fail to see his cures as a dramatic form of preaching the good news that the kingdom of God had arrived and that those who wished might enter it.

Here for the first time Luke mentions the kingdom of God, which was the main theme of Jesus' preaching. In one sense, of course, God is eternally King. The twin pillars of Israel's faith were that history had a purpose and that Israel was the agent of that purpose, that God was King of all creation and especially King of those who accepted his rule. But facts were constantly belying this faith: pagan nations maintained their despotic and immoral rule unchecked, and Israel herself failed to be the holy nation she had undertaken to be. The Jews therefore looked forward to the day when God would openly assume his royal power. Jesus could claim that this reign or kingdom had come in him, because through him God's power was working to overthrow all evil things and to redress all wrongs, and because this power could work perfectly only through such utter obedience as he was prepared to give.

The first two cures were performed on the sabbath. This was contrary to the Pharisaic interpretation of the Law, which allowed a doctor to work on the sabbath only when life was in danger. The crowds were more scrupulous than Jesus and waited until sunset when the sabbath ended, before taking advantage of his healing powers. The demons, with their preternatural knowledge, were not allowed to hail Jesus as Messiah, partly because he did not value such testimony, partly because he did not want popular enthusiasm to make him the leader of a national uprising.

ಙಙ

44

The reading 'Galilee' is a correction by a scribe who did not realize
that Luke regularly used 'Judea' for Palestine (cf. 1^5, 6^{17}, 7^{17}, 23^5, Acts
10^{37}).

5^{1-11} POPULARITY: (2) FISHERS OF MEN

*5 While the people pressed upon him to hear the word of God, he was
standing by the lake of Gennesaret. ²And he saw two boats by the lake; but
the fishermen had gone out of them and were washing their nets. ³Getting
into one of the boats, which was Simon's, he asked him to put out a little
from the land. And he sat down and taught the people from the boat. ⁴And
when he had ceased speaking, he said to Simon, 'Put out into the deep and
let down your nets for a catch.' ⁵And Simon answered, 'Master, we toiled
all night and took nothing! But at your word I will let down the nets.' ⁶And
when they had done this, they enclosed a great shoal of fish; and as their nets
were breaking, ⁷they beckoned to their partners in the other boat to come and
help them. And they came and filled both the boats, so that they began to
sink. ⁸But when Simon Peter saw it, he fell down at Jesus' knees, saying,
'Depart from me, for I am a sinful man, O Lord.' ⁹For he was astonished,
and all that were with him, at the catch of fish which they had taken; ¹⁰and
so also were James and John, sons of Zebedee, who were partners with
Simon. And Jesus said to Simon, 'Do not be afraid; henceforth you will be
catching men.' ¹¹And when they had brought their boats to land, they left
everything and followed him.*

The crowds pressed upon Jesus because of his words of authority and
his deeds of power. But there were some upon whom he made a
deeper and more permanent impression, who found in him something
transcendent, numinous, utterly compelling. The first to experience
this humbling and exhilarating awe was Simon. Sitting in his boat on
the Lake of Gennesaret (elsewhere called the Sea of Galilee or the Sea
of Tiberias), he listened to the teaching of Jesus and it won him heart
and soul. Common sense, reason, and fisherman's lore bade him go
home to bed; but Jesus said, 'Let down your nets', and he obeyed.

Whether Luke supposed the amazing catch of fish to involve control over nature or supernatural insight, who can say? The point of his story is Jesus' miraculous influence with dispirited men, wearied by a night of profitless toil. These were the men he needed as his disciples, men disciplined by labour and hardship, but with the impetuous loyalty to say, 'If you give the order, I will do it.' On Simon at least the impact he made was a profoundly moral one, resulting in a sense of sin. It was not the miracle that brought him to his knees but the grandeur of sheer goodness.

இஅ

This incident is in some respects similar to the one recorded in John 21, and it has been conjectured that the two accounts are variants of a single story, which came to Luke without any indication of its original setting. The differences, however, are far more striking than the similarities. This is part of the very complex problem of the relation between the third and fourth Gospels (see Introduction). One possibility is that two independent stories have in the course of oral transmission interacted on one another, as in the case of the two stories of the anointing of Jesus (Luke 7³⁶⁻³⁸; Mark 14³⁻⁹; John 12¹⁻⁸).

5^{12-16} POPULARITY: (3) THE UNTOUCHABLE

¹²*While he was in one of the cities, there came a man full of leprosy; and when he saw Jesus, he fell on his face and besought him, 'Lord, if you will, you can make me clean.' ¹³And he stretched out his hand, and touched him, saying, 'I will; be clean.' And immediately the leprosy left him. ¹⁴And he charged him to tell no one; but 'go and show yourself to the priest, and make an offering for your cleansing, as Moses commanded, for a proof to the people.'ᵃ*
¹⁵*But so much the more the report went abroad concerning him; and great multitudes gathered to hear and to be healed of their infirmities. ¹⁶But he withdrew to the wilderness and prayed.*

a Greek *to them*

Leprosy is a term which in the Bible covers a variety of skin diseases; but whatever the precise nature of his malady, the leper was an outcast – *he shall . . . cry, 'Unclean, unclean' . . . he shall dwell alone in a habitation outside the camp* (Lev. 13⁴⁵⁻⁴⁶). The distinction between clean and unclean may have had some connexion with primitive hygiene, but primarily it was a religious distinction. Israel had been called to be holy, and the Old Testament religion was based on the assumption that the way to be holy was to avoid defilement by contact with uncleanness, physical, ceremonial, or moral. Jesus believed that true holiness could not be contaminated by anything from outside (11³⁷⁻⁴⁰; cf. Mark 7¹⁵), and that to be holy was to be like God, merciful to the afflicted. He therefore did what no Jew would do – he touched the leper, and, instead of incurring uncleanness, made the man clean.

As in the case of the sabbath Law, so here Jesus had no compunction about disregarding regulations which interfered with his carrying out of God's commission.* But he did not encourage laxity in religious observance. Only a priest could officially declare the leper clean, and the cure was not complete until the outcast was formally received back into society. The need to carry out the proper rites thwarted Jesus' desire for secrecy, and the first phase of his ministry came to an end in an embarrassing popularity. He withdrew to the wilderness to avoid sensation-hunters, to recuperate his energies of body and spirit, and to pray. Prayer in the life of Jesus was never just a means to an end. What he did in the solitude was as much the work of God as what he did among the crowds.

5¹⁷⁻²⁶ CONFLICT: (I) THE FORGIVENESS OF SINS

¹⁷*On one of those days, as he was teaching, there were Pharisees and teachers of the law sitting by, who had come from every village of Galilee and Judea and from Jerusalem; and the power of the Lord was with him to heal.ᵃ* ¹⁸*And behold, men were bringing on a bed a man who was paralysed, and they sought to bring him in and lay him before Jesus,ᵇ* ¹⁹*but finding no way to bring him in, because of the crowd, they went up on the roof and let him*

* For further examples of Jesus' attitude to the Law see 6¹⁻¹¹, 10²⁵⁻³⁷, 11³⁷⁻⁵⁴, 13¹⁰⁻²¹, 16¹⁶.

down with his bed through the tiles into the midst before Jesus. ²⁰*And when he saw their faith he said, 'Man, your sins are forgiven you.'* ²¹*And the scribes and the Pharisees began to question, saying, 'Who is this that speaks blasphemies? Who can forgive sins but God only?'* ²²*When Jesus perceived their questionings, he answered them, 'Why do you question in your hearts?* ²³*Which is easier, to say, "Your sins are forgiven you," or to say, "Rise and walk?"* ²⁴*But that you may know that the Son of man has authority on earth to forgive sins'* – *he said to the man who was paralysed* – '*I say to you, rise, take up your bed and go home.'* ²⁵*And immediately he rose before them, and took up that on which he lay, and went home, glorifying God.* ²⁶*And amazement seized them all, and they glorified God and were filled with awe, saying, 'We have seen strange things today.'*

a Other ancient authorities read *was present to heal them*
b Greek *him*

The first opposition to Jesus came from the religious leaders. The Pharisees were a small but influential sect, numbering about six thousand, who took with desperate earnestness the duty of Israel to be the holy people of God. Their name means 'segregationists', probably because they endeavoured to separate themselves from contact with defilement of any kind; but they called themselves *Haberim* (associates), because they banded together in holy societies, called *Haburoth*. They made it their object to live a life covered in every aspect by the regulations of the Law of Moses. Each Commandment was elaborately defined, so as to show its application to every conceivable circumstance, and these elaborations were handed down from one generation to another in an oral tradition to which they accorded the same reverence as to the Law itself. To guard against sins of ignorance and omission they 'put a hedge about the Law', i.e. left a margin of safety, by going at all points a little further than the Law required. *Teachers of the law* is Luke's name for the men who are usually called scribes. They were the legal experts, who therefore had much in common with the Pharisaic sect to which many of them belonged. Because Judaism made no distinction between religious and civil law, they combined the functions of theologian and lawyer.

It is worth noting that Jesus pronounces the man's sins to be forgiven because of the faith of his friends. Interdependence and corporate solidarity, though somewhat foreign to modern individualism, are part of the stuff of biblical thought, and without them there could be no Gospel. The words of Jesus to the paralytic do not imply that all illness is caused by sin, but only that he has diagnosed this particular ailment as psychosomatic (i.e. a physical disease with a mental or emotional cause); and there is no gainsaying the logic of his argument that, where illness is caused by sin, a cure is proof of forgiveness. His critics are justified in their premise that only God can forgive sins, but not in their conclusion that a man who claims this divine prerogative is a blasphemer; for God may delegate his authority. Jesus declares that as Son of man he has this delegated authority, and proves his point by performing a cure.

The expression *Son of man* is used in Jewish literature in a variety of allied senses. In the prophecies of Ezekiel it means simply 'a human being', a man in his weakness and insignificance. In Psalm 8 it means man, weak and insignificant, but destined for authority second only to that of God. In Psalm 80 it denotes Israel, made strong out of weakness. In the visions of Daniel, after four beasts which symbolize successive despotic empires, comes *one like a son of man*, symbolizing 'the saints of the Most High', to whom God is about to entrust his judgement and his kingdom (Dan. $7^{13, 22}$). In the *Similitudes of Enoch* this representative figure becomes less of a symbol and more of an individual. In the Gospels the term occurs many times, always on the lips of Jesus. There are a few places where it is due to editorial insertion (e.g. Matt. 16^{13}), but in general there is adequate evidence that it was Jesus' own choice of title, perhaps a deliberately mysterious and ambiguous one.* It enabled him, without actually claiming to be Messiah, to indicate his essential unity with mankind, and above all with the weak and humble, and also his special function as predestined representative of the new Israel and bearer of God's judgement and kingdom. Even when he used it as a title, its strongly corporate overtones made it not merely a title, but an invitation to others to join him in the destiny he had accepted.† And when he

---

* For a different view see the commentary on St Mark in this series by D. E. Nineham.

† See T. W. Manson, *The Teaching of Jesus*, pp. 211–36; 'The Son of Man in Daniel, Enoch, and the Gospels', *Bulletin of the John Rylands Library*, XXXII (1950), pp. 171–93.

spoke of the glory of the Son of man he was predicting not so much his own personal victory as the triumph of the cause he served.

ᏬᏬ

19

Luke has taken the story of the paralytic from Mark and adapted it slightly for his Gentile readers. In Mark's version the house was a Palestinian house with a turf roof, in Luke's it is a Roman house with a tiled roof and a central opening.

5^{27-32} CONFLICT: (2) BAD COMPANY

27After this he went out, and saw a tax collector, named Levi, sitting at the tax office; and he said to him, 'Follow me.' 28And he left everything, and rose and followed him.

29And Levi made him a great feast in his house; and there was a large company of tax collectors and others sitting at table^a with them. 30And the Pharisees and their scribes murmured against his disciples, saying, 'Why do you eat and drink with tax collectors and sinners?' 31And Jesus answered them, 'Those who are well have no need of a physician, but those who are sick; 32I have not come to call the righteous, but sinners to repentance.'

a Greek reclining

Not all tax collectors were in the direct employ of Rome, for Antipas had been left some powers of taxation; and Levi and his friends were probably his underlings. But the stigma of the collaborator attached to the whole profession, inasmuch as all were in regular contact with Gentile officials and merchants. Moreover, the current method of collecting import and export duties, harbour and market dues, and other customs, left ample room for extortion. Tax collectors were banned from the synagogue and treated as the dregs of society, which indeed they often were since no respectable Jew would accept such employment. At the other end of the social scale were the Pharisees, who regarded as sinners all who did not adopt their own meticulous attitude to the Law. They avoided social contact with sinners, lest their own sanctity be sullied, and were especially careful not to eat with any who neglected the laws of cleanness and tithing. It was a serious threat to their *modus vivendi* that anyone as popular as Jesus should break down their carefully erected barriers by eating with the grossest of sinners. But Jesus had an answer for them which was the *reductio ad absurdum* of their whole position. They were insisting that the doctor associate only with healthy people, for fear that he should catch an infection. Sinners were not criminals to be placed under a legal penalty, but sick people to be healed. Salvation from the contagion of sin was not to be found in spiritual quarantine regulations but in carrying to those who needed it the healing power of God's forgiveness.

5³³⁻³⁹   CONFLICT: (3) FEASTING AND FASTING

³³*And they said to him, 'The disciples of John fast often and offer prayers, and so do the disciples of the Pharisees, but yours eat and drink.'* ³⁴*And Jesus said to them, 'Can you make wedding guests fast while the bridegroom is with them?* ³⁵*The days will come, when the bridegroom is taken away from them, and then they will fast in those days.'* ³⁶*He told them a parable also: 'No one tears a piece from a new garment and puts it upon an old garment; if he does, he will tear the new, and the pieces from the new will not match the old.* ³⁷*And no one puts new wine into old wineskins; if he does, the new wine will burst the skins and it will be spilled, and the skins will be destroyed.* ³⁸*But new wine must be put into fresh wineskins.*

³⁹*And no one after drinking old wine desires new; for he says, "The old is good." 'ᵃ*

a Other ancient authorities read *better*

From early times fasting was a normal expression of sorrow, contrition, or need. The later Judaism had systematized this practice and had turned it into a religious exercise to be valued for its own merit. Besides observing the regular public fasts, the Pharisees fasted voluntarily twice a week (18¹²). The disciples of John had more reason than others to fast, for their master was in prison and his vision of imminent judgement remained unfulfilled. Those who impose upon themselves a régime of self-discipline are always in danger of resenting, envying, or despising the liberty of others. The way of life which Jesus exemplified and taught was spontaneous, natural, and gay; he shocked 'religious' people. But he was able to justify his conduct by a simple analogy.

Wedding celebrations in Palestine usually lasted a week. The groom and bride were king and queen and ruled over the festivities of their guests. By common consent all members of the wedding party were exempt from other obligations like fasting, which would interfere with the general merriment. There would be ample time for such sombre duties when the week was over. Jesus claims for his disciples a similar exemption, on the ground that they are guests at the greater banquet of the messianic age.

The early Church had a way of reading into the parables of Jesus, meanings which he did not intend, by treating them as allegories. A parable is a picture from ordinary life, which illustrates a spiritual lesson, and the shorter parables of Jesus have only a single point of comparison. An allegory is a story so constructed that every detail has a meaning. In the present parable the one point was: if fasting is out of place during a wedding, how much more out of place is it when the kingdom of God has arrived! In v. 35 allegorical interpretation has been at work, identifying the bridegroom with Jesus, so as to create a prediction of his death and a validation of fasting in the Church (cf. *Didache*, v i i i, i), both of which are out of keeping with the original purpose of the parable, since the joyous celebration of the kingdom had come to stay.

That parables of Jesus sometimes suffered in the course of transmission may be seen from the next example (cf. Matt. 22¹⁻¹⁰). Mark's original version begins, '*No one sews a piece of unshrunk cloth on an old garment.*' This was a lesson every housewife had to learn; but no woman in her senses would do what Luke suggests – tear a piece from a new garment to patch an old one. The parables of Jesus were always true to life, and Luke has destroyed the realism in the interests of allegory. The double parable of the patch and the wineskins was a warning against compromise between the old order of Judaism and the new order of the kingdom. The old cloak could not be patched with new cloth, the new ferment could not be contained within the old institutions. To his Marcan material Luke has added from another source the parable of the old and new wine, which was a warning against the dangers of tradition: those who are satisfied with the old ways are not likely to be enthusiastic supporters of revolutionary change.

CONFLICT: (4) THE SABBATH

6 *On a sabbath,ᵃ while he was going through the grainfields, his disciples plucked and ate some ears of grain, rubbing them in their hands. ²But some of the Pharisees said, 'Why are you doing what is not lawful to do on the sabbath?' ³And Jesus answered, 'Have you not read what David did when he was hungry, he and those who were with him: ⁴how he entered the house of God, and took and ate the bread of the Presence, which it is not lawful for any but the priests to eat, and also gave it to those with him?' ⁵And he said to them, 'The Son of man is Lord of the sabbath.'*

⁶On another sabbath, when he entered the synagogue and taught, a man was there whose right hand was withered. ⁷And the scribes and the Pharisees watched him, to see whether he would heal on the sabbath, so that they might find an accusation against him. ⁸But he knew their thoughts, and he said to the man who had the withered hand, 'Come and stand here.' And he rose and stood there. ⁹And Jesus said to them, 'I ask you, is it lawful on the sabbath to do good or to do harm, to save life or to destroy it?' ¹⁰And he looked around on them all, and said to him, 'Stretch out your hand.' And he did so, and his hand was restored. ¹¹But they were filled with fury and discussed with one another what they might do to Jesus.

a Other ancient authorities read *On the second first sabbath* (on the second sabbath after the first)

Of all the Jewish institutions the sabbath was the most important for the survival of Judaism in a predominantly Gentile world. Other requirements of the law could be performed – or omitted – in private, but the sabbath commandment obliged the Jew week by week to make a public profession of faith by abstaining from work. The rabbis had enumerated thirty-nine activities which were to be considered work within the intention of the Law, so that everyone should know exactly how far his obligation extended. Any threat to the sabbath was bound to evoke strenuous opposition, yet Jesus not only broke these regulations but often seems to have gone out of his way to break them.

The disciples were accused of breaking the sabbath by reaping and threshing. Jesus defended them by referring to the story of 1 Samuel 21$^{1-6}$. The bread of the Presence consisted of twelve loaves placed in the Temple every sabbath on a special table. Only the priests were allowed to eat this consecrated bread (Lev. 24^9). David's action therefore provided good scriptural precedent for Jesus' argument that need overrides the outward forms of religion. At their best the Pharisees would have admitted this, but they could hardly have been prepared for Jesus' next statement that the Son of man is Lord of the sabbath. Here he is going behind the scribal regulations, behind the Law itself, to ask what was the purpose for which God instituted the sabbath, and to claim that as Son of man, the agent of God's authority and purpose, he is the one true arbiter of the proper use of the sabbath.

In the second incident Jesus, sensing a trap, took the initiative with a question which cut the ground from under his adversaries' feet. Is it lawful on the sabbath to do good or to do harm? Which is keeping the spirit of the sabbath better, he with his deed of mercy or they with their malicious designs? The question needs no answer: it is always right to do good, and what better day than the sabbath could there be for doing the works of God!

In all four of these controversies there is a common factor. The Pharisees recognized in Jesus a threat to all they held most dear. What they did not recognize was that in him the promised kingdom of God had arrived, bringing pardon to the sinful, healing to the spiritually sick, joy in the place of mourning, and blessedness of which the sabbath rest had been but a shadowy foretaste. If their zeal for the Law had been prompted by any genuine understanding of God's purpose, they would have seen in Jesus one more dedicated to that purpose than themselves. But they loved their system more than they loved God. They were wrong to think that Jesus intended to break or abrogate the Law; he was the servant of a higher loyalty which, in transcending the letter of the Law, fulfilled its intention (Matt. 5$^{16-20}$, Luke 16^{16}).

¹²*In these days he went out into the hills to pray; and all night he continued in prayer to God.* ¹³*And when it was day, he called his disciples, and chose from them twelve, whom he named apostles;* ¹⁴*Simon, whom he named Peter, and Andrew his brother, and James and John, and Philip, and Bartholomew,* ¹⁵*and Matthew, and Thomas, and James the son of Alphaeus, and Simon who was called the Zealot,* ¹⁶*and Judas the son* ᵃ *of James, and Judas Iscariot, who became a traitor.*

¹⁷*And he came down with them and stood on a level place, with a great crowd of his disciples and a great multitude of people from all Judea and Jerusalem and the seacoast of Tyre and Sidon, who came to hear him and to be healed of their diseases;* ¹⁸*and those who were troubled with unclean spirits were cured.* ¹⁹*And all the crowd sought to touch him, for power came forth from him and healed them all.*

  a Or *brother*

Jesus must now decide how to act in view of the mounting hostility of the Pharisees, and Luke, characteristically, tells us that he faced the decision in a night of prayer. He emerged from solitude with his path clear and his resolution strong. The next step is to inaugurate the new Israel – for the appointment of the twelve is just that. They are to be twelve to correspond to the twelve tribes of the old Israel (22³⁰). Luke is guilty of an anachronism in calling them apostles. Mark does not use this word except when they are sent out on their preaching mission, and then he uses it only in a non-technical sense, meaning 'missionaries'. In the early Church there were more apostles than twelve (1 Cor. 15⁷, Gal. 1¹, ¹⁹, Acts 14⁴, Rom. 16⁷), and it was only towards the end of the first century that the name was restricted to the twelve (Rev. 21¹⁴). Whatever other functions these men may later have acquired, their present call was to be twelve, to be the symbolic nucleus of the new people of God.

Jesus' choice fell on ordinary men. With one or two exceptions we hear little more of them as individuals. In later centuries legends grew up, purporting to preserve their subsequent histories, but when the Gospels were written there was not even complete certainty about their identity. Judas the son of James does not appear in the lists of Mark and Matthew, where his place is taken by Thaddaeus-Lebbaeus. To the early Church the number was more important than the names.

6^{20-49} The New Israel: (2) The Inaugural Sermon

Luke's sermon is the counterpart of Matthew's Sermon on the Mount. Both begin with the Beatitudes and end with the parables of the Two Houses, and almost the whole of Luke's material is found also in Matthew. The common material was drawn from Q. But Matthew has combined the Q sermon with excerpts from other parts of Q and also with other material drawn from a different source, perhaps even a second sermon, which also began with Beatitudes and overlapped at other points with Q. Luke has reproduced the sermon as it stood in Q. There is, however, some question whether the Woes should be ascribed to Jesus. They interrupt the address to the disciples, so that an awkward resumption is necessary in v. 27, and they are in any case only an inverted form of the Beatitudes which might have been added by the early Church by way of commentary.

6^{20-26} THE BEATITUDES

²⁰*And he lifted up his eyes on his disciples and said:*
    'Blessed are you poor, for yours is the kingdom of God.
    ²¹*'Blessed are you that hunger now, for you shall be satisfied.*
    'Blessed are you that weep now, for you shall laugh.
    ²²*'Blessed are you when men hate you, and when they exclude you and*
    revile you, and cast out your name as evil, on account of the Son of man!
    ²³*'Rejoice in that day, and leap for joy, for behold, your reward is great*
    in heaven; for so their fathers did to the prophets.
    ²⁴*'But woe to you that are rich, for you have received your consolation.*
    ²⁵*'Woe to you that are full now, for you shall hunger.*
    'Woe to you that laugh now, for you shall mourn and weep.

²⁶'*Woe to you, when all men speak well of you, for so their fathers did to the false prophets.*'

The sermon is a description of the life of the new Israel, which is also life in the kingdom of God. In its fullness the kingdom belongs to the End, when God's purposes are complete, and so throughout the Beatitudes there runs a contrast between the conditions of the present and the conditions of the future. But the good news which Jesus proclaimed was that the kingdom was already breaking in upon the present, so that men could here and now begin to enter into the ultimate blessedness. Thus the Beatitudes were not merely a promise but an invitation.

The first characteristic of the new life is a complete reversal of the world's values. What is the recipe for happiness? 'Why,' says Mr Worldly Wiseman, 'prosperity, comfort, peace of mind, and popularity.' Jesus pronounces his blessing on those who have failed to find their satisfaction in these worldly goals. But his words must not be misunderstood. They are not a general benediction upon misfortune, as though poverty, hunger, grief, and public resentment were in themselves guarantees of eternal bliss. It is only in the presence of a magnificent banquet that the hungry man is more blessed than the well-fed; and it is because Jesus has proclaimed the presence of the kingdom that the advantage belongs to those who approach it with the greatest need and capacity for its inexhaustible riches, undistracted by the spurious consolations of the world.

Matthew has tried to make this point clear by spiritualizing the Beatitudes. In his version the promises are not to the poor and hungry but to those who have a sense of spiritual need and a hunger for the vindication of the right cause; but this shift of emphasis leads to another possible source of misunderstanding. We might suppose from the Matthean Beatitudes that Jesus was setting an ethical standard for entry into the kingdom, and that men must earn their blessedness by being humble, merciful, and pure of heart. Luke's simpler version guards against this misinterpretation. The one thing that Jesus requires in his disciples is an emptiness that God can fill, a discontent with the world which will lead them to the wealth, the satisfaction, the consolation, the comradeship of the kingdom.

The great reward exists in heaven, ready to be enjoyed. It is not mercenary to expect a reward, for there is a reward which is the enjoyment of the results of our conduct. One boy does his piano practice because his parents bribe him, another because he wants to enjoy music. One man makes friends because they are useful to him in business, another because he enjoys friendship. The joys of the kingdom of God are the result of being a certain sort of person, one who will enjoy being for ever with God because he has already found in God his exceeding great reward.

²⁷'But I say to you that hear. Love your enemies, do good to those who hate you, ²⁸bless those who curse you, pray for those who abuse you. ²⁹To him who strikes you on the cheek, offer the other also; and from him who takes away your cloak do not withhold your coat as well. ³⁰Give to every one who begs from you; and of him who takes away your goods, do not ask them again. ³¹And as you wish that men would do to you, do so to them.

³²'If you love those who love you, what credit is that to you? For even sinners love those who love them. ³³And if you do good to those who do good to you, what credit is that to you? For even sinners do the same. ³⁴And if you lend to those from whom you hope to receive, what credit is that to you? Even sinners lend to sinners, to receive as much again. ³⁵But love your enemies, and do good, and lend, expecting nothing in return;ᵃ and your reward will be great, and you will be sons of the Most High; for he is kind to the ungrateful and the selfish. ³⁶Be merciful, even as your Father is merciful.

³⁷'Judge not, and you will not be judged; condemn not, and you will not be condemned; forgive, and you will be forgiven; ³⁸give, and it will be given to you; good measure, pressed down, shaken together, running over, will be put into your lap. For the measure you give will be the measure you get back.'

a Other ancient authorities read despairing of no man

The second characteristic of the new life is love. The Greek language has three words for love, which enable us to distinguish Christian love (*agapê*) from passionate devotion (*eros*) and warm affection (*philia*). Jesus did not tell his disciples to fall in love with their enemies or to feel for them as they felt for their families and friends. *Agapê* is a gracious, determined, and active interest in the true welfare of others, which is not deterred even by hatred, cursing, and abuse, not limited by calculation of deserts or results, based solely on the nature of God. Love does not retaliate (vv. 27–31), seeks no reward (vv. 32–36), is not censorious (vv. 37–38).

The men who were bidden to love their enemies were living in enemy-occupied territory, where resentment was natural and provocation frequent. They were not just to submit to aggression, but to rob it of its sting by voluntarily going beyond its demands. To those who believe in standing up for their individual or national rights this teaching has always seemed idealistic, if not actually immoral. But those who are concerned with the victory of the kingdom of God over the kingdom of Satan can see that it is the only realism. He who retaliates thinks that he is manfully resisting aggression; in fact, he is making an unconditional surrender to evil. Where before there was one under the control of evil, now there are two. Evil propagates by contagion. It can be contained and defeated only when hatred, insult, and injury are absorbed and neutralized by love.

The Golden Rule (v. 31) appears in many religions and philosophies in a negative form. The Rabbi Hillel, for example, was asked to recite the whole law while he stood on one leg, and answered, 'What is hateful to you, do not to your fellow. That is the whole law and all the rest is commentary.' But an ethical programme which consists in not-doing, especially when it has to be expounded in a vast commentary of rules and ceremonies, can hardly be compared with one which calls for positive and unlimited benevolence.

Most people – even sinners – have a rough-and-ready ethic based on common sense, enlightened self-interest, give-and-take; and they can claim to be as good as their neighbours. But the followers of Jesus must go further. The Christian ethic is Ethics Part II. Other systems distinguish what is right from what is wrong: Jesus distinguishes what is good from what is merely right, and urges his disciples not to be content with the lower standard. Duty is not enough. Duty obeys the rules, but love grasps opportunities. Duty acts under constraint, love is spontaneous and therefore gracious. Duty expects to be recompensed or at least recognized, love expects nothing in return. To love like that is to be sons of the Most High; for likeness is proof of parentage. *'Be merciful'* might appear to be less exacting than Matthew's *'You, therefore, must be perfect'* (Matt. 5⁴⁸). In the Old Testament, however, to be perfect means to be completely loyal and is a normal human virtue, but mercy is the very character of God. The son must inherit the attributes of his Father.

Generosity in giving must be matched by generosity of judgement. The rule of measure for measure does not mean that God deals with men on a basis of strict justice – the rest of the sermon belies that – but that intake is in proportion to output. He who gives and forgives sparingly receives sparingly. The gifts of God, including his mercy, come most freely to those who most freely pass them on to others.

בסמ

38
The metaphor from the grain market is not improved by the use of the modern lap to replace the older bosom; for the bosom was a fold of the robe pulled out above the girdle to form a pocket, and a bosomful of grain would be more manageable than a lapful.

³⁹*He also told them a parable: 'Can a blind man lead a blind man? Will they not both fall into a pit?* ⁴⁰*A disciple is not above his teacher, but every one when he is fully taught will be like his teacher.* ⁴¹*Why do you see the speck that is in your brother's eye, but do not notice the log that is in your own eye?* ⁴²*Or how can you say to your brother, "Brother, let me take out the speck that is in your eye," when you yourself do not see the log that is in your own eye? You hypocrite, first take the log out of your own eye, and then you will see clearly to take out the speck that is in your brother's eye.*

⁴³*'For no good tree bears bad fruit, nor again does a bad tree bear good fruit;* ⁴⁴*for each tree is known by its own fruit. For figs are not gathered from thorns, nor are grapes picked from a bramble bush.*

⁴⁵*'The good man out of the good treasure of his heart produces good, and*

the evil man out of his evil treasure produces evil; for out of the abundance of the heart his mouth speaks.'

We have here a group of originally unrelated utterances which in Matthew's Gospel are found in a variety of contexts with considerable divergence of interpretation (Matt. 15¹⁴, 10²⁴⁻²⁵, 7¹⁸⁻¹⁹, 12³³⁻³⁵). In the present context the connecting link is the relation between character and influence. The disciples have been told that, whatever their social position, in the ethical field they are to be leaders of men. But the leader can guide only if he first sees the way. The teacher can impart only what he himself has learned. The only critic who profits others is the self-critic. Sound influence is the fruit growing on the tree of sound character, the overflow of an inner abundance.

The parable of the log and the speck is an example of the humorous hyperbole with which Jesus so often administered gentle reproof (cf. 18²⁵, Matt. 23²⁴). The ban on speck-hunting does not, of course, mean that Christians must condone evil or refrain from forming moral judgements. This is a parable about personal relationships. Pseudo-religion, which Jesus calls hypocrisy, is for ever trying to make other people better; and the cure for it is a mirror.

6⁴⁶⁻⁴⁹   THE TWO HOUSES

⁴⁶'Why do you call me "Lord, Lord", and not do what I tell you?
    ⁴⁷'Every one who comes to me and hears my words and does them, I will show you what he is like: ⁴⁸he is like a man building a house, who dug deep, and laid the foundation upon rock; and when a flood arose, the stream broke against that house, and could not shake it, because it had been well built.ᵃ ⁴⁹But he who hears and does not do them is like a man who built a house on the ground without a foundation; against which the stream broke, and immediately it fell, and the ruin of that house was great.'

a Other ancient authorities read *founded upon the rock*

The final characteristic of the new life is obedience, not, as in Judaism, to a set of rules, but to a person. The title Lord contains in itself a whole history of New Testament thought about Jesus. On the lips of the early Christians it expressed successively respect to their Teacher, loyalty to their Messiah, homage to the risen and ascended King, worship to the divine Saviour. But at every stage there was the same need for a reminder that undisciplined emotion readily masquerades as true faith and that Lordship is the right to command obedience.

Luke's parable of the two houses is slightly different from Matthew's. In Matthew the parable has its original Palestinian setting: the one man finds rock to build on, the other chooses an attractive stretch of sand, not realizing that it is a dry *wadi* which in winter will become a raging torrent. Luke has adapted the parable to Gentile geography and climate. In his version the sensible man digs down through the soil to the underlying rock; the short-sighted one builds on the surface, and the damage to his house is done by the flooding of the river. But the meaning is the same in each case. The man who hears and does is safe against every crisis, while the man who only hears is inviting disaster.

7$^{1-10}$ LOVE IN ACTION: (I) THE GENTILE

7 *After he had ended all his sayings in the hearing of the people he entered Capernaum. ²Now a centurion had a slave who was dear to him,ᵃ who was sick and at the point of death. ³When he heard of Jesus, he sent to him elders of the Jews, asking him to come and heal his slave. ⁴And when they came to Jesus, they besought him earnestly, saying, 'He is worthy to have you do this for him, ⁵for he loves our nation, and he built us our synagogue.' ⁶And Jesus went with them. When he was not far from the house, the centurion sent friends to him, saying to him, 'Lord, do not trouble yourself, for I am not worthy to have you come under my roof; ⁷therefore I did not presume to come to you. But say the word, and let my servant be healed.*

⁸*'For I am a man set under authority, with soldiers under me: and I say to one, "Go", and he goes; and to another, "Come", and he comes; and to my slave, "Do this", and he does it.' ⁹When Jesus heard this he marvelled at him, and turned and said to the multitude that followed him, 'I tell you,*

*not even in Israel have I found such faith.' * [10] *And when those who had been sent returned to the house, they found the slave well.*

  a Or *valuable*

It must have given Luke great pleasure to record that the highest praise ever uttered by Jesus was addressed to a Gentile. He was an officer, presumably in the army of Antipas. According to Luke, he never met Jesus, but communicated with him first through the elders of the synagogue and then through a group of friends. He was one of the many Gentiles who, attracted to Judaism by its high moral standards, had hesitated to identify himself fully with the Jewish nation by becoming a proselyte. He knew enough to realize that a Jew might shrink from entering the house of a Gentile and was courteous enough to respect such scruples. He must have been a wealthy man, for he had built the local synagogue; and his care for his slave shows that he was also a humane one.

The interest of the story, however, is in the message of the centurion which called forth the final commendation of Jesus. In his parables Jesus was constantly inviting his listeners to learn lessons about God from the analogy of their daily life, and the centurion did this for himself without having to be prompted. From his experience of army discipline he knew how a word of command could produce results, and he was confident that a word from Jesus would be even more effective. But he also knew that his commands were obeyed because he was under authority, because he held a commission from Antipas; and this enabled him to recognize in Jesus one who also derived his authority from a higher source. Others had been astonished at Jesus' authority and had entrusted themselves to his healing power; but this was not what Jesus meant by faith. Faith was to recognize that in Jesus the kingdom of God was exercising its power.

This story is found also at Matt. 8$^{5-13}$. The dialogue there is almost identical, but the narrative setting is as different as it could be. It is possible that only the dialogue stood in Q, with the briefest indication of attendant circumstances.

^{11}*Soon afterwards^a he went to a city called Nain, and his disciples and a great crowd went with him.* ^{12}*As he drew near to the gate of the city, behold, a man who had died was being carried out, the only son of his mother, and she was a widow; and a large crowd from the city was with her.* ^{13}*And when the Lord saw her, he had compassion on her, and said to her, 'Do not weep.'* ^{14}*And he came and touched the bier, and the bearers stood still. And he said, 'Young man, I say to you, arise.'* ^{15}*And the dead man sat up and began to speak. And he gave him to his mother.* ^{16}*Fear seized them all; and they glorified God, saying, 'A great prophet has arisen among us!' and 'God has visited his people!'* ^{17}*And this report concerning him spread through the whole of Judea and all the surrounding country.*

a Other ancient authorities read *Next day*

The story of the centurion is a typical pronouncement story, i.e. a story treasured for the saying of Jesus which formed the climax of it; in this case the saying was to Gentile Christians like a charter of Church membership. The story of the widow of Nain is a typical miracle story, recording the serious situation, the word of command, the success of the miracle, and the effect on the bystanders. But Luke has inserted the story at this point in his Gospel, not as an act of power, but as an act of compassion, a further example of Jesus' gracious concern for the helpless in which once again the law of uncleanness yields to the high law of mercy (Num. 19^{11}). His concern throughout is for the woman, not for her son: '. . . the only son of his mother and she was a widow . . . he had compassion on her . . . he gave him to his mother.' These last words are a quotation from the story of Elijah and the widow of Zarephath (1 Kings 17^{23}) and explain the reaction of the crowd. Jesus was a great prophet because he had done what Elijah and Elisha did.

The resuscitation of the dead is as well attested as any of the other miracles of Jesus. Luke drew this story from his private source L, the story of Jairus' daughter from Mark, and from Q a saying of Jesus which includes the raising of the dead among the achievements of the ministry (7²²). There is, of course, no way of proving to the satisfaction of a sceptic that the people concerned were in fact dead, and not just in a cataleptic trance which Jesus was able to recognize; but there can be no doubt about the conviction of the early Church that Jesus had reclaimed to life those whom others had declared dead.

7¹⁸⁻³⁵   LOVE IN ACTION: (3) THE PRISONER

¹⁸ *The disciples of John told him of all these things.* ¹⁹*And John, calling to him two of his disciples, sent them to the Lord, saying, 'Are you he who is to come, or shall we look for another?'* ²⁰*And when the men had come to him, they said, 'John the Baptist has sent us to you, saying, "Are you he who is to come, or shall we look for another?"'* ²¹*In that hour he cured many of diseases and plagues and evil spirits, and on many that were blind he bestowed sight.* ²²*And he answered them, 'Go and tell John what you have seen and heard: the blind receive their sight, the lame walk, lepers are cleansed, and the deaf hear, the dead are raised up, the poor have good news preached to them.* ²³*And blessed is he who takes no offence at me.'*

²⁴*When the messengers of John had gone, he began to speak to the crowds concerning John: 'What did you go out into the wilderness to behold? A reed shaken by the wind?* ²⁵*What then did you go out to see? A man clothed in soft raiment? Behold, those who are gorgeously apparelled and live in luxury are in kings' courts.* ²⁶*What then did you go out to see? A prophet? Yes, I tell you, and more than a prophet.* ²⁷*This is he of whom it is written,*

"Behold, I send my messenger before thy face,
who shall prepare thy way before thee."

²⁸*'I tell you, among those born of women none is greater than John; yet he who is least in the kingdom of God is greater than he.'*

²⁹*(When they heard this all the people and the tax collectors justified God, having been baptized with the baptism of John;* ³⁰*but the Pharisees and the lawyers rejected the purpose of God for themselves, not having been baptized by him.)*

³¹*'To what then shall I compare the men of this generation, and what are they like?* ³²*They are like children sitting in the market place and calling to one another,*

> "*We piped to you, and you did not dance;*
> *we wailed, and you did not weep.*"
> ³³'*For John the Baptist has come eating no bread and drinking no wine; and you say, "He has a demon." ³⁴The Son of man has come eating and drinking; and you say, "Behold, a glutton and a drunkard, a friend of tax collectors and sinners!" ³⁵Yet wisdom is justified by all her children.*'

Another attractive facet in the personality of Jesus is seen in his dealings with John the Baptist. In spite of the deep gulf that separated his radiant friendliness from John's forbidding austerity, he had a profound appreciation of his grim herald. He admired his unshakeable honesty and his disregard of comfort and luxury; and, at the risk of reprisals from Antipas, he gave public testimony to his prophetic greatness. Though John had professed himself unworthy to untie the sandals of the Coming One, Jesus treated him as a colleague in God's service, as one of Wisdom's children who had done great credit to his mother.

John's question to Jesus was an echo of his own preaching: Is Jesus the Coming One, whose way he had been sent to prepare? He might as well have asked whether Jesus was the Messiah; but, like Jesus, he was accustomed to avoid the term for fear of its being misconstrued by his hearers. The question has been interpreted both as the rise of doubt and as the dawn of faith. Matthew, who believed that John recognized Jesus as Messiah at the time of his baptism, of necessity took the former view; and it has usually and unwarrantably been assumed that Luke agreed with him. Luke has told us that Jesus was related to John, but also that, notwithstanding the remarkable events described in the birth and infancy narratives, his kinsfolk were the slowest to understand him. Even his closest disciples did not declare their faith in his Messiahship until after John's death (9^{7, 20}). It was quite natural, then, that John should not have begun to think of Jesus as Messiah until he heard about the impression he was making wherever he went.

There are two clear indications that this is the correct reading of the situation. John still had disciples, who remained aloof from the new movement of Jesus. If he had accepted Jesus as Messiah, he would certainly have persuaded his followers to transfer their allegiance. Secondly, Jesus said of John, '*he who is least in the kingdom of God is greater than. he'*. He was not denying him a place in the ultimate kingdom, where many from the four corners of the earth will sit at table with patriarch and prophet (13$^{28-29}$); for to that company John assuredly belonged. The kingdom in which John had no part was the present kingdom which had arrived with Jesus, and into which men entered by becoming his disciples. John belonged to the old order – the greatest man that ever lived before the coming of the kingdom (cf. 16^{16}).

Jesus knew how much it had cost John to ask his question. He must have heard that Jesus was keeping company with the very *'chaff'* on whom he had called down the fire of God. He had looked for imminent judgement, the overthrow of wrong and the vindication of justice; and nothing that Jesus had done so far had brought promise of his own release from prison. The ministry of Jesus had impressed him, but was this all that was to be expected from the Mighty One of God? The words *'blessed is he who takes no offence at me'* show that Jesus was deeply sensitive to John's perplexity. If he was to be rescued from disillusionment and despair, he must somehow be brought to the conviction that God's promises to him had already come true, though not in the way he had expected. All that Jesus could do to help him was to point to the facts of his own ministry in language which would remind him of the pictures of the messianic age in the Book of Isaiah (29$^{18-19}$, 35$^{5-6}$, 61^{1}).

John had indeed prepared the way for Jesus, for those who had listened to the one would listen to the other as well. The tax collectors who accepted baptism justified God, i.e. admitted that he was right and they had been wrong, and were ready for the richer message of the gospel. But there were some who would listen to neither John nor Jesus. Jesus compared them to spoilt, bad-tempered children whom nothing ever pleases; when their playmates are in serious mood, they whine that they do not want to play anything but festivals, and when others are gay, nothing but funerals will do. Even so, there were Jews who found John too unsociable to be sane and Jesus too sociable to be moral.

చిళి

27

The quotation, which appears in almost identical form in Mark 1^{2}, is a hybrid, produced by crossing Malachi 3^{1} – '*Behold, I send my messenger*

(Elijah) *to prepare the way before me'* – with Exod. 23²⁰ – *'Behold, I send an angel* (Moses) *before you, to guard you on the way.'* The result is a fusion of two messianic traditions, one which said that Elijah would appear as herald of the day of the Lord, and one which said that God would raise up in Israel a prophet, a second Moses (Deut. 18¹⁵⁻¹⁹; cf. John 1²¹, 6¹⁴, 7⁴⁰). John has inherited both the staff of Moses and the mantle of Elijah. It used to be thought that this revision of the Old Testament text in the interests of Christian doctrine was the work of some collector of 'testimonies' or proof texts in the early Church; but it is far more likely that such a synthesis of ideas as this had its origin in the creative mind of Jesus, for we shall find Moses and Elijah together again as the forerunners of Jesus in the story of the transfiguration (9³⁰; cf. Rev. 11 ³⁻¹³).

7³⁶⁻⁵⁰   LOVE IN ACTION: (4) THE PENITENT

³⁶*One of the Pharisees asked him to eat with him, and he went into the Pharisee's house, and sat at table.* ³⁷*And behold, a woman of the city, who was a sinner, when she learned that he was sitting at table in the Pharisee's house, brought an alabaster flask of ointment,* ³⁸*and standing behind him at his feet, weeping, she began to wet his feet with her tears, and wiped them with the hair of her head, and kissed his feet, and anointed them with the ointment.*

³⁹*Now when the Pharisee who had invited him saw it, he said to himself, 'If this man were a prophet, he would have known who and what sort of woman this is who is touching him, for she is a sinner.'* ⁴⁰*And Jesus answering said to him, 'Simon, I have something to say to you.' And he answered, 'What is it, Teacher?'* ⁴¹*'A certain creditor had two debtors; one owed five hundred denarii, and the other fifty.* ⁴²*When they could not pay, he forgave them both. Now which of them will love him more?'* ⁴³*Simon answered 'The one, I suppose, to whom he forgave more.' And he said to him, 'You have judged rightly.'* ⁴⁴*Then turning towards the woman he said to Simon, 'Do you see this woman? I entered your house, you gave me no water for my feet, but she has wet my feet with her tears and wiped them with her hair.* ⁴⁵*You gave me no kiss, but from the time I came in she has not ceased to kiss my feet.* ⁴⁶*You did not anoint my head with oil, but she has anointed my feet with ointment.*

7³⁶⁻⁵⁰

47'*Therefore I tell you, her sins, which are many, are forgiven, for she loved much; but he who is forgiven little, loves little.*' 48*And he said to her, 'Your sins are forgiven.*' 49*Then those who were at table with him began to say among themselves, 'Who is this, who even forgives sins?*' 50*And he said to the woman, 'Your faith has saved you; go in peace.*'

Simon respected Jesus enough to call him Rabbi and half thought he might be a prophet; he was sufficiently interested in him to invite him to dinner, but received him with formal politeness, without any of the little gestures – the footbath, the kiss, the perfume – which would have betokened a warm welcome. At an oriental banquet the guests left their sandals at the door and reclined on low couches with their feet behind them. It was not uncommon for the doors to be left open to admit all sorts of people, from beggars in search of food to a rabbi's admirers in search of intellectual entertainment. There is no reason to suppose that the woman who came to stand behind Jesus had ever spoken with him; she had seen and heard him from the fringe of the crowd, and that had been enough to soften the hardness of her heart and to set her back on the road to self-respect. She had been a woman of evil ways and evil reputation: the reputation remained, but the ways were changed. Now she came to make a magnificent gesture of gratitude; but tears came before she could get the stopper out of her bottle of perfume, and, forgetting that this was something a decent woman never did in public, she let her hair down to wipe them away. Through all this Jesus did not turn; for he had no need; all that he needed to know about the uninvited guest he could read in the mirror of Simon's shocked face, and all he needed to do for the woman he could do by accepting motionless the homage of her penitent love – Simon in his place would have flinched from contact with the unclean.

Simon was conceited enough to think that a prophet would see in the woman exactly what the Pharisee saw; but where he saw only a sinner, Jesus saw a sinner pardoned and restored. By the parable of the Two Debtors he drew from his reluctant host the admission that great love can be the product of great forgiveness and showed how, from the woman's display of affection and gratitude, he himself had deduced her many sins and the magnitude of her pardon. '*I tell you, her sins . . . are forgiven, for she loved much*' does not mean that she has earned her forgiveness by her love; it was her faith, not her love, that saved her. Her love was not the ground of a pardon she had come to seek, but the proof of a pardon she had come to acknowledge. It may not, however, have been as obvious to her as it was to him that she was already pardoned before ever she entered the house. Jesus often knew people better than they knew themselves, and surprised them by the generosity with which he read their character.

༚

37
There is no excuse for confusing the nameless woman of this episode either with Mary Magdalene or with Mary of Bethany (8^2, Mark 14^{3-9}, John 12^{1-8}), though it is possible that the two stories of the anointing of Jesus by a woman have interacted on one another (cf. especially John 12^3 with Luke 7^{38}).

48-49
These verses introduce an entirely new subject, which has only a slight connexion with the main theme, and it is possible that they have crept in during the oral period from another part of the tradition (cf. 5^{21}).

8^{1-3} ITINERANT MINISTRY: (I) ITS SUPPORTERS

8 *Soon afterwards he went on through cities and villages, preaching and bringing the good news to the kingdom of God. And the twelve were with him, ²and also some women who had been healed of evil spirits and infirmities: Mary, called Magdalene, from whom seven demons had gone out, ³and Joanna, the wife of Chuza, Herod's steward, and Susanna, and many others, who provided for them^a out of their means.*

   a Other ancient authorities read *him*

The character of Jesus' ministry now changed; on this Mark and Luke agree, though they disagree about the precise nature and cause of the change. According to Mark, it was the growing enmity of the leaders and the almost embarrassing enthusiasm of the crowds that prompted Jesus to abandon the more settled ministry of the synagogue and to make the sloping seashore his auditorium. Luke, even where he is following Mark, has contrived to eliminate from his version much of the Marcan atmosphere of mounting tension; instead, he implies that it was no outer compulsion of circumstance but the inner necessity of his own missionary programme that drove Jesus to undertake a systematic visitation of the smaller townships and villages. Luke is here relying on a good tradition, which was known in another form to Mark, although he did not use it at this point, but only alluded to it in connexion with the women at the tomb (Mark 15⁴¹).

When at a slightly later date Jesus began to send his disciples out in twos on preaching tours, he gave them instructions to rely on hospitality; but now, when he was travelling with them all together, they were too large a group to be provided for in that way. The expenses of the mission were met by a number of well-to-do women, all of whom had one thing in common, that they had been cured by Jesus. They may also have been prominent members of the Palestinian Church in Luke's own day; if he had met Joanna, this would explain how he received his information about the court of Herod Antipas (23⁶⁻¹²). Mary's seven demons must have been a very stubborn form of mental illness.

8⁴⁻²¹   ITINERANT MINISTRY:
          (2) ENCOURAGEMENT AND WARNING

⁴*And when a great crowd came together and people from town after town came to him, he said in a parable:* ⁵*'A sower went out to sow his seed; and as he sowed, some fell along the path, and was trodden under foot, and the birds of the air devoured it.* ⁶*And some fell on the rock; and as it grew up, it withered away, because it had no moisture.* ⁷*And some fell among thorns; and the thorns grew with it and choked it.* ⁸*And some fell into good soil and grew, and yielded a hundredfold.' As he said this, he called out, 'He who has ears to hear, let him hear.'*

⁹*And when his disciples asked him what this parable meant,* ¹⁰*he said, 'To you it has been given to know the secrets of the kingdom of God; but for others they are in parables, so that seeing they may not see, and hearing they may not understand.*

¹¹'*Now the parable is this: The seed is the word of God.* ¹²*The ones along the path are those who have heard; then the devil comes and takes away the word from their hearts, that they may not believe and be saved.* ¹³*And the ones on the rock are those who, when they hear the word, receive it with joy; but these have no root, they believe for a while and in time of temptation fall away.* ¹⁴*And as for what fell among the thorns, they are those who hear, but as they go on their way they are choked by the cares and riches and pleasures of life, and their fruit does not mature.* ¹⁵*And as for that in the good soil, they are those who, hearing the word, hold it fast in an honest and good heart, and bring forth fruit with patience.*

¹⁶'*No one after lighting a lamp covers it with a vessel, or puts it under a bed, but puts it on a stand, that those who enter may see the light.* ¹⁷*For nothing is hid that shall not be made manifest, nor anything secret that shall not be known and come to light.* ¹⁸*Take heed then how you hear; for to him who has will more be given, and from him who has not, even what he thinks he has will be taken away.*'

¹⁹*Then his mother and his brothers came to him, but they could not reach him for the crowd.* ²⁰*And he was told, 'Your mother and your brothers are standing outside, desiring to see you.'* ²¹*But he said to them, 'My mother and my brothers are those who hear the word of God and do it.'*

The idea of instruction as a seed which takes root in the hearts of men has been employed by many teachers before and after Jesus. But the parables of Jesus were not meant to convey ethical commonplaces; they were designed to bring home to his hearers the realities of the situation with which they were confronted through the coming of the kingdom. The parable of the sower had a double purpose: to assure the disciples in a time of discouragement that, in spite of all setbacks, frustrations, and disappointments, the preaching of the Gospel could be trusted to bring in a rich harvest; and to warn others that the true quality of their lives would stand revealed by the reception they gave to the word of God.

All truth is clear, self-evident, and compelling to those who have seen the point, and mystery to those who have not. It is hardly surprising then that Jesus should have spoken of the secrets of the kingdom of God. It was not that he deliberately veiled the truth from the many and disclosed it to the chosen few. His secret – his new conception of the meaning of the kingdom – was open for everyone to see and hear, but even an open secret remains a secret from those who do not wish to learn it. Jesus told parables partly to accommodate profound truth to simple minds, partly to elicit from his hearers a decision about the story which would at the same time be a decision about their own lives, partly to distinguish the percipient, who were open to receive the secrets of the kingdom, from the dull of understanding, to whom the parables were stories and nothing more.

The allegorical explanation of the parable looks like an attempt by the early Church to adapt it to the needs of a more settled community. In view of what has just been said about the purpose of parables, it is unlikely that Jesus ever explained his parables (an explained parable is as flat as an explained joke). The need for explanation arose only when the Church, living in circumstances quite different from the critical urgency of the Galilean ministry, asked, What has this parable to say to us today? The result is a homily full of sound advice to the new convert on the dangers of superficial enthusiasm, unstable faith, and preoccupation with worldly affairs.

In their present context the following sayings are clearly meant to be variations on the theme of the parable of the sower. When God kindles a light in the lives of men, they must let it shine for the benefit of others. God's revelation begins as a private discovery and ends as a public trust. It grows with sharing, and those who try to keep it for themselves find they have lost even what they thought they had. Israel had been entrusted with God's light, but only in order to be a light to the Gentiles (Isa. 49⁶); and, instead of allowing the light to shine, she had concentrated her efforts on protecting the flame from extinction.

The passage ends with a forceful reminder that the rich harvest of God's word and the bright shining of God's light involve obedience. Those who are brothers and sisters to Jesus must be sons and daughters to God, and to be that they must do the will of their Father. Luke has here softened what in Mark's Gospel is a rebuke to Jesus' family; for Mark tells us that the family of Jesus came looking for him to restrain him, thinking he had taken leave of his senses, and in that context the words of Jesus have an added measure of sternness (Mark 3²¹, ³¹⁻³⁵).

ॐ

16–18

This passage presents an interesting study in synoptic origins. It consists of three sayings which Luke has taken over from Mark 4^{21-25} with only slight modifications. But all three are doublets, i.e. there is another version of them elsewhere in the Gospel, in widely separated contexts and with considerable difference of meaning (see Introduction). The three sayings must have circulated as isolated texts before being taken up into the various collections of teaching which formed the sources of the Gospels. In 11^{33} the saying about the lamp and the lampstand follows immediately on a denunciation of sign-seekers, and the inference is that the lamp stands for the illumination which has come into the world through Jesus, the one sure sign of God's activity. In 12^2 the saying about hidden things is part of a warning to the Pharisees and those likely to be influenced by them that the day is coming when all secrets will be laid bare before the light of God's judgement. In 19^{26} the saying about the haves and the have-nots is an admonition concerning the correct use of spiritual gifts.

16

It is interesting to note the different interpretations which Matthew and Luke have placed upon the parable of the lamp by editorial alteration of Mark's original version. Matthew's lamp is to 'give light to all in the house' – he is thinking of a reform within Judaism; Luke's lamp is placed, as in a Roman house, in the vestibule, *'that those who enter* [i.e. the Gentiles] *may see the light'*.

19

Mark tells us (6^3) that Jesus had four brothers and an unspecified number of sisters. In the interests of the belief in the perpetual virginity of Mary, about which nothing is said in the Bible, it has been argued that they were children of Joseph by a previous marriage or even cousins (so Jerome); but there is no justification for evading the plain meaning of Mark's words, that they were younger children of Joseph and Mary. The present passage would lose much of its point if this were not so.

8^{22-39} ITINERANT MINISTRY:
(3) DOMINION OVER TEMPEST AND DEMONS

^{22}*One day he got into a boat with his disciples, and he said to them, 'Let us* go across to the other side of the lake.' So they set out, ²³and as they sailed he fell asleep. And a storm of wind came down on the lake, and they were filling with water, and were in danger. ²⁴And they went and woke him, saying, 'Master, Master, we are perishing!' And he awoke and rebuked the wind and the raging waves; and they ceased, and there was a calm. ²⁵He said to them, 'Where is your faith?' And they were afraid, and they marvelled, saying to one another, 'Who is this then, that he commands even wind and water, and they obey him?'

²⁶Then they arrived at the country of the Gerasenes,ᵃ which is opposite Galilee. ²⁷And as he stepped out on land, there met him a man from the city who had demons; for a long time he had worn no clothes, and he lived not in a house but among the tombs. ²⁸When he saw Jesus, he cried out and fell down before him, and said with a loud voice, 'What have you to do with me, Jesus, Son of the Most High God? I beseech you, do not torment me.' ²⁹For he had commanded the unclean spirit to come out of the man. (For many a time it had seized him; he was kept under guard, and bound with chains and fetters, but he broke the bonds and was driven by the demon into the desert.) ³⁰Jesus then asked him, 'What is your name?' And he said, 'Legion'; for many demons had entered him. ³¹And they begged him not to command them to depart into the abyss. ³²Now a large herd of swine was feeding there on the hillside; and they begged him to let them enter these. So he gave them leave. ³³Then the demons came out of the man and entered the swine, and the herd rushed down the steep bank into the lake and were drowned.

³⁴When the herdsmen saw what had happened, they fled, and told it in the city and in the country. ³⁵Then people went out to see what had happened, and they came to Jesus, and found the man from whom the demons had gone, sitting at the feet of Jesus, clothed and in his right mind; and they were afraid. ³⁶And those who had seen it told them how he who had been possessed with demons was healed.

³⁷Then all the people of the surrounding country of the Gerasenesᵃ asked him to depart from them; for they were seized with great fear; so he got into the boat and returned. ³⁸The man from whom the demons had gone begged that he might be with him; but he sent him away, saying, ³⁹'Return to your home, and declare how much God has done for you.' And he went away, proclaiming throughout the whole city how much Jesus had done for him.

a Other ancient authorities read *Gadarenes*, others *Gergesenes*

Modern writers have tended to assign these two miracles to different categories, the one being a nature miracle, the other a miracle of healing; but by biblical standards they belong together as examples of Jesus' authority over the chaos in nature and in man. The biblical view of man is that God intended him to be lord of nature (Gen. 1²⁶; Ps. 8), and because he has by sin forfeited his viceregal throne, nature displays signs of disorder parallel to those in human life; the sovereignty of God is challenged not merely by human sin, but by disease and death, the unclean and the demonic, the desolation of the wilderness and the turbulence of the sea. In the Creation story God had subdued by his word of power the waters of the Great Deep, the primeval ocean (Ps. 93, 104⁵⁻⁹); and in the imagery of Old Testament thought the sea continued to be the symbol of all those hostile forces which had not yet been brought beneath the rule of God,

> *who dost still the roaring of the seas,*
> *the roaring of their waves,*
> *the tumult of the peoples* (Ps. 65⁷; cf. 89⁹⁻¹⁰, 46³)

From this intimate association of man and nature in their relation to the mystery of iniquity it followed that the redemption of man would be accompanied by the restoration of paradise: the wolf would dwell with the lamb and the desert would blossom as the rose (Isa. 11⁶⁻⁹, 35, 55¹²⁻¹³). The miracles of Jesus were all 'miracles of the kingdom', evidence that God's sovereignty was breaking in, with a new effectiveness, upon the confusion of a rebellious world. The question of his disciples – '*Who then is this?*' – admitted of only one answer: this is the man to whom God has entrusted the authority of his kingdom.

From the calming of the seas we pass on to the calming of a deranged mind. In the madman of Gerasa we have a typical case of disintegrated personality. All the symptoms described have the note of authenticity: the morbid preoccupation with graves, the abnormal strength, the insensitivity to pain, the refusal to wear clothes, and the multiple and fluctuating self. The man conceived himself to be possessed by a whole regiment of demons; like the country he lived in, he was enemy-occupied territory, and it may well be that his condition arose out of a traumatic experience associated with the Roman occupation. The cure was accompanied by a violent and obstreperous convulsion, which caused a nearby herd of pigs to stampede in disastrous panic. The onlookers, who shared the common belief that there was an affinity between unclean demons and unclean beasts, and that both together might be found haunting unhallowed spots (cf. Isa. 13$^{20-22}$, 34$^{8-17}$), naturally assumed that the demons, deprived of their former residence, had found a new and more suitable one in the unclean pigs; and that, this being so, it must have happened with the consent of Jesus.

ຄວຄ

26
Gerasa was probably the small village of Khersa on the eastern shore of the lake. It is not to be confused with Gerasa in Perea, forty miles farther south. The variant readings 'Gadarenes' and 'Gergesenes' were probably scribal attempts (by scribes who knew of the Perean Gerasa but not of the lakeshore village) to correct what appeared to be an error in topography.

30
A legion was a division of the Roman army, consisting of 6,000 infantrymen, together with auxiliary troops; and at this time the province of Syria, including the principalities of Palestine, was held by four legions.

32
The presence of pigs is a reminder that Jesus was here in the predominantly Gentile territory of the Decapolis. To the Jew the pig was an unclean animal, and the eating of pork expressly forbidden in the Law (Lev. 11$^{7-8}$).

840-56   ITINERANT MINISTRY:
(4) DOMINION OVER SICKNESS AND DEATH

^{40}*Now when Jesus returned, the crowd welcomed him, for they were all waiting for him.* ^{41}*And there came a man named Jairus, who was a ruler of the synagogue; and falling at Jesus' feet he besought him to come to his house,* ^{42}*for he had an only daughter, about twelve years of age, and she was dying.*

As he went, the people pressed round him. ^{43}*And a woman, who had had a flow of blood for twelve years^a and could not be healed by any one,*

⁴⁴*came up behind him, and touched the fringe of his garment; and immediately her flow of blood ceased.* ⁴⁵*And Jesus said, 'Who was it that touched me?' When all denied it, Peter said,*[b] *'Master, the multitudes surround you and press upon you!'* ⁴⁶*But Jesus said, 'Someone touched me; for I perceive that power has gone forth from me.'* ⁴⁷*And when the woman saw that she was not hidden, she came trembling, and falling down before him declared in the presence of all the people why she had touched him, and how she had been immediately healed.* ⁴⁸*And he said to her, 'Daughter, your faith has made you well; go in peace.'*

⁴⁹*While he was still speaking, a man from the ruler's house came and said, 'Your daughter is dead; do not trouble the Teacher any more.'* ⁵⁰*But Jesus on hearing this answered him, 'Do not fear; only believe, and she shall be well.'* ⁵¹*And when he came to the house, he permitted no one to enter with him, except Peter and John and James, and the father and mother of the child.* ⁵²*And all were weeping and bewailing her; but he said, 'Do not weep; for she is not dead but sleeping.'* ⁵³*And they laughed at him, knowing that she was dead.* ⁵⁴*But taking her by the hand he called, saying, 'Child, arise.'* ⁵⁵*And her spirit returned, and she got up at once; and he directed that something should be given her to eat.* ⁵⁶*And her parents were amazed; but he charged them to tell no one what had happened.*

a Other ancient authorities add *and had spent all her living upon physicians*
b Other ancient authorities add *and those who were with him*

Back in Galilee Jesus found a great crowd waiting to receive him. Luke, like Mark, gives us the impression that throughout his Galilean ministry, whatever may have been the attitude of the religious leaders, Jesus never lost his popularity with the common people, and that he was often as much embarrassed by the exacting and untutored enthusiasm of his friends as he was by the impenetrable dogmatism of his antagonists. On this occasion, however, it was one of the leaders, the president of the local council of elders, who made a public profession of his faith in Jesus' healing powers; and, in view of the rising tide of official disapproval, it must have required both courage and humility on his part to make the approach. Luke has slightly heightened the pathos of Mark's story by making the girl an only daughter (cf. 7¹², 9³⁸). By the time Jesus reached the house the girl was dead, and the professional mourners were in attendance, giving to the bereaved the meagre consolation of having conformed to the demands of convention. These mourners, knowing that the girl was dead, mocked Jesus, because they thought he was disputing the fact of death; but his assertion that she was only sleeping was simply an assurance of his unlimited confidence in his own ability to wake her from the sleep of death.

The story of Jairus is interrupted by the story of a woman, who resembles him in this respect that she was driven to Jesus by the extremity of her need. She had an illness (menorrhagia – a continuous menstruation) which was probably psychological in origin, but none the less distressing and debilitating in its effects; and in Jewish society it had the further devastating consequence that it rendered her permanently unclean, and so unfit for any human contact (Lev. 15¹⁹⁻³⁰). It was a serious offence for her to touch another person, because her touch would impart to him something of her uncleanness. Small wonder, then, that she dared to seek the healing touch of Jesus only furtively under cover of the crowd. The reaction of Jesus is interesting for three reasons: first, as the disciples suggest, only a person of extraordinarily acute perception could have distinguished between the pressure of the crowd and the deliberate, though faltering, touch of a woman in quest of healing; secondly, it appears that every cure Jesus performed cost him something in spiritual energy, so that he was capable of feeling spent and in need of renewal; and thirdly, there is the fact that Jesus felt it necessary to embarrass the woman by publicity. If she had been allowed to slip away in a comfortable obscurity, one of two things would have happened: either she would have suffered a relapse, brought on by a sense of guilt at having broken the laws of uncleanness; or she would have enjoyed a permanent cure, but without seeing in it the gateway to a richer and more abundant life under the grace and fatherhood of God. She needed the blessing of Jesus on the cure which she had gained by stealth and his assurance that she owed her new health not to a magical power but to her own faith in the saving activity of God.

ഇഇ

43
The words 'and had spent all her living upon physicians' do not occur in Codex Vaticanus, Codex Bezae, or the Sinaitic Syriac version. They

were probably added to the Lucan text by a harmonizer to make it agree with Mark 5²⁶. Luke omitted this slighting reference to doctors either from professional pride or simply because, like Matthew, he was abbreviating Mark.

9¹⁻⁹   JESUS AND HIS DISCIPLES: (I) MISSION

9 *And he called the twelve together and gave them power and authority over all demons and to cure diseases, ²and he sent them out to preach the kingdom of God and to heal. ³And he said to them, 'Take nothing for your journey, no staff, nor bag, nor bread, nor money; and do not have two tunics. ⁴And whatever house you enter, stay there, and from there depart. ⁵And wherever they do not receive you, when you leave that town shake off the dust from your feet as a testimony against them.' ⁶And they departed and went through the villages, preaching the gospel and healing everywhere.*

⁷*Now Herod the tetrarch heard of all that was done, and he was perplexed, because it was said by some that John had been raised from the dead, ⁸by some that Elijah had appeared, and by others that one of the old prophets had risen. ⁹Herod said, 'John I beheaded; but who is this about whom I hear such things?' And he sought to see him.*

The ministry of Jesus, already carried far afield by his own travels, from which Luke has given us a few typical excerpts, was now further enlarged by the mission of the twelve. Because we know the end of the gospel story, we are inclined to think of Jesus as a solitary figure, always a little apart from the rest of mankind, his disciples included; and this, no doubt, is an important part of the truth. But he preferred to think of himself as the servant of the kingdom, sharing that service with those who had answered its call: they were to share his intimate knowledge of the Father (10²¹⁻²²), his task and authority, even his sufferings (9²³⁻²⁷). It was an integral part of his own mission, then, that his disciples should participate in it, proclaiming by both word and deed the arrival of the kingdom. But this new development was also dictated by circumstances: the unremitting demands of the crowds meant that Jesus alone could not hope to cover all the territory of Israel (cf. Matt. 10²³), and the growing threat of official interference meant that his time was likely to be short. Accordingly, the disciples are instructed to conduct their missionary tour in haste, carrying not an ounce of superfluous equipment, relying entirely on hospitality, and wasting no time upon the inhospitable and unreceptive. It was the practice among strict Jews, on leaving Gentile soil, to shake from their feet the dust of Gentile pollution: the disciples are bidden to adopt this symbolic act as a declaration that those who will not accept God's kingdom no longer belong to his people.

The new sense of urgency and foreboding which came upon Jesus at the height of his Galilean popularity appears to have been occasioned by the death of John the Baptist. John's death is mentioned only incidentally at this point by Mark and Luke, but it must have been a recent occurrence: he was alive, though in prison, when Jesus began to preach (Mark 1¹⁴); some time must have elapsed before he sent his message of doubtful inquiry to Jesus (Luke 7¹⁸); and now, less than a year after his imprisonment, he was dead. Mark and Luke attribute John's execution to the vengeful malice of Herodias, Josephus to Herod's fear of a messianic uprising; but, whatever the reason for it, it undoubtedly gave Jesus a premonition of the fate in store for himself (Mark 9⁹⁻¹³).

The little story of Herod's qualms over the common gossip about Jesus is extraordinarily revealing. Jesus had all the qualities of grace, friendliness, and compassion which were lacking in John's make-up; but in the public estimate the two men were of the same mould, and even Herod was apprehensive lest the dead John should be returning to haunt him. A man who could be confused with Elijah and John the Baptist must have had a mighty vein of granite in his character.

9^{10–17}   JESUS AND HIS DISCIPLES:
(2) THE FAREWELL BANQUET

¹⁰*On their return the apostles told him what they had done. And he took them and withdrew apart to a city called Bethsaida. ¹¹When the crowds learned it, they followed him; and he welcomed them and spoke to them of the kingdom of God, and cured those who had need of healing. ¹²Now the day*

began to wear away; and the twelve came and said to him, 'Send the crowd away, to go into the villages and country round about, to lodge and get provisions; for we are here in a lonely place.' [13]*But he said to them, 'You give them something to eat.' They said, 'We have no more than five loaves and two fish – unless we are to go and buy food for all these people.'* [14]*For there were about five thousand men. And he said to his disciples, 'Make them sit down in companies, about fifty each.'* [15]*And they did so, and made them all sit down.* [16]*And taking the five loaves and the two fish he looked up to heaven, and blessed and broke them, and gave them to the disciples to set before the crowd.* [17]*And all ate and were satisfied. And they took up what was left over, twelve baskets of broken pieces.*

In the Jewish literature one of the symbols for the messianic age was the great Banquet, the coronation feast of God (Isa. 25[6-8]); it was natural that a people who had lived with privation should picture God's brave new world in such imagery, sometimes even to the point of discussing the menu (2 Bar. 29[4], 4 Ezra 6[52]). In his popular preaching Jesus made frequent use of this symbol, to denote either the presence of the kingdom with its rich invitation (5[34], 6[21], 14[16-24]) or its ultimate, heavenly fulfilment (13[29-30], 22[15-18]). The Last Supper was, as we shall see, a dramatic anticipation of the heavenly feast; but it was not the only meal to which Jesus gave this symbolic significance. On the eve of his departure from Galilee with the twelve into the comparative safety of Philip's tetrarchy – Bethsaida was just outside the territory of Antipas – he took leave of a great multitude of his followers in a meal which is best explained as a sacramental foretaste of the messianic Banquet. From very early times this meal was associated in Christian tradition with the Lord's Supper, so that even in Mark's Gospel it is described in eucharistic terms (compare Mark 6[41] with Mark 14[22]). As the story now stands it is a miracle story, but it is noteworthy that in none of the six versions found in the four Gospels is it said that Jesus multiplied the loaves; the miracle enters the story only with the twelve baskets of broken pieces. We must allow, then, for the possibility that oral tradition has turned into miracle what was originally an impressive act of prophetic symbolism.

ॐ

17

At this point there occurs Luke's 'Great Omission'. From 8^4 to 9^{50} he follows Mark; but he leaves out Mark 6^{45}–8^{26}. There is no need to suppose that he was using a mutilated copy of Mark. He simply omitted this section, along with many other shorter ones, because he did not wish to use it: some of its duplicated material he had already used, Mark 7^{1-23} was of little interest to Gentiles, and the story of the Syro-Phoenician woman could be taken to show an anti-Gentile bias. The omission, however, certainly improves the sequence of events, and it is quite possible that Luke has unwittingly restored the original order, which Mark had disrupted by inserting a long, independent cycle of stories at this point in his main source.

9^{18-27} JESUS AND HIS DISCIPLES:
(3) SHADOW OF THE CROSS

^{18}Now it happened that as he was praying alone the disciples were with him; and he asked them, 'Who do the people say that I am?'
^{19}And they answered, 'John the Baptist; but others say, Elijah; and others, that one of the old prophets has risen.' ^{20}And he said to them, 'But who do you say that I am?' And Peter answered, 'The Christ of God.' ^{21}But he charged and commanded them to tell this to no one, saying, ^{22}'The Son of man must suffer many things, and be rejected by the elders and chief priests and scribes, and be killed, and on the third day be raised.'
^{23}And he said to all, 'If any man would come after me, let him deny himself and take up his cross daily and follow me. ^{24}For whoever would save his life will lose it; and whoever loses his life for my sake, he will save it. ^{25}For what does it profit a man if he gains the whole world and loses or forfeits himself? ^{26}For whoever is ashamed of me and of my words, of him will the Son of man be ashamed when he comes in his glory and the glory of the Father and of the holy angels.
^{27}'But I tell you truly, there are some standing here who will not taste of death before they see the kingdom of God.'

The question which Jesus put to his disciples implies that they had recently been in closer touch with public opinion than he; Luke is therefore probably correct in thinking that it followed quickly upon their return from their missionary tour. But the question is important in another way also: no other recorded saying of Jesus speaks more eloquently than this of his inner consciousness of a unique vocation; not only is he aware that people are asking questions about him, but he assumes that such questions are inescapable, and that on the answers people give to them will depend their eternal destiny.

Peter's answer shows how far the disciples have come in the past year. They find it possible to accept Jesus as Messiah, not because he has shown any signs of conforming to the traditional conceptions of Messiah, but because by his words and works he has recast their inherited ideas in the mould of his own interpretation. The process is not indeed complete; but Jesus accepts the title from Peter, believing that he has at least begun to appreciate its true significance. The disciples are warned not to mention the title in public, because it would certainly mean something disastrously different to the populace. Having penetrated the first of Jesus' secrets, the disciples must now be initiated into the second and harder one, that the Messiah must suffer. This word 'must' is used frequently by Luke, and less frequently by the other evangelists, to denote a divine necessity, an obligation imposed by God's plan of redemption and foreshadowed in the Old Testament scriptures. Jesus himself had arrived at the conclusion that the Messiah must suffer by meditation on the scriptures, out of which there had arisen in his mind a fusion of three Old Testament figures – the Messiah, the Son of man, and the Servant of the Lord.

In origin these figures were distinct: the Messiah was the Davidic king who was to restore the glories of David's reign and introduce God's rule of justice and peace; the Son of man was the symbolic figure of Daniel's vision (Dan. 7^{13}), representing the empire to be given at the last to the persecuted 'saints of the Most High'; and the Servant of the Lord was Israel, or a small, faithful remnant of Israel, who through vicarious suffering and death would bring the nations to the knowledge of God (Isa. 52^{13}–53^{12}). The three figures had, however, two things in common which enabled the creative mind of Jesus to reduce them to a unity: they were all concerned with the establishment of God's kingdom and with the realization of Israel's destiny to be the holy people of God. The king must be the embodiment of his people, and king and people must share, under God, a common vocation. This is why it is never quite clear whether Jesus, in speaking of the Son of man, was thinking of himself as symbolic head of the people of God or of the people of God with himself at their head. This, too, is why his mind moved inevitably from his own future sufferings to those of his disciples; indeed, it is likely that at this time he still did not think of his sufferings and theirs as two separate stages in the divine economy, but rather expected that they would share with him the redemptive sufferings of the Son of man.

It is in the light of these corporate associations of Jesus' triple role that we must interpret the prediction of resurrection on the third day. Because Jesus died on Friday and was seen alive by many witnesses on the following Sunday, it has been assumed by some that the prediction was an example of supernatural prescience, by others that it was a *vaticinium ex eventu*. There is, however, a third possibility – that the prophecy was a genuine one, but meant something different when it was uttered from what it came to mean through the Christian experience of Easter. According to an early credal formula received by Paul, Jesus *was raised on the third day in accordance with the scriptures* (1 Cor. 15⁴). The only scripture which speaks of resurrection on the third day is Hos. 6², and this has to do, not with the revival of a dead person, but with the restoration of Israel to nationhood after national obliteration. If, then, as seems likely, Jesus was basing his prediction on the Old Testament, he meant simply that the new Israel, represented by him and perhaps also by his disciples, must pass through humiliation and death, and shortly afterwards – that is all the third day means in Hosea – be vindicated and restored. The interpretation is in keeping with the final saying of the passage (9²⁷); in view of the atmosphere of imminent violence which pervades the whole context, it is unlikely that Jesus was contemplating a far-off event due to happen in the extreme old age of the youngest bystanders; rather he was promising that, although some of them will share with him in the death which God has decreed for the Son of man, others will survive to see the triumph of God's kingdom which that death will secure.

JESUS AND HIS DISCIPLES:
              (4) THE VISION OF GLORY

28*Now about eight days after these sayings he took with him Peter and John
and James, and went up on the mountain to pray.* 29*And as he was praying,
the appearance of his countenance was altered, and his raiment became
dazzling white.* 30*And behold, two men talked with him, Moses and Elijah,*
31*who appeared in glory and spoke of his departure, which he was to accomplish at Jerusalem.* 32*Now Peter and those who were with him were
heavy with sleep but kept awake, and they saw his glory and the two men
who stood with him.* 33*And as the men were parting from him, Peter said to
Jesus, 'Master, it is well that we are here; let us make three booths, one for
you and one for Moses and one for Elijah' – not knowing what he said.*
34*As he said this, a cloud came and overshadowed them; and they were
afraid as they entered the cloud.* 35*And a voice came out of the cloud, saying,
'This is my Son, my Chosen;*[a] *listen to him!'* 36*And when the voice had
spoken, Jesus was found alone. And they kept silence and told no one in
those days anything of what they had seen.*

a Other ancient authorities read *my Beloved*

According to Mark it was in the neighbourhood of Caesarea Philippi
that Peter declared Jesus to be Messiah. Immediately to the north of
Caesarea lay Mount Hermon, and it is likely that this was the mountain to which Jesus resorted a week later with three of his friends. The
mention of a precise interval by Mark and Luke indicates that in their
opinion the two events were intimately related. For the three witnesses their experience on the mountain provided an impressive confirmation of the new teaching they had received at Caesarea. There
Jesus, in response to Peter's confession, had made a threefold disclosure:
that the Messiah must suffer, that his disciples must be prepared to
share his suffering, and that his suffering and theirs must be seen against
a background of ultimate and certain glory. Now they have a pre-
vision of the glory to come and hear a voice from heaven bidding
them heed the words of God's Son. The form of the words spoken
from heaven shows that the transfiguration of Jesus is to be linked
also with his baptism. Then Jesus had accepted God's commission to

be both Messiah and Servant of the Lord, and the voice from heaven had come to him to confirm him in the course he had chosen. Now he has begun to reveal to his disciples the secret of his calling, and the same voice comes to them to confirm his instruction.

But the transfiguration cannot be understood simply as a stage in the education of the disciples; it must also have been a crisis in the religious life of Jesus. Luke draws our attention to this point in his usual manner: Jesus, he tells us, was praying; and his comment is borne out by the researches of Evelyn Underhill and others, who have shown that the intense devotions of saint and mystic are often accompanied by physical transformation and luminous glow (further partial parallels are supplied by the accounts of the changed appearance of writers, artists, composers, and scientists, when the creative inspiration is upon them). Many scholars, past and present, have treated the transfiguration story with suspicion, regarding it either as a misplaced resurrection story or as a legendary product of later Christian piety. But the account may be accepted as literal truth, if we suppose that Jesus underwent an experience so profound that his companions, in the susceptible state between sleep and waking, were drawn into it. The very fact that Jesus took with him the three men who were later to accompany him into Gethsemane suggests that, now as then, he expected some trial of his spiritual stamina in which he would be glad of their companionship. Luke gives us a clue to the nature of the trial when he tells us that Moses and Elijah appeared and spoke of his departure which he was to accomplish at Jerusalem. This was not the first time, according to Luke, that Jesus had contemplated the prospect of death in the service of God. From the outset he had accepted the prophecy of the suffering Servant of the Lord as the blue-print of his ministry. But it is one thing to believe that obedience to God's decree will lead ultimately to rejection and death; it is quite another thing to embrace rejection and death as immediate, human possibilities. The Greek word which Luke uses for death is an unusual one – *exodos*; and it is clear that he used it because of its Old Testament associations with divine deliverance. At Jerusalem Jesus was to accomplish the New Exodus, leading God's people from a greater bondage than that of Egypt into the promised land of the kingdom. Like Moses of old, he was now standing on the brink of a great sea, the ocean of iniquity through which he must pass and in which he must accomplish another baptism (12^{50}). He has always obeyed the Father, but the road he has travelled hitherto has been well marked by the feet of prophets and forerunners, like Moses and Elijah. Now God is about to lead him into a path never before trodden by human foot, a path which will lead him to Gethsemane and Calvary. Henceforth, as pioneer of our salvation (Heb. 2^{10}, 12^2), he must journey alone, and not even Moses and Elijah can bear him company. Others, indeed, like John the Baptist, have suffered and died in God's service, but the death that awaits this man is more than martyrdom.

Peter's proposal to build three booths, or tabernacles, was a plausible one, though Mark and Luke, from their vantage point of superior knowledge, judged it to be ill-considered. He saw three men, each one a manifestation of the divine glory, and he wanted to capture the fleeting and stupendous moment by providing for each one a tabernacle such as Israel had built in the wilderness to enshrine the glory of the Lord. Perhaps it confirmed his faith in Jesus to see him in such company: for Moses had spoken with God as a man speaks with his friend, so that his face shone as he received the law at God's hand, and, like Elijah, he had stood alone as the champion of God's people; both men had made such an impression on their fellows that they were believed to have been translated bodily to heaven, and both were regarded as forerunners of the kingdom. What Peter did not realize was that Moses and Elijah belonged, with John the Baptist, to the old order that was passing away, and that a moment later he would see them vanish, leaving Jesus alone, and hear a voice say, 'This is my Son, my Chosen; listen to him!' (cf. Deut. 18^{15}). There was no need for three tabernacles: the divine glory, imperfectly and partially revealed under the old dispensation, was now being gathered up in the sole person of this Jesus who had set his face to go to Jerusalem. He stood alone, and the cloud of the divine presence overshadowed him and his.

JESUS AND HIS DISCIPLES:
              (5) REBUKES AND WARNINGS

³⁷*On the next day, when they had come down from the mountain, a great crowd met him.* ³⁸*And behold, a man from the crowd cried, 'Teacher, I beg you to look upon my son, for he is my only child;* ³⁹*and behold, a spirit seizes him, and he suddenly cries out; it convulses him till he foams, and shatters him, and will hardly leave him.* ⁴⁰*And I begged your disciples to cast it out, but they could not.'*

⁴¹*Jesus answered, 'O faithless and perverse generation, how long am I to be with you and bear with you? Bring your son here.'* ⁴²*While he was coming, the demon tore him and convulsed him. But Jesus rebuked the unclean spirit, and healed the boy, and gave him back to his father.* ⁴³*And all were astonished at the majesty of God.*

But while they were all marvelling at everything he did, he said to his disciples, ⁴⁴*'Let these words sink into your ears; for the Son of man is to be delivered into the hands of men.'* ⁴⁵*But they did not understand this saying, and it was concealed from them, that they should not perceive it; and they were afraid to ask him about this saying.*

⁴⁶*And an argument arose among them as to which of them was the greatest.* ⁴⁷*But when Jesus perceived the thought of their hearts, he took a child and put him by his side,* ⁴⁸*and said to them, 'Whoever receives this child in my name receives me, and whoever receives me receives him who sent me; for he who is least among you all is the one who is great.'*

⁴⁹*John answered, 'Master, we saw a man casting out demons in your name, and we forbade him, because he does not follow with us.'* ⁵⁰*But Jesus said to him, 'Do not forbid him; for he that is not against you is for you.'*

The magnificent isolation of Jesus in his moral and spiritual grandeur, symbolized by the vanishing of Moses and Elijah from the mount of vision, is now further emphasized by four incidents which betray the weak faith, the slow comprehension, the self-seeking, and the intolerance of the disciples. First, a distracted father brings to Jesus his son, whom the disciples have been unable to cure of epilepsy. The contrast between this scene and the previous one has been well brought out by Plummer: 'the chosen three blinded by the light, the remaining nine baffled by the powers of darkness'. But the main interest of the story lies in the impatient ejaculation of Jesus, *'how long am I to be with you?'* The ministry of Jesus has taken on a new urgency; he has a rendezvous to keep at Jerusalem, and the slowness of his disciples irks him (cf. 12⁴⁹⁻⁵⁰).

A second prediction of the Passion found the disciples equally unprepared. Luke, by abbreviating Mark's version, has made it more mysterious and awesome, but he has also added a comment which in some measure exonerates the disciples – *it was concealed from them, that they should not perceive it.* Luke the universalist is not afraid of pre-destination (cf. 8¹²). He and his contemporaries knew that it was through the Cross alone, and not through any prediction of it, that the disciples came to know the secret plan of God. Not until they had seen acted out, in all their grim glory, the redemptive sorrows of the Son of man could they appreciate the warnings which had formerly fallen on uncomprehending ears. But that which God intends to reveal effectively in the future may be said for the present to be con-cealed by him.

But the disciples could not be totally acquitted. Humanly speaking, there was a reason for their obtuseness, as the third incident makes clear. They could not understand Jesus because to him the only greatness worthy of the name was the greatness of humble service rendered even to the undeserving, while their hearts were set on recognition and precedence. *'How can you believe, who receive glory from one another, and do not seek the glory that comes from the only God?'* (John 5⁴⁴). Self-assertion can never understand the self-forgetful love which takes delight in serving those from whom no return can be expected. Yet the one sure path into God's presence is to love those whom he loves. To receive a child in Jesus' name means to act as Jesus' representative, to do what Jesus himself would do, to be the agent of the Father's love; and this is to receive both Jesus and the Father.

Where there is self-importance, jealousy and intolerance will not be far away. The episode of the unauthorized exorcist contains a rebuke not only to John, but to all those who in later days have sought by priestcraft or persecution, by Acts of Uniformity or sectarian tests, to confine the activity of God to the 'proper channels'.

Jesus' refusal to question the stranger's credentials is consistent with his regular response to those who questioned his own: the word of God and the works of God are self-authenticating. He who really knows and loves God will always be ready to acknowledge as an ally anyone who is obviously doing God's work.

Luke 9^{51}-19^{28}

The Road to Jerusalem

The next ten chapters consist chiefly of teaching, but Luke has attempted to provide a narrative framework by casting the whole section in the form of a journey towards Jerusalem (9^{51}, 13^{22}, 17^{11}, 19^{28}). The result is a somewhat artificial structure, full of topographical inconsistencies: Jesus starts out from Galilee by the short route through Samaria, but arrives by the longer route through Jericho; and in between he is first in Bethany, a few miles from Jerusalem, and later on the borders of Samaria and Galilee (10^{38}, 17^{11}). In view of Luke's affinities with the fourth Gospel, it is possible that he had received a vague and incomplete version of the Johannine tradition that Jesus, during the final year of his ministry, made repeated visits to Jerusalem for the great festivals; but, however that may be, his main purpose was to preserve the dramatic tension of his story by constant reminders of the crisis which lay ahead, just as John does by his repeated references to the hour which had not yet come.

9^{51-62} THE MEANING OF DISCIPLESHIP:
            (I) TRAVELS THROUGH SAMARIA

^{51}*When the days drew near for him to be received up, he set his face to go to Jerusalem. And he sent messengers ahead of him,*

^{52}*who went and entered a village of the Samaritans, to make ready for him; ^{53}but the people would not receive him, because his face was set toward Jerusalem. ^{54}And when his disciples James and John saw it, they said, 'Lord, do you want us to bid fire come down from heaven and consume them?'^{a} ^{55}But he turned and rebuked them.^{b} ^{56}And they went on to another village.*

^{57}*As they were going along the road, a man said to him, 'I will follow you wherever you go.' ^{58}And Jesus said to him, 'Foxes have holes, and birds of the air have nests; but the Son of man has nowhere to lay his head.' ^{59}To another he said, 'Follow me.' But he said, 'Lord, let me first go and bury my* *father.'* ⁶⁰*But he said to him, 'Leave the dead to bury their own dead; but as for you, go and proclaim the kingdom of God.'* ⁶¹*Another said, 'I will follow you, Lord; but let me first say farewell to those at my home.'* ⁶²*Jesus said to him, 'No one who puts his hand to the plough and looks back is fit for the kingdom of God.'*

> *a* Other ancient authorities add *as Elijah did*
>
> *b* Other ancient authorities add *and he said, 'You do not know what manner of spirit you are of; for the Son of man came not to destroy men's lives but to save them.'*

As with the use of the word *exodos* in the transfiguration story, so here Luke packs a whole theology into the word *analempsis*, which means an assumption, a reception up into heaven. The word contains a strong echo of the Elijah motif which has already figured so prominently in the Gospel (cf. 2 Kings 2⁹⁻¹¹). But Luke uses the word here in a thoroughly Johannine fashion to cover the whole complex of events by which Jesus made the transit from earth to heaven – crucifixion, resurrection, and ascension (cf. John 3¹⁴, 8²⁸, 12³²⁻³⁴).

The Elijah theme is again in evidence in the story of the inhospitable Samaritans. The long-standing feud between Jews and Samaritans had many causes, racial and political as well as religious, but the symbols of their intransigent hostility were the rival temples of Jerusalem and Mount Gerizim, each claiming to be the one true sanctuary of the Deuteronomic law (Deut. 12). Samaritan antipathy towards Jews was directed most strongly against pilgrims going from Galilee to Jerusalem (Josephus, *Jewish War*, II, 12, 3) for the festivals, and most pilgrims preferred the longer route through Perea. James and John wanted to emulate Elijah (2 Kings 1⁹⁻¹⁶); but we must recognize that in this respect Elijah was typical of the whole Old Testament, which knew no other way of dealing with the enemies of Israel than to call down God's curse upon them. This is why Elijah had to disappear from the mountain to give place to Jesus, with his new way of loving his enemies and dying for them, and to the new conception of God which that way implied. It is, however, an impressive testimony to the power of Jesus that the two brothers did not doubt their own ability in his name to call down fire from heaven.

The three aspirants to discipleship are warned to count the cost and, in particular, to reckon with the conflict of loyalties which disciple-

ship inevitably brings. In normal circumstances it is good that a man
should have a home of his own in which he can perform his acts of
filial piety to his parents, whether in life or in death, and show affection to his kindred and friends. All this is part of that family life which
God has graciously appointed for his children. But a man must be
prepared to sacrifice security, duty, and affection, if he is to respond
to the call of the kingdom, a call so urgent and imperative that all
other loyalties must give way before it. The most difficult choices in
life are not between the good and the evil, but between the good and
the best.

54-56
The longer text of these verses, given in the R.S.V. margin, is found in
Codex Bezae and many later manuscripts, but not in the most important codices. The additions are quite in keeping with the spirit of the
incident, and must be regarded as the attempt of an intelligent scribe to
turn the story into a pronouncement story by ending it with a telling
saying of Jesus.

IO$^{1-20}$ THE MEANING OF DISCIPLESHIP:
                 (2) THE SEVENTY

IO *After this the Lord appointed seventy^a others, and sent them on ahead
of him, two by two, into every town and place where he himself was about
to come.* ^{2}*And he said to them, 'The harvest is plentiful, but the labourers
are few; pray therefore the Lord of the harvest to send out labourers into
his harvest.* ^{3}*Go your way; behold, I send you out as lambs in the midst of
wolves.* ^{4}*Carry no purse, no bag, no sandals; and salute no one on the road.*
^{5}*Whatever house you enter, first say, "Peace be to this house!"* ^{6}*And if a
son of peace is there, your peace shall rest upon him; but if not, it shall return
to you.* ^{7}*And remain in the same house, eating and drinking what they
provide, for the labourer deserves his wages; do not go from house to house.*
^{8}*Whenever you enter a town and they receive you, eat what is set before
you;* ^{9}*heal the sick in it and say to them, "The kingdom of God has come
near to you."* ^{10}*But whenever you enter a town and they do not receive you,
go into its streets and say,* ^{11}*"Even the dust of your town that clings to our*

feet, we wipe off against you; nevertheless know this, that the kingdom of God has come near." ¹²I tell you it shall more be tolerable on that day for Sodom than for that town.

¹³*'Woe to you, Chorazin! woe to you, Bethsaida! for if the mighty works done in you had been done in Tyre and Sidon, they would have repented long ago, sitting in sackcloth and ashes. ¹⁴But it shall be more tolerable in the judgement for Tyre and Sidon than for you.*

¹⁵*'And you, Capernaum, will you be exalted to heaven? You shall be brought down to Hades.*

¹⁶*'He who hears you hears me, and he who rejects you rejects me, and he who rejects me rejects him who sent me.'*

¹⁷*The seventy^a returned with joy, saying, 'Lord, even the demons are subject to us in your name!' ¹⁸And he said to them, 'I saw Satan fall like lightning from heaven. ¹⁹Behold, I have given you authority to tread upon serpents and scorpions, and over all the power of the enemy; and nothing shall hurt you. ²⁰Nevertheless do not rejoice in this, that the spirits are subject to you; but rejoice that your names are written in heaven.'*

a Other ancient authorities read *seventy-two*

The missionaries are bidden to fulfil their task with the utmost haste: they are to carry not even the simplest impedimenta, to avoid the time-consuming futilities of oriental wayside etiquette, to waste no time on the heedless, and to leave behind them any scruples they may have about the ritual cleanness of food, which would certainly hamper their effective progress. Their mission is an urgent one because they are harvesters: Israel is ripe for the sickle and must be gathered into the garner of the kingdom while the brief season lasts. '*The kingdom of God has come near to you*' does not mean that the arrival of the kingdom is a future crisis about which men must be warned during the interval that remains; it means that the kingdom is present and men must be summoned to enter it before the opportunity goes by for ever. The real presence of the kingdom is to be proclaimed by word of mouth and also actively demonstrated by the healing of the sick and by the bestowal of heavenly peace, a blessing so solid that it must either find a worthy recipient (a son of peace) to rest on or recoil upon the head of its bearer. Whether men like it or not, whether they believe it or not, the kingdom is inexorably present, a reign of peace to those who accept it and a sentence of doom to those who do not. The time is short because the opposition is gathering its forces, so that even now the disciples go out as lambs in the midst of wolves.

The judgement of Jesus is pronounced against whole towns and cities, which implies that he is now looking for a corporate rather than an individual response to the gospel message. He has come to recall Israel to her true vocation as the holy people of God, and the cities of Israel must choose between his way of humble, self-denying service and the other way of defiant and contemptuous nationalism. Again and again in the succeeding chapters we shall find Jesus warning Israel that to reject him is to choose disaster on that day -- the day when God's transcendent judgement takes historical form and is worked out by human agents of destruction.

While the missionaries are away, enjoying their own success as exorcists, Jesus has one of his ecstatic experiences, this time a vision of Satan falling from heaven. The vision is prophetic: the exorcisms of Jesus and his disciples were not themselves the decisive victory over Satan, but only tokens of a victory yet to be won through the Cross. Up to this point, it should be noted, Satan is still in heaven. He owes his place there partly to his original office of prosecuting counsel in the divine lawcourt (Job 1, Zech. 3^{1-5}), the ruthless accuser who mis-represents God's purpose by pressing the claims of his justice to the complete exclusion of his mercy; partly to the commonly accepted idea that all earthly realities and events have their counterpart in heaven, so that even the sum total of earthly evil must have its heaven-ly representative (cf. Heb. 9^{23}, where even the heavenly temple requires to be cleansed by sacrifice). The ejection of Satan means that God's redemptive mercy has delivered men both from the sentence that hung over them and from the guilt and power of sin that held them captive (Rev. 12^{7-12}). But it is important to realize that this is simply a mythological way of talking about earthly realities and of investing them with eternal significance; the victory is won on earth, not in heaven. It was the earthly success of the disciples that occasioned Jesus' vision of heavenly triumph. God's purpose is being worked out in history, and in history it must be vindicated; the earthly dominion of Satan and all his brood of serpents must be effectively broken (cf. Gen. 3^{15}). Yet even so the disciples are warned not to count on this earthly vindication for themselves. The ultimate triumph of the kingdom is assured, but the individual servant of the kingdom must be content to know that his name is written in heaven and to leave results in the hands of God. For even the defeat of Satan is not an end in itself: it is the removal of obstacles to God's purpose of creating people fit for his heavenly kingdom, in which the disciples are already enrolled as citizens.

ഇ

I

The sending out of the seventy (or seventy-two) is recorded by Luke alone, and it raises for us some difficult questions. Did Luke find the number in one of his sources or is it his own editorial contribution? The charge to the missionaries he drew partly from Q (vv. 2–3, 8–16) and partly from L (vv. 4–7, 17–20). It is unlikely that Q contained any mention of the seventy, because the same material is placed by Matthew in his charge to the twelve (Matt. 9^{37-38}, $10^{7-16, 40}$). The L tradition may have mentioned the seventy; but on the other hand the instructions here given clearly belong with 22^{35-38}, where it is assumed that this charge was originally delivered to the twelve. Whether it be fact or fiction, the number is symbolic: but what does it symbolize? The Gentile nations listed in Genesis 10 were reckoned by the rabbis to number seventy (or seventy-two), so that Luke could have regarded this mission as a symbolic anticipation of the mission to the Gentiles. The elders appointed to assist Moses were also seventy in number (or seventy-two, including Eldad and Medad). The balance of probability seems to lie with the theory that we have here a piece of deliberate symbolism by Luke, whereby he sought to sustain the Moses and Elijah theme; Jesus, like a second Moses, was sharing the burden of his work with his seventy assistants. Since they are said to be sent to prepare for the coming of Jesus, we must conclude that Luke calls them seventy *others*, not to distinguish them from the twelve – by hypothesis he wrote this part of the Gospel before he came across Mark – but in contrast with the messengers mentioned in 9^{51-52}.

10^{21-24} THE MEANING OF DISCIPLESHIP:
(3) THE KNOWLEDGE OF GOD

[21]*In that same hour he rejoiced in the Holy Spirit and said, 'I thank thee, Father, Lord of heaven and earth, that thou hast hidden these things from the wise and understanding and revealed them to babes; yea, Father, for*

such was thy gracious will.^a ²²*All things have been delivered to me by my Father; and no one knows who the Son is except the Father, or who the Father is except the Son and any one to whom the Son chooses to reveal him.'*

²³*Then turning to the disciples he said privately, 'Blessed are the eyes which see what you see! ²⁴For I tell you that many prophets and kings desired to see what you see, and did not see it, and to hear what you hear, and did not hear it.'*

a Or *so it was well-pleasing before thee*

The return of the seventy is the occasion for an inspired and exultant utterance by Jesus, which contains a succinct summary of most of his teaching. The prayer of thanksgiving, here as in the psalter, is the strongest possible form of credal asseveration. Jesus thanks the Father that his disciples have been allowed to experience the presence and power of the kingdom and to discover for themselves what it means to be a Son of God, even though the learned leaders of the nation have turned their backs on this privilege. This has happened in accordance with God's eternal purpose of grace: the only conditions God has established for entry into the kingdom are sincerity, humility, and faith, and those who insist on erecting other standards of intellectual or moral achievement only blind themselves to the simplicity and universality of God's plan. Now, perhaps for the first time, Jesus realizes how completely God's eternal purpose has been entrusted to his hands. Since his baptism his life has been controlled by the consciousness that he has been designated Son of God, and he has lived in intimate mutual understanding with his Father, sharing the Father's concerns and the Father's love. Now it is borne in upon him that others, whatever their religious profession, do not in fact share this intimate relationship. To know a man as father one must be his son, and to know God as Father one must be his Son; and sonship is a gift which the Father has kept within his own authority. When Jesus says that no one knows who the Son is (Matt. 11²⁷: '*no one knows the Son*') except the Father, he does not mean that the identity of the Son is a secret known only to God; he means that God alone has the right to determine who is his Son and who is not, for God's knowledge is always prescient and determinative (cf. Amos 3², where to know is almost the equivalent of to choose; and Mark 13^{32}, where God's knowledge of the last day does not mean that the date is fixed and known only to God, but rather that God alone can determine when his purposes have reached their goal). Only he himself, to whom God has said, 'Thou art my Son', really understands what it means to call God Father. But the gracious purpose which God has so wholly committed to him is that he should share this knowledge with others, and he thanks God that this blessing is already being imparted to the babes who are his disciples. For this event the whole course of Israel's history has been a preparation, and in it the aspirations of prophets and kings find their fulfilment. But the purpose of which Jesus speaks is not merely the purpose for which God called Israel into existence; it is the purpose of the whole creation. The Father is also the Lord of heaven and earth, and the whole magnificent cosmos is but the workshop in which the divine Artificer is producing his masterpiece – sons who know and love their Father.

בבב

21-22
Many scholars have doubted whether Jesus could really have made the claims attributed to him in this passage. Hase described it as 'an aerolite from the Johannine heaven', the implication being that such a theological affirmation has no place in the more terrestrial narrative of the Synoptic Gospels, that the historical Jesus could not have used the terms Father and Son in this absolute fashion (cf. Mark 13^{32}). Modern scholars would be a little more hesitant about the assumption that sayings found in John's Gospel are necessarily unhistorical. If we find a 'Johannine' saying in Q, the oldest strand of the synoptic tradition, the natural inference is, not that Q is untrustworthy, but that John had access to a reliable sayings source. The whole passage abounds in semitic turns of phrase and follows the rhythms of Hebrew verse, so that it cannot be regarded as a theological product of the Greek-speaking Church. Nor is the passage unique even in the Q tradition, for it contains little which is not at least implicit in the stories of the baptism and temptation of Jesus. In the setting of semitic thought the terms Father and Son denote not a metaphysical unity of essence ('of one substance with the Father'), but an ethical unity of character and purpose (cf. Matt. 5^{45}, where to be a son means to take after one's father). When Jesus calls himself the Son, he is not claiming to be God – he emphatically subordinates himself to the Father – but he is claiming that God has

singled him out for special privilege and responsibility, so that he stands in a unique relationship to God into which others can enter only through his mediation.*

10$^{25-37}$ THE MEANING OF DISCIPLESHIP:
         (4) THE LAWYER'S QUESTION

^{25}And behold, a lawyer stood up to put him to the test, saying, 'Teacher, what shall I do to inherit eternal life?' ^{26}He said to him, 'What is written in the law? How do you read?' ^{27}And he answered, 'You shall love the Lord your God with all your heart, and with all your soul, and with all your strength, and with all your mind; and your neighbour as yourself.' ^{28}And he said to him, 'You have answered right; do this, and you will live.'

^{29}But he, desiring to justify himself, said to Jesus, 'And who is my neighbour?' ^{30}Jesus replied, 'A man was going down from Jerusalem to Jericho, and he fell among robbers, who stripped him and beat him, and departed, leaving him half-dead. ^{31}Now by chance a priest was going down that road; and when he saw him he passed by on the other side. ^{32}So likewise a Levite, when he came to the place and saw him, passed by on the other side. ^{33}But a Samaritan, as he journeyed, came to where he was; and when he saw him, he had compassion, ^{34}and went to him and bound up his wounds, pouring on oil and wine; then he set him on his own beast and brought him to an inn, and took care of him.

^{35}'And the next day he took out two denarii^{a} and gave them to the innkeeper, saying, "Take care of him; and whatever more you spend, I will repay you when I come back." ^{36}Which of these three, do you think, proved neighbour to the man who fell among the robbers?'

^{37}He said, 'The one who showed mercy on him.' And Jesus said to him, 'Go and do likewise.'

    a The denarius was worth about a shilling

The conversation between Jesus and the lawyer perfectly illustrates the difference between the ethics of law and the ethics of love. To the

* For a different view see the note on Matt. 11$^{25-27}$ in *The Gospel of St. Matthew* by J. C. Fenton in the series.

lawyer eternal life is a prize to be won by the meticulous observance of religious rules: to Jesus love to God and neighbour is in itself the life of the heavenly kingdom, already begun on earth. The lawyer wants moral duties limited and defined with a rabbinic thoroughness: Jesus declines to set any limits to the obligations of love. Religion to the one is a set of restrictive regulations, to the other a boundless series of opportunities.

The lawyer asks his question, not because he wishes to know the answer, but because he wishes to test Jesus' competence as an expositor of scripture. Jesus turns the tables on him, first by showing that he already knew the answer to his own question, then by compelling him to measure his own life against the standard which he had been prepared to use as a weapon in an intellectual sparring match. In Mark 12$^{28-32}$ it is Jesus who sums up the whole duty of man in the two great commandments, and we might get the impression that Jesus was the first to bring together Deut. 6^5 and Lev. 19^{18} as a summary of the Law. Luke, however, is probably right in thinking that the rabbis had already reached the same conclusion. But between the rabbis and Jesus there were far-reaching differences of interpretation. They thought the whole Law, with all its 613 commandments, was the prescribed way of showing love to God, and he was convinced that love to God meant devotion to God's purpose of grace and redemption. They regarded neighbour as a term of limited liability, and end-lessly debated what classes of men were excluded by it from the scope of the commandment (Gentiles certainly, probably others as well). Jesus refuses to enter this debate. He tells the story of the Good Samaritan, not to answer the question 'Who is my neighbour?' but to show that it is the wrong question. The proper question is, 'To whom can I be a neighbour?'; and the answer is, 'To anyone whose need constitutes a claim on my love.' It is neighbourliness, not neighbourhood, that makes a neighbour.

It is essential to the point of the story that the traveller was left half-dead. The priest and the Levite could not tell without touching him whether he was dead or alive; and it weighed more with them that he might be dead and defiling to the touch of those whose business was with holy things than that he might be alive and in need of care. Jesus deliberately shocks the lawyer by forcing him to consider the possibility that a semi-pagan foreigner might know more

about the love of God than a devout Jew blinded by preoccupation
with pettifogging rules.

10^{38-42} THE MEANING OF DISCIPLESHIP:
          (5) THE DANGER OF SELF-CONCERN

38*Now as they went on their way, he entered a village; and a woman
named Martha received him into her house.* 39*And she had a sister called
Mary, who sat at the Lord's feet and listened to his teaching.*

40*But Martha was distracted with much serving; and she went to him and
said, 'Lord, do you not care that my sister has left me to serve alone? Tell
her then to help me.'* 41*But the Lord answered her, 'Martha, Martha, you
are anxious and troubled about many things;*

42*one thing is needful.*a *Mary has chosen the good portion, which shall
not be taken away from her.'*

  a Other ancient authorities read *few things are needful, or only one*

Few stories in the Gospels have been as consistently mishandled as
this one. It is regularly referred to as the story of Mary and Martha,
though Luke's introductory sentence makes it quite plain that this is
Martha's story, not Mary's. The Middle Ages found here dominical
authority for preferring the contemplative to the active life, and even
modern scholars have tended to assume that the good part chosen by
the spiritual Mary and missed by the worldly Martha was the kingdom of God. Mary has been quite unjustifiably identified with Mary
Magdalene and credited with her passionate devotion. The idealizing
of Mary set in so early that it has even left its mark on the text of
vv. 41–42, where there are no less than five variant readings (see
below). All reference to the one or few things needful should be
omitted, on the evidence of the Western text, as an early gloss. There
is then no comparison between the two sisters; Mary is defended, not
praised to the disparagement of Martha: it is meat and drink to Jesus
to have an appreciative audience, and Mary is not to be deprived of
the one thing she can do well.

Martha, then, is the central figure; she is the hostess, and who, having just read the story of the Good Samaritan, can doubt that she is a stronger character and a more mature disciple than her sister (cf. John 11$^{20-44}$). She is full of good works and entirely free from the selfishness that seeks its own pleasure – a fault which she thinks she detects in Mary. But she earns a gentle reproof from Jesus because she has not yet learned that unselfishness, service, and even sacrifice can be spoiled by self-concern and self-pity, that good works which are not self-forgetful can become a misery to the doer and a tyranny to others.

ﬡﬡ

41–42

There are five variant readings of the reply of Jesus to Martha:

(i) 'Martha, Martha, Mary has chosen, etc.'

(ii) 'Martha, Martha, you are troubled; Mary has chosen, etc.'

(iii) 'Martha, Martha, you are anxious and troubled about many things; but few things are needful: for Mary has chosen, etc.'

(iv) 'Martha, Martha, you are anxious and troubled about many things; one thing is needful. Mary has chosen, etc.'

(v) 'Martha, Martha, you are anxious and troubled about many things; but few things are needful, or only one: for Mary has chosen etc.'

In such a case the backing of even the best MSS. means very little, and the last three readings should all be regarded as variants of an early gloss.

II$^{1-13}$ THE MEANING OF DISCIPLESHIP:
(6) PRAYER

I I *He was praying in a certain place, and when he ceased, one of his disciples said to him, 'Lord, teach us to pray, as John taught his disciples.'* *²And he said to them, 'When you pray, say:*

'Father, hallowed be thy name. Thy kingdom come. ³Give us each ⁴day our daily bread;ᵃ and forgive us our sins, for we ourselves forgive everyone who is indebted to us; and lead us not into temptation.'

⁵And he said to them, 'Which of you who has a friend will go to him at midnight and say to him, "Friend, lend me three loaves;

⁶*for a friend of mine has arrived on a journey, and I have nothing to set before him"; ⁷and he will answer from within, "Do not bother me; the door is now shut, and my children are with me in bed; I cannot get up and give you anything"? ⁸I tell you, though he will not get up and give him anything because he is his friend, yet because of his importunity he will rise and give him whatever he needs. ⁹And I tell you, Ask, and it will be given you; seek, and you will find; knock, and it will be opened to you. ¹⁰For every one who asks receives, and he who seeks finds, and to him who knocks it will be opened. ¹¹What father among you, if his son asks for*ᵇ *a fish, will instead of a fish give him a serpent; ¹²or if he asks for an egg, will give him a scorpion? ¹³If you then, who are evil, know how to give good gifts to your children, how much more will the heavenly Father give the Holy Spirit to those who ask him?'*

a Or *our bread for the morrow*
b Other ancient authorities insert *a loaf, will give him a stone; or if he asks for*

In many manuscripts of Luke's Gospel the Lord's Prayer has been amplified to make it conform to Matthew's longer version, but there is no doubt that the shorter form is what Luke wrote. A comparison of the two versions shows that at some points the one is more original and at some points the other. The clauses in Matthew which have no parallel in Luke can be regarded as liturgical additions. On the other hand, in the petitions for bread and forgiveness, Matthew's precise and particular form is more likely to be original than the generalized form of Luke. Matthew has altered by addition, Luke by modification. The prayer of Jesus may tentatively be reconstructed as follows:

Father, hallowed be thy name.
Thy kingdom come.
Give us this day our daily bread:
and forgive us our debts, as we have also forgiven our debtors.
And lead us not into temptation.

The recovery of the original form is a matter of some importance. Any Jew could have prayed, 'Our Father, who art in heaven ...', using the formal and exclusively religious *Abinu*. But when Jesus prayed, he used the word *Abba* with which a child addressed his human father. He transformed the Fatherhood of God from a theological doctrine into an intense and intimate experience; and he taught his disciples to pray with the same family intimacy.

The Lord's Prayer covers all that a son needs to say to his Father. Before he comes to his own personal needs he shares the Father's larger concerns and plans. God's name is his whole nature and purpose, and it is hallowed when that nature and purpose are known and held in reverence. The first petition, then, is primarily a prayer that God will act to display his holiness and love (cf. Ezek. 36²³); but since God's acts require human agents and a human response, it is also a dedication. The second petition is similarly a double one: for God's kingdom is his rule of righteousness and love, and it is established by his free, unconditioned grace, but it is also a demand for men's faith and obedience. There is no contradiction between this prayer for the future coming of the kingdom and the repeated proclamation of the gospel that the kingdom had already arrived. The rule of God is perfectly present in Jesus and to some extent already in his disciples, but it must grow and spread until it embraces all peoples. But the Lord of history can also be trusted to provide for the needs of individuals; he gives them bread enough for the coming day, pardons their wrong-doings, unless by resentment against others they have closed their hearts to his mercy, protects them from any trial that would prove too much for their strength of character.

The parable of the friend at midnight not only encourages importunity in prayer, but explains why it is necessary. The traveller depended for accommodation on hospitality and, if he made his journey in the evening to avoid the midday heat, might arrive late and unannounced; but the laws of hospitality imposed on his host a solemn obligation to provide for him. No less a reason would justify a man in rousing his neighbour once the door was shut, for the family slept close together on mats on the floor, and nobody could get up without waking the household. His importunate knocking not only got the man the loaves he needed, but also showed how much store he set by getting them. God does not have to be waked or cajoled into giving us what we need – many gifts he bestows on the ungodly and ungrateful; but his choicest blessings are reserved for those who will value them and who show their appreciation by asking until they receive.

Jesus does not promise his disciples that they will always get what they ask, but he does assure them that they cannot ask, seek, or knock in vain. If an earthly father with all his faults and follies provides for the needs of his child, the heavenly Father in all the perfection of his love can be relied on not to play bad jokes on his children. The Father is worthy of absolute trust, and Jesus is prepared to say this without qualification; but we are not to suppose that this saying contains all that he ever had to say about human wants and sufferings. He knew that God often allows some men to suffer the consequences of their own sin and stupidity. He knew that God sometimes subjects others to privation in order that they may inherit a richer blessing (4⁴). The point is that, no matter what God may send, his children must persist in the confidence that he knows what he is about. It was in that trust that Jesus went to the Cross.

מאו

11
In Matt. 7⁹⁻¹⁰ the corresponding terms are loaf–stone, fish–serpent; in the best text of Luke they are fish–serpent, egg–scorpion. The clause about giving a stone for a loaf in some manuscripts of Luke is a harmonizer's attempt to assimilate the text to that of Matthew.

13
The promise of the Holy Spirit is due to the editorial hand of Luke. Matthew (7¹¹) has '*good things*'.

11^{14-26} JESUS AND HIS OPPONENTS:
                    (I) THE TWO KINGDOMS

¹⁴*Now he was casting out a demon that was dumb; when the demon had gone out, the dumb man spoke, and the people marvelled.* ¹⁵*But some of them said, 'He casts out demons by Beelzebul, the prince of demons';*
  ¹⁶*while others, to test him, sought from him a sign from heaven.*
  ¹⁷*But he, knowing their thoughts, said to them, 'Every kingdom divided against itself is laid waste, and house falls upon house.* ¹⁸*And if Satan also is divided against himself, how will his kingdom stand? For you say that I*

cast out demons by Beelzebul. ¹⁹*And if I cast out demons by Beelzebul, by whom do your sons cast them out? Therefore they shall be your judges.* ²⁰*But if it is by the finger of God that I cast out demons, then the kingdom of God has come upon you.* ²¹*When a strong man, fully armed, guards his own palace, his goods are in peace;* ²²*but when one stronger than he assails him and overcomes him, he takes away his armour in which he trusted, and divides his spoil.* ²³*He who is not with me is against me, and he who does not gather with me scatters.*

²⁴'*When the unclean spirit has gone out of a man, he passes through waterless places seeking rest; and finding none he says, "I will return to my house from which I came."* ²⁵*And when he comes he finds it swept and put in order.* ²⁶*Then he goes and brings seven other spirits more evil than himself, and they enter and dwell there; and the last state of that man becomes worse than the first.*'

Jesus is accused of being in league with the devil and of performing cures by black magic. He answers the charge with three arguments. First, the devil is not such a fool as to allow civil war among his servants; mental and physical disease are part of the control which he holds over human life, and he cannot be expected to provide the means of relaxing it. Secondly, there are other exorcists besides Jesus, who know that Satan's minions can be overpowered only by God's strength, and who therefore convict Jesus' critics of blasphemous slander. Thirdly, his detractors should know that the only power capable of breaking the grip of Satan is '*the finger of God*' (Exod. 8¹⁹), and should draw the inevitable conclusion that Satan's kingdom is being invaded by the kingdom of God.

The name Baalzebub (lord of flies) occurs in 2 Kings 1² as a corrupted form of Baalzebul (lord of the house) – the name of the god of Ekron. Neither name occurs in Jewish literature as a title for Satan, but there was a general tendency to identify pagan deities with evil spirits. The name prompts Jesus to draw a picture of Satan as lord of a fortified mansion, keeping his ill-gotten possessions intact until he is overpowered by one who is stronger than he. Thus we are bidden to think of the world as enemy-occupied territory: it belongs by right to God, but through the sin of man it has fallen under the tyranny of Satan, who keeps it in a grip that no power of man can break; and the good news of the gospel is that into this embattled fortress has broken the first champion and representative of an invading and liberating power, the kingdom of God. The two kingdoms confront one another in a war that knows neither truce nor neutrality; he who does not side with Jesus sides with Satan, and he who does not fight for the forces of unity fights for the forces of disruption.

The parable of the empty house presents the same lesson in microcosm. The heart of man is a house which must have an occupant, and the only way to ensure that it is not taken over by disreputable squatters is to see that it is inhabited by the God who made it for himself. Exorcism is not enough: the spiritual world, like the natural, abhors a vacuum.

11²⁷⁻³⁶   JESUS AND HIS OPPONENTS:
              (2) THE FAITHLESS GENERATION

²⁷*As he said this, a woman in the crowd raised her voice and said to him, 'Blessed is the womb that bore you, and the breasts that you sucked!'* ²⁸*But he said, 'Blessed rather are those who hear the word of God and keep it!'*

²⁹*When the crowds were increasing, he began to say, 'This generation is an evil generation; it seeks a sign, but no sign shall be given to it except the sign of Jonah.* ³⁰*For as Jonah became a sign to the men of Nineveh, so will the Son of man be to this generation.* ³¹*The queen of the South will arise at the judgement with the men of this generation and condemn them; for she came from the ends of the earth to hear the wisdom of Solomon, and behold, something greater than Solomon is here.* ³²*The men of Nineveh will arise at the judgement with this generation and condemn it; for they repented at the preaching of Jonah, and behold, something greater than Jonah is here.*

³³*'No one after lighting a lamp puts it in a cellar or under a bushel, but on a stand, that those who enter may see the light.*

³⁴*'Your eye is the lamp of your body; when your eye is sound, your whole body is full of light; but when it is not sound, your body is full of darkness.* ³⁵*Therefore be careful lest the light in you be darkness.* ³⁶*If then your whole body is full of light, having no part dark, it will be wholly bright, as when a lamp with its rays gives you light.'*

The words of the woman in the crowd were a common form of extravagant compliment; but Jesus dismissed them as sheer sentimentality, for the danger of pious effusions is that they are readily enjoyed for their own sake and become a substitute for the one proper response to God's word. The compiler of Q, by placing the story in its present context, has registered his opinion that sentimentality is a form of unbelief.

The rather obscure saying about the sign of Jonah is followed by one explanation here and by quite a different one in Matt. 12⁴⁰. It is probable that in each case the explanation is the work of the evangelist; and of the two Luke's is preferable. Those who asked for a sign wanted some spectacular proof that Jesus was the emissary of God he claimed to be. He replied that the only proof of his credentials he was prepared to give was that which Jonah offered to the Ninevites; Jonah called them to repentance, and in his words they recognized the authentic demand of God. The same demand was present in the preaching of Jesus, and those who were deaf to it were not likely to be convinced by any other form of authentication. They were an evil generation who had proved by their lack of response that, for all their religiosity, they could not recognize the voice of God when they heard it. The Queen of Sheba and the city of Nineveh had responded to the best revelation of God available in their day; and these foreigners would compare favourably on the day of judgement with the chosen people of God who had turned their backs on the greatest of all opportunities.

The final paragraph consists of a series of detached sayings on the theme of light, all with a bearing on spiritual perspicacity and dullness. Israel had been called to be God's light to illumine the world; but, instead of allowing her lamp to shine, she had covered it up to keep it from being blown out, and now had come to the point where she forgot what God's light looked like. Her condition was like that of a man who is unaware that his eyesight is impaired, and who walks blithely into disaster under the impression that he can see where he is going (cf. John 9⁴⁰⁻⁴¹). The last sentence as it stands is hopelessly platitudinous, and C. C. Torrey (*The Four Gospels*, p. 309) has suggested that it is a mistranslation of the Aramaic words of Jesus, and should run: 'If however your whole body is lighted up, with no dark part, then all about you will be light, just as the lamp lights you with its brightness.' Those who allow the light of God to enter their lives become a lamp to dispel the darkness for others.

JESUS AND HIS OPPONENTS:
              (3) PHARISEES AND LAWYERS

^{37}*While he was speaking, a Pharisee asked him to dine with him, so he went in and sat at table. * ^{38}*The Pharisee was astonished to see that he did not first wash before dinner. * ^{39}*And the Lord said to him, 'Now you Pharisees cleanse the outside of the cup and of the dish, but inside you are full of extortion and wickedness. * ^{40}*You fools! Did not he who made the outside make the inside also? * ^{41}*But give for alms those things which are within; and behold, everything is clean for you.*

^{42}*'But woe to you Pharisees! for you tithe mint and rue and every herb, and neglect justice and the love of God; these you ought to have done, without neglecting the others. * ^{43}*Woe to you Pharisees! for you love the best seat in the synagogues and salutations in the market places. * ^{44}*Woe to you! for you are like graves which are not seen, and men walk over them without knowing it.'*

^{45}*One of the lawyers answered him, 'Teacher, in saying this you reproach us also.' * ^{46}*And he said, 'Woe to you lawyers also! for you load men with burdens hard to bear, and you yourselves do not touch the burdens with one of your fingers. * ^{47}*Woe to you! for you build the tombs of the prophets whom your fathers killed. * ^{48}*So you are witnesses and consent to the deeds of your fathers; for they killed them, and you build their tombs. * ^{49}*Therefore also the Wisdom of God said, "I will send them prophets and apostles, some of whom they will kill and persecute," * ^{50}*that the blood of all the prophets, shed from the foundation of the world, may be required of this generation,*

^{51}*from the blood of Abel to the blood of Zechariah, who perished between the altar and the sanctuary. Yes, I tell you, it shall be required of this generation. * ^{52}*Woe to you lawyers! for you have taken away the key of knowledge; you did not enter yourselves, and you hindered those who were entering.'*

^{53}*As he went away from there, the scribes and the Pharisees began to press him hard, and to provoke him to speak of many things,*

^{54}*lying in wait for him, to catch at something he might say.*

It is unlikely that Jesus ever delivered a single great harangue such as this against the Pharisees, and still more unlikely that he did it while a guest in a Pharisee's house. The Woes (vv. 42–52) are a collection made by the compiler of Q, perhaps for use in the continuing debate between Church and synagogue; and Luke has attached them to a similar story drawn from his source L (vv. 37–41, 53–54). The result is a series of seven criticisms of Pharisaism.

i. (vv. 37–41) To the Pharisees religion meant obedience to law. But law can regulate only what a man does, not what he is; and in any legal religion there is a tendency to concentrate on those aspects of conduct – always the most superficial – which can readily be reduced to a code of regulations. Jesus declares that this is like washing the outside of a cup or dish and leaving the inside dirty. 'Give for alms those things which are within' is almost certainly a mistranslation of the Aramaic, and the sentence should read: 'Cleanse the inside and behold all is clean for you.' Where there is inner purity, outward conduct can be allowed to look after itself.

ii. (v. 42) Legal religion concentrates on not doing wrong instead of on active and positive goodness. Dr Johnson's remark to the abbess of a convent – 'Madam, you are here, not for the love of virtue, but the fear of vice' – perfectly fits the Pharisee, who in order to avoid an unwitting transgression of any commandment left a margin of safety round each of them, so that, for example, though the law of tithing obviously applied only to agricultural produce, they paid tithes on their herb gardens just to be on the safe side. Such scrupulosity can flourish only where men have lost their sense of proportion.

iii. (v. 43) Concentration on the great moral obligations, which no one can claim to have adequately fulfilled, produces humility: concentration on minor pieties, which are well within the compass of an enthusiast, leads to self-satisfaction, vanity, and a demand for recognition.

iv. (v. 44) Contact with death made a man ceremonially unclean (Num. 19¹⁶), and graves were frequently whitened to warn all comers of the risk of defilement. Jesus calls the Pharisees unmarked graves, because their reputation for holiness concealed from men the insidious quality of their influence. Matthew (23²⁷) appears to have misunderstood this saying and gives it in a radically different form.

v. (v. 46) The great mass of legislation which the legal experts believed to be binding on every Israelite formed a burden that few men were able to carry. Jesus does not accuse the lawyers of setting up a standard for others which they themselves evaded, but he does accuse them of loading a burden on the weak and not helping them to carry it. A system which makes religion burdensome must be a misrepresentation of the Father's will for his children.

vi. (vv. 47–51) Those who believe that in the Law God has said all that he ever wants to say are not likely to listen to a new revelation from the lips of a living prophet. Legalists are quite prepared to build monuments to dead prophets, but their veneration of tradition commonly goes hand in hand with the same spirit of intolerance that brought the prophets to their death. God in his wisdom has foreseen and provided against this hostile reception of his messengers, and his purpose will not be thwarted by it. But the final crisis of Israel's history has arrived: the present generation must either break with the past by a thorough-going repentance or pay the penalty for the accumulated guilt of past generations. Abel is the first martyr and Zechariah (2 Chron. 24^{22}) the last in the Hebrew canon of scripture.

vii. (v. 52) The function of the scribes was to unlock the scriptures, so that men could find in them the knowledge of God; and instead, by their concentration on the secondary and the peripheral, they have locked the book and thrown away the key.

12$^{1-12}$ FALSE AND TRUE SECURITY:
(I) THE FEAR OF MAN AND THE FEAR OF GOD

12 *In the meantime, when so many thousands of the multitude had gathered together that they trod upon one another, he began to say to his disciples first, 'Beware of the leaven of the Pharisees, which is hypocrisy. ²Nothing is covered up that will not be revealed, or hidden that will not be known. ³Whatever you have said in the dark shall be heard in the light, and what you have whispered in private rooms shall be proclaimed upon the housetops.*

⁴*'I tell you, my friends, do not fear those who kill the body,*

⁵*and after that have no more that they can do. But I will warn you whom to fear: fear him who, after he has killed, has power to cast into hell;ᵃ yes,*

I tell you, fear him! ⁶Are not five sparrows sold for two pennies? And not one of them is forgotten before God. ⁷Why, even the hairs of your head are all numbered. Fear not; you are of more value than many sparrows.

⁸'And I tell you, everyone who acknowledges me before men, the Son of man will also acknowledge before the angels of God; ⁹but he who denies me before men will be denied before the angels of God. ¹⁰And everyone who speaks a word against the Son of man will be forgiven; but he who blasphemes against the Holy Spirit will not be forgiven.

¹¹'And when they bring you before the synagogues and the rulers and the authorities, do not be anxious how or what you are to answer or what you are to say; ¹²for the Holy Spirit will teach you in that very hour what you ought to say.'

a Greek *Gehenna*

The last chapter ended with a diatribe against the Pharisees: this chapter begins by making them an object lesson for the disciples. The whole case against them can be summed up in one word – hypocrisy. Jesus nowhere said that all Pharisees were hypocrites, nor that all hypocrites were Pharisees; but he found more hypocrisy among them than in any other group, and regarded it as the natural product of their teaching. The hypocrite is one who, consciously or unconsciously, has sacrificed truth to appearance: he is more taken up with what people think of him than with the actual state of his soul; he is so busy living up to his reputation that he has no time to be himself; he must always be justifying himself to others, to himself, or to God. He may succeed in deceiving himself and others, but not God; and the day is coming when all pretence will be exposed. The opposite of hypocrisy is repentance, which means accepting the truth about oneself, facing oneself as one really is.

In time of persecution the disciples may be tempted to purchase security by pretending to be other than they are. But there is a limit to what men can say about them or do to them. Their lives are at all times in the hands of God, who alone is to be feared; and the fear of God casts out all other fears. For the fear of God is of quite a different quality from the fear of men; it is not the fear of danger, but the humble acknowledgement of his sovereignty. To him who has no fear of God, no reverence for his majesty and holiness, no appreciation of his grace and mercy, the presence of God could hardly be other than a consuming fire – and what is that but to be cast into hell?

Every man, then, must be loyal to the truth as it has come to him, and for the disciples the truth is embodied in Jesus. In vv. 8–9 Jesus appears to distinguish between himself and the Son of man, possibly because in the Son of man he means to include all who with him belong to the true Israel. Those who are not ashamed or afraid to acknowledge their loyalty to Jesus on earth will be accepted in heaven as members of the people of God. The following saying (v. 10), as it stands, is in flat contradiction to this one, and a comparison with Mark 3²⁸⁻²⁹ indicates that both versions of the saying have suffered in course of transmission. In place of 'the Son of man' here we should read 'the sons of men': every injury and insult offered to men can be forgiven, but not blasphemy against the Holy Spirit; for the Spirit is the bringer of truth to the hearts of men, and to sin against the Spirit is to treat as false that which one knows to be true. This is the un-pardonable sin, not because God is ever unwilling to pardon a penitent, but because an inner dishonesty makes a man incapable of that honest appraisal of himself which is repentance. But those who keep faith with God will find that, even in the utmost crisis, God through his Holy Spirit will keep faith with them, putting into their mouths the simple avowal of the truth which is the only defence they need.

12¹³⁻³⁴   FALSE AND TRUE SECURITY:
(2) EARTHLY AND HEAVENLY TREASURE

¹³One of the multitude said to him, 'Teacher, bid my brother divide the inheritance with me.' ¹⁴But he said to him, 'Man, who made me a judge or divider over you?' ¹⁵And he said to them, 'Take heed, and beware of all covetousness; for a man's life does not consist in the abundance of his pos-sessions.' ¹⁶And he told them a parable, saying, 'The land of a rich man brought forth plentifully; ¹⁷and he thought to himself, "What shall I do, for I have nowhere to store my crops?" ¹⁸And he said, "I will do this: I will pull down my barns, and build larger ones; and there I will store all my grain and my goods. ¹⁹And I will say to my soul, Soul, you have ample

goods laid up for many years; take your ease, eat, drink, be merry." 20But God said to him, "Fool! This night your soul is required of you; and the things you have prepared, whose will they be?" 21So is he who lays up treasure for himself, and is not rich toward God.'

22And he said to his disciples, 'Therefore I tell you, do not be anxious about your life, what you shall eat, nor about your body, what you shall put on. 23For life is more than food, and the body more than clothing. 24Consider the ravens: they neither sow nor reap, they have neither storehouse nor barn, and yet God feeds them. Of how much more value are you than the birds! 25And which of you by being anxious can add a cubit to his span of life?ᵃ 26If then you are not able to do as small a thing as that, why are you anxious about the rest? 27Consider the lilies, how they grow; they neither toil nor spin;ᵇ yet I tell you, even Solomon in all his glory was not arrayed like one of these. 28But if God so clothes the grass which is alive in the field today and tomorrow is thrown into the oven, how much more will he clothe you, O men of little faith? 29And do not seek what you are to eat and what you are to drink, nor be of anxious mind. 30For all the nations of the world seek these things; and your Father knows that you need them. 31Instead, seek hisᶜ kingdom, and these things shall be yours as well.

32'Fear not, little flock, for it is your Father's good pleasure to give you the kingdom. 33Sell your possessions, and give alms; provide yourselves with purses that do not grow old, with a treasure in the heavens that does not fail, where no thief approaches and no moth destroys. 34For where your treasure is, there will your heart be also.'

    a Or *to his stature*
    b Other ancient authorities read *Consider the lilies; they neither spin nor weave*
    c Other ancient authorities read *God's*

It was natural for a plaintiff to bring his case to a religious leader; for the Mosaic code embraced without distinction criminal, civil, ecclesiastical, and moral law, and the rabbi was expected to be proficient in all its departments. This confusion of morality with positive law was one of the weaknesses of Judaism which Jesus constantly sought to correct. Here he declines to act as judge or arbitrator: the maintenance of justice belongs to the realm of Caesar, whereas he is concerned with the higher standards of the kingdom of God. Law may lay a restraint on sinful men, so as to make them law-abiding citizens, but it cannot make them good. On the other hand, when men have become good by entering the kingdom and living by its moral standards and its spiritual resources, legislation ceases to be relevant to them (cf. Mark 10^{1-12}, where the law of divorce is said to be irrelevant for those who have entered the kingdom). Thus in the present instance Jesus points out that there could be no dispute to bring before an arbitrator if it were not for covetousness. Better to be a victim of injustice than to fall into the error of thinking that abundance of life is to be found in material possessions (cf. 1 Cor. 6^{7-8}).

The rich fool in the parable discovered too late that material wealth is not a permanent possession. Because he had devoted all his energy to amassing property, he had nothing he could call his own, and death disclosed his essential poverty. The only possessions worthy of man's striving are those death cannot take away.

Wealth is a peril to those who have it but also to those who do not. Jesus denounces anxiety as absurd, pointless, pagan; but his reason for doing so is that it may be an insidious threat to the disciples' loyalty. A courageous man will brace himself against persecution, but insecurity, when it is a constant companion, can engross the attention and sap the resolve. Nothing is more likely to distract the disciples from whole-hearted devotion to the kingdom than worry. Yet it is absurd to worry: would God have given man the gift of life without providing the smaller gifts of food and clothing that are necessary for the maintenance of life, or would he lavish so much care and artistry on improvident birds and transient flowers, only to neglect those whom he has destined to be his children? It is pointless to worry: as the rich fool learnt, anxiety cannot postpone for one hour the approach of death, nor is it any more effective in other matters. It is pagan to worry: it implies that we do not really believe that God is our Father. But the real cure for worry is to put first things first, to care more about God's kingdom than about personal needs. Those who do so, find that God provides for his servants, but they also find that the necessities of life are fewer and simpler than selfishness supposes.

Even devotion to the kingdom is capable of breeding worry. The servant of the kingdom may exchange his worldly cares for a confidence that his individual destiny is in God's keeping and that he has a treasure secure against theft and damage; but what of the future of the cause he serves? Jesus knows that to his little flock the enterprise he is sharing with them must appear formidable and the hope of victory remote. They have to learn to think of the kingdom not as an other-worldly dream or as a distant goal of history, but as a present possession, realized not by their own achievement but by the Father's gift, and guaranteed to them by his good pleasure, his eternal purpose of grace.

৩৩

25
The ambiguous word here can mean either age or height. But a cubit is the distance from elbow to fingertip; and not many people spend their lives fretting about adding eighteen inches to their stature. Hence the translation in the text is to be preferred. The poet Mimnermus uses the cubit to denote a brief span of time, and the Psalmist speaks of his whole life as '*a few handbreadths*' (Ps. 39⁵).

27
The reading of Codex Bezae – 'they neither spin nor weave' – is accepted by many scholars on the ground that the better-attested reading is a harmonization of Luke's text with Matthew's.

12³⁵⁻⁴⁸   THE IMMINENT CRISIS:
                 (I) FOR THE DISCIPLES

³⁵'*Let your loins be girded and your lamps burning,* ³⁶*and be like men who are waiting for their master to come home from the marriage feast, so that they may open to him at once when he comes and knocks.* ³⁷*Blessed are those servants whom the master finds awake when he comes; truly, I say to you, he will gird himself and have them sit at table, and he will come and serve them.* ³⁸*If he comes in the second watch, or in the third, and finds them so, blessed are those servants!* ³⁹*But know this, that if the householder had known at what hour the thief was coming, he would have been awake and*ᵃ *would not have left his house to be broken into.* ⁴⁰*You also must be ready; for the Son of man is coming at an hour you do not expect.*'

⁴¹*Peter said, 'Lord, are you telling this parable for us or for all?'* ⁴²*And the Lord said, 'Who then is the faithful and wise steward, whom his master*

will set over his household, to give them their portion of food at the proper time? 43Blessed is that servant whom his master when he comes will find so doing. 44Truly I tell you, he will set him over all his possessions. 45But if that servant says to himself, "My master is delayed in coming," and begins to beat the menservants and the maidservants, and to eat and drink and get drunk, 46the master of that servant will come on a day when he does not expect him and at an hour he does not know, and will punishᵇ him, and put him with the unfaithful. 47And that servant who knew his master's will, but did not make ready or act according to his will, shall receive a severe beating. 48But he who did not know, and did what deserved a beating, shall receive a light beating. Every one to whom much is given, of him will much be required; and of him to whom men commit much they will demand the more.'

a Other ancient authorities omit *would have been awake and*
b Or *cut him in pieces*

We have here a series of warnings to the disciples to be on the alert for an impending emergency – the coming of the Son of man: they are to keep their long robes tucked up into their girdles in readiness for immediate and energetic action; like loyal servants keeping an all-night vigil in case their master should return from the protracted festivities of a wedding, they must be sure that the decisive moment does not catch them napping; they must not be taken unawares, like the householder who is asleep when the thief breaks through the mud wall of his house. But what is the nature of the crisis for which Jesus wishes his friends to be prepared?

Matthew and Luke disagree about the answer to this question. Matthew has placed two of these parables in the fifth of his great discourses, which is devoted to the parousia or Second Coming of Christ. Luke, on the other hand, follows this passage with one about the approaching climax of Jesus' ministry and another dealing with the judgement which is about to overtake the nation of Israel; and the juxtaposition of these three themes indicates that in his mind they were intimately related. Jesus, he would have us understand, was expecting a single great crisis, which would mean death for himself, a searching test for his disciples, and judgement for Israel; and this event, contrary to all appearances of defeat and failure, was to be the great triumph prophesied by Daniel (7^{13}), in which God would bestow world dominion on the Son of man, the symbolic representative of the people of God.

There can be little doubt that Luke's interpretation is right and Matthew's wrong. Whatever Jesus may have had to say about his own return and the consummation of history, it is hardly credible that he should have required his disciples during his lifetime to be on guard night and day for an emergency which, to say the least of it, could not happen for some time after his death. If, however, he did not know when to expect the final and fatal outbreak of official hostility to his ministry, it was inevitable that he should repeatedly and earnestly warn his friends to be ready at all times for the clash, in which they themselves might well be involved, and by which Israel would seal her own destiny. Yet Luke helps us to detect the process by which Matthew's reinterpretation arose. When the crucifixion had become a distant memory, the parables of watchfulness were still preserved along with other teaching of Jesus, and Christians were bound to ask whether these warnings were intended only for the twelve as they faced the historic crisis that brought the Master to his death, or whether they had a more general and permanent application (cf. Mark 13^{37}). Matthew's answer was to edit all such warnings so as to make them into predictions of the parousia. Luke, always more conservative, has simply hinted at the problem. Peter's question (v. 41) was not part of the tradition which Luke derived from Q, and is best regarded as his own editorial addition. He has, in fact, made Peter spokesman for the Church of his own day, and his answer is that Christians need not speculate about dates as long as they remain loyal and dutiful servants (cf. Acts 1$^{7-8}$).

❧

39
The words 'would have been awake and' are omitted by Codex Sinaiticus, Codex Bezae, and a few other manuscripts, and should probably be regarded as a harmonistic addition from Matt. 24^{43}.

I2$^{49-53}$ THE IMMINENT CRISIS: (2) FOR JESUS

^{49}*'I came to cast fire upon the earth; and would that it were already kindled!* ^{50}*I have a baptism to be baptized with; and how I am constrained until it is accomplished!* ^{51}*Do you think that I have come to give peace on earth? No, I tell you, but rather division;* ^{52}*for henceforth in one house there will be five divided, three against two and two against three;* ^{53}*they will be divided, father against son and son against father, mother against daughter and daughter against her mother, mother-in-law against her daughter-in-law and daughter-in-law against her mother-in-law.'*

The imagery which Jesus here uses has a long history. In the Old Testament we frequently read of men passing through the fire of testing and judgement or overwhelmed in a sea of troubles (Ps. 66^{12}, 69$^{2-3}$, Isa. 43^2). But baptism is not an Old Testament word. In using it, here and elsewhere (Mark 10^{38}), to describe his own death, Jesus was consciously echoing the teaching of John the Baptist, and incidentally demonstrating how great a gulf lay between him and the greatest of his predecessors. John had prophesied the coming of one who should baptize with the fire of the divine judgement: it had never occurred to him that the Coming One might be the first to undergo that baptism. Jewish inter-testamental literature was full of descriptions of the 'woes' which would overwhelm the world as a prelude to the establishment of God's kingdom: but there had never been any suggestion that the Messiah must pass through these deep waters. An earlier writer had depicted the break-up of family life as one of the symptoms of Israel's degeneracy which called for punishment (Mic. 7^6): he would have been astonished to be told that God would deliberately bring about such a state of affairs in the working out of his purpose.

This rare glimpse into the inner mind of Jesus reveals an agonizing mixture of impatience and reluctance. Convinced that God's redemptive plan requires him to bring upon the earth the fiery baptism of judgement, not by inflicting it on others but by undergoing it himself, he feels handicapped and thwarted until this mission can be accomplished. But he knows also that his death will be caused not only by 'the definite plan and foreknowledge of God' but by the free choice of Israel's leaders, and he is loath to force their hands, to bring upon his people the inevitable conflict of loyalties, to compel them to choose once and for all between God's kingdom and their own nationalism; for he knows that, in rejecting him, they will be rejecting their last chance of national safety.

12^{54}–13^9 THE IMMINENT CRISIS:
(3) FOR ISRAEL

^{54}*He also said to the multitudes, 'When you see a cloud rising in the west, you say at once, "A shower is coming"; and so it happens.*

^{55}*'And when you see the south wind blowing, you say, "There will be scorching heat"; and it happens.* ^{56}*You hypocrites! You know how to interpret the appearance of earth and sky; but why do you not know how to interpret the present time?*

^{57}*'And why do you not judge for yourselves what is right?* ^{58}*As you go with your accuser before the magistrate, make an effort to settle with him on the way, lest he drag you to the judge, and the judge hand you over to the officer, and the officer put you in prison.*

^{59}*'I tell you, you will never get out till you have paid the very last copper.'*

13 *There were some present at that very time who told him of the Galileans whose blood Pilate had mingled with their sacrifices.*

^{2}*And he answered them, 'Do you think that these Galileans were worse sinners than all the other Galileans, because they suffered thus?*

^{3}*'I tell you, No; but unless you repent you will all likewise perish.*

^{4}*'Or those eighteen upon whom the tower in Siloam fell and killed them, do you think that they were worse offenders than all the others who dwelt in Jerusalem?* ^{5}*I tell you, No; but unless you repent you will all likewise perish.'*

^{6}*And he told this parable: 'A man had a fig tree planted in his vineyard; and he came seeking fruit on it and found none.* ^{7}*And he said to the vine-dresser, "Lo, these three years I have come seeking fruit on this fig tree, and I find none. Cut it down; why should it use up the ground?"* ^{8}*And he answered him, "Let it alone, sir, this year also, till I dig about it and put on manure.* 9*And if it bears fruit next year, well and good; but if not, you can cut it down."* ʼ

When a small cloud appeared over the Mediterranean, or when the wind veered round to the south, the weatherwise Israelites knew how to draw the proper conclusion; but when the storm clouds were racing before high winds on the political horizon, they remained unconcerned. This criticism tells us as much about Jesus as it does about Israel. His premonitions of disaster were based in part on his understanding of God's purpose for him, laid down in the pages of scripture, but in part also on his ability to interpret the present time. His gospel was not a political manifesto, but it had political implications: as Messiah he had summoned Israel to reconsider the meaning of her vocation as people of God and to repent of the national pride which interpreted that vocation in terms of privilege and worldly greatness. To reject the way of Jesus was to choose the path leading directly to conflict with Rome and subsequent catastrophe. In the mounting hostility to his own mission, in the strained relations between Jew and Gentile, in the frequent outbreaks of patriotic frenzy, and in the growing severity with which these outbreaks were suppressed, Jesus read the signs of the times, which he believed should be equally legible to others. As in the days of Isaiah God had used Assyria as the rod of his anger (Isa. 10⁵ff.), so now he was about to use Rome as the agent of his judgement upon his people; and only immediate repentance could save them.

The urgency of the need is brought out in the three paragraphs that follow. The insolvent debtor makes every effort to settle his case out of court, rather than face the utter ruin of being jailed for debt, with no prospect either of earning money to pay his creditor or of being released until the debt is paid. Similarly Israel, faced with the Great Assize, would do well to settle her account with God by admitting her spiritual bankruptcy and casting herself upon his mercy. The victims of tragedy, whether it is due to the vindictive severity of Pilate (cf. Josephus, *Jewish War*, II, 9, 4) or to unforeseeable accident, must not be regarded as outstanding sinners specially singled out for divine retribution, but provide nevertheless a salutary reminder that the whole nation is heading for a more comprehensive disaster. Like the unfruitful fig tree which is given one last chance to respond to special treatment, Israel must use the respite which God in his mercy has given her to bring about a national reformation, or find that there is a limit to the divine forbearance.

13¹⁰⁻²¹   THE PRESENCE OF THE KINGDOM

¹⁰*Now he was teaching in one of the synagogues on the sabbath.*

¹¹*And there was a woman who had had a spirit of infirmity for eighteen years; she was bent over and could not fully straighten herself.* ¹²*And when Jesus saw her, he called her and said to her, 'Woman, you are freed from your infirmity.'* ¹³*And he laid his hands upon her, and immediately she was made straight, and she praised God.* ¹⁴*But the ruler of the synagogue, indignant because Jesus had healed on the sabbath, said to the people, 'There are six days on which work ought to be done; come on those days and be healed, and not on the sabbath day.'* ¹⁵*Then the Lord answered him, 'You hypocrites! Does not each of you on the sabbath untie his ox or his ass from the manger, and lead it away to water it?* ¹⁶*And ought not this woman, a daughter of Abraham whom Satan bound for eighteen years, be loosed from this bond on the sabbath day?'* ¹⁷*As he said this, all his adversaries were put to shame; and all the people rejoiced at all the glorious things that were done by him.*

¹⁸*He said therefore, 'What is the kingdom of God like? And to what shall I compare it?* ¹⁹*It is like a grain of mustard seed which a man took and sowed in his garden; and it grew and became a tree, and the birds of the air made nests in its branches.'*

²⁰*And again he said, 'To what shall I compare the kingdom of God?*

²¹*'It is like leaven which a woman took and hid in three measures of meal, till it was all leavened.'*

The episode of the cripple woman has much in common with earlier controversies about the sabbath. Jesus is accused of breaking the Law by healing on the sabbath when there was no danger of death. He replies that, since rabbinic regulations allow a man to provide for his domestic animals on the sabbath, it is inconsistent to be more merciful to a beast than to a fellow human being. But there is also a new note in Jesus' answer – it was necessary that this woman be loosed from her bond on the sabbath. The word used for 'necessary' (*dei*) is the same that was used to express the divine necessity of the Cross (9²²). Jesus is acting in obedience to a necessity which takes precedence over all other obligations, including the sabbath law. The kingdom of God has broken in upon the kingdom of Satan, and the work of liberating the victims of Satan's tyranny must go on seven days a week. So far from being the wrong day, the sabbath was actually the best day for such works of mercy. For the sabbath – the day which God had given to Israel as a weekly release from the bondage of labour – was also a weekly foretaste of the rest which awaited the people of God in the kingdom, the final release from all bondage. To liberate men and women from the reign of Satan and to bring them under the gracious reign of God was therefore to fulfil the purpose of the sabbath, not to profane it.

The parables that follow explain in what sense Jesus thought of the kingdom as a present reality. From the tiny mustard seed grows a plant which can reach a height of ten or twelve feet. From a small lump of yeast comes a ferment which can permeate a basinful of meal. In the same way, the small triumphs of Jesus' preaching and healing ministry seem insignificant in comparison with the immense and pervasive power of evil; yet in them the kingdom of God is present in germinal and dynamic form, which holds a guarantee of future results out of all proportion to its present size. The tree which supplies a home for the birds is a common Old Testament picture representing the great empire which gives security to the nations of the world (Ezek. 17²³, 31⁶, Dan. 4¹²).

13²²⁻³⁵   THE PENALTY OF REFUSAL

²²*He went on his way through towns and villages, teaching and journeying towards Jerusalem.* ²³*And someone said to him, 'Lord, will those who are saved be few?'* ²⁴*And he said to them, 'Strive to enter by the narrow door; for many, I tell you, will seek to enter and will not be able.* ²⁵*When once the householder has risen up and shut the door, you will begin to stand outside and to knock at the door, saying, "Lord, open to us." He will answer*

you, "I do not know where you come from." ²⁶Then you will begin to say, "We ate and drank in your presence, and you taught in our streets." ²⁷But he will say, "I tell you, I do not know where you come from; depart from me, all you workers of iniquity!" ²⁸There you will weep and gnash your teeth, when you see Abraham and Isaac and Jacob and all the prophets in the kingdom of God and you yourselves thrust out. ²⁹And men will come from east and west, and from north and south, and sit at table in the kingdom of God. ³⁰And behold, some are last who will be first, and some are first who will be last.'

³¹At that very hour some Pharisees came, and said to him, 'Get away from here, for Herod wants to kill you.' ³²And he said to them, 'Go and tell that fox, "Behold, I cast out demons and perform cures today and tomorrow, and the third day I finish my course. ³³Nevertheless, I must go on my way today and tomorrow and the day following; for it cannot be that a prophet should perish away from Jerusalem."

³⁴'O Jerusalem, Jerusalem, killing the prophets and stoning those who are sent to you! How often would I have gathered your children together as a hen gathers her brood under her wings, and you would not! ³⁵Behold, your house is forsaken. And I tell you, you will not see me until you say, "Blessed be he who comes in the name of the Lord."'

The question whether many or few would be saved was much discussed (cf. 4 Ezra 7⁴⁵⁻⁹²²). Jesus refuses to speculate about matters that are better left to the wisdom and mercy of God. Idle speculation can only distract men's attention from the one clear and urgent fact, that the kingdom of God is present and the door open. The door is not so wide that men may saunter casually in at their own convenience; it is a narrow opening through which they must thrust themselves with determination. It will not remain open indefinitely, and those who miss the present opportunity may find that they are too late. The master of the house expects his household to be indoors by locking-up time and will not after hours be wheedled into admitting others who have ignored the door while it stood open, and who now come knocking with the flimsy pretext of superficial acquaintance. All who enter by the open door are members of God's family, but those who wait till the door is shut prove themselves strangers to him.

When the Jews were under foreign domination, without possibility of physical retaliation, many of them found compensation in the thought that in the world to come they would be honoured guests at the messianic Banquet, and that one ingredient of their bliss would be the exclusion of their Gentile oppressors. Jesus reverses this popular fancy: those who refuse the invitation of the gospel will find themselves on the outside looking in, doubly mortified by their own exclusion and by the inclusion of the Gentiles. The standards of the heavenly kingdom are so different from those of earth that there are bound to be many surprises.

The Pharisees who came to warn Jesus of Herod's intentions posed as friends, but they might have guessed that he would be suspicious of their unwonted solicitude for his safety and would recognize that they were actually in collusion with Herod. Herod earned himself the title of fox because, not daring to take direct action against Jesus at the height of his Galilean popularity, he tried to drive him from his tetrarchy by this devious intimidation, subtly disguised as friendship. Jesus' retort is that he will not be deflected by threats from the course he has set himself. When the time comes for him to leave Herod's territory – and the day cannot be long delayed – he will move on towards Jerusalem, driven not by threats but by the inner compulsion of his mission. In the meantime he is in no danger: Herod has no right to usurp the position, which Jerusalem occupies by long usage, as killer of the messengers of God.

Luke has inserted the story of Herod's stratagem from L at this point in an otherwise solidly Q context, because, like the passage that follows, it speaks of Jerusalem as the murderer of prophets. But the link is quite artificial. The one saying is full of savage irony, the other of passionate regret. The lament over Jerusalem is full of Old Testament allusions. The gathering of the scattered children of Jerusalem is one of the most frequently reiterated themes of messianic expectation (e.g. Isa. 60⁴, Zech. 10⁶⁻¹⁰). The house may mean Jerusalem (Jer. 12⁷) or the temple (Ezek. 8-11), but in either case it is said to be forsaken because God has withdrawn his protective presence and abandoned his people to their enemies. The final quotation is taken from Psalm 118, one of the psalms used by pilgrims to the great festivals: it describes the deliverance of Israel from her enemies by the intervention of God, and could readily be interpreted as a prediction of the final deliverance. The whole passage has been used as evidence that Jesus made frequent visits to Jerusalem which are not recorded in the Synoptic Gospels; but this interpretation makes it almost impossible to give any satisfactory meaning to the words, '*You will not see me until you say* . . .' The difficulty disappears if we suppose God to be the speaker, as in similar expressions of thwarted affection in the prophetic writings (Hos. 11$^{8-9}$, Isa. 65$^{1-2}$). It is God who has sent his prophets with patient persistence, who gathers his people under the shadow of his wings (Deut. 32^{11}, Ruth 2^{12}, Ps. 57^{1}, 61^{4}, 91^{4}), who abandons Israel's house to destruction by his own departure, who hides his face from his people until they are ready to welcome their Messiah.

14$^{1-14}$ DINNER-TABLE DISCOURSES:
(1) AT A PHARISEE'S TABLE

14 *One sabbath when he went to dine at the house of a ruler who belonged to the Pharisees, they were watching him. ²And behold, there was a man before him who had dropsy. ³And Jesus spoke to the lawyers and Pharisees, saying, 'Is it lawful to heal on the sabbath, or not?'*

⁴But they were silent. Then he took him and healed him, and let him go. ⁵And he said to them, 'Which of you, having an ass^{a} or an ox that has fallen into a well, will not immediately pull him out on a sabbath day?' ⁶And they could not reply to this.

⁷Now he told a parable to those who were invited, when he marked how they chose the places of honour, saying to them, ⁸'When you are invited by anyone to a marriage feast, do not sit down in a place of honour, lest a more eminent man than you be invited by him; ⁹and he who invited you both will come, and say to you, "Give place to this man," and then you will begin with shame to take the lowest place. ¹⁰But when you are invited, go and sit in the lowest place, so that when your host comes he may say to you, "Friend, go up higher"; then you will be honoured in the presence of all who sit at table with you. ¹¹For every one who exalts himself will be humbled, and he who humbles himself will be exalted.'

¹²He said also to the man who had invited him, 'When you give a dinner or a banquet, do not invite your friends or your brothers or your kinsmen or rich neighbours, lest they also invite you in return, and you be repaid. ¹³*But when you give a feast, invite the poor, the maimed, the lame, the blind,* ¹⁴*and you will be blessed, because they cannot repay you. You will be repaid at the resurrection of the just.*'

a Other ancient authorities read *a son*

Many of the sayings of Jesus came to Luke without any indication of the context in which they were spoken, and he has consistently tried to supply such 'orphaned' traditions with a narrative setting. The arrangement of the present section seems somewhat artificial, inasmuch as Luke has used an episode at a Pharisee's dinner-table as the setting for three different discourses on the subject of feasting. There is, however, more coherence between the discourses and their setting than appears on the surface; for all are part of the continuing debate between Jesus and the Pharisees.

First there is a story about sabbath observance – the fourth recorded by Luke. There is no reason to suppose that the man with dropsy was the bait in a Pharisaic trap – he could have been a tolerated intruder like the woman with the ointment (7^{36ff.}) – but his presence created a tense situation which Jesus could not ignore. By his first question he grasped the initiative; his table companions could not answer yes or no without appearing either lax in their attitude to the Law or harsh and unsympathetic towards suffering; but by refusing to express a legal opinion they forfeited the right to criticize afterwards. The second question carried the dispute to the superior court of conscience. As an academic exercise rabbis might discuss the case of the domestic animal in the well and come to different conclusions (*Zad. Fr.* 13²³), but to the man whose property was involved the answer would not be in doubt. Yet if the law of mercy may take precedence over the sabbath law in the case of a beast, how much more in the case of a person.

The advice about precedence at table (vv. 7–11) could be paralleled over and over again from Jewish sources; but, as Luke points out, Jesus intended it to be taken as a parable. That is, he was using a familiar home-truth about good manners to convey a religious lesson which the Pharisees particularly needed to learn. As in social etiquette, so in the spiritual realm, recognition eludes those who demand it and accrues to those who think more highly of others than of themselves.

True dignity is always unconscious dignity, and true honour, whether conferred by man or God, is always unexpected.

The rule for hosts was also peculiarly applicable to Pharisees. It is a common human characteristic to cultivate the society only of one's own kind, but the Pharisees had elevated this tendency into a spiritual principle, refusing all social contact with those who did not share their standards of piety. Whatever earthly satisfaction they may have derived from their mutual benefit society, they missed the heavenly blessedness that comes to those who show hospitality and kindness where there is no possibility of recompense. It may seem strange that Jesus should have spoken of reward for disinterested goodness, for one cannot be unselfish with an eye to heavenly gain; yet the reward is real. The loving service of the helpless and needy, which Jesus himself exemplified, is the very life of the kingdom of God, and those who learn on earth to enjoy such a life will enjoy the perfection of it in heaven.

ഇരുന

5
The Chester Beatty Papyrus (P⁴⁵), Codex Vaticanus, Codex Alexandrinus, and other manuscripts read 'son' for 'ass'. If this reading is adopted, then the argument is that the rule of mercy is not to be applied only when self-interest is involved.

14^{15-24} DINNER-TABLE DISCOURSES:
                (2) THE GREAT BANQUET

¹⁵*When one of those who sat at table with him heard this, he said to him,* '*Blessed is he who shall eat bread in the kingdom of God!*'

¹⁶*But he said to him,* '*A man once gave a great banquet, and invited many;* ¹⁷*and at the time for the banquet he sent his servant to say to those who had been invited, "Come; for all is now ready." *¹⁸*But they all alike began to make excuses. The first said to him, "I have bought a field, and I must go out and see it; I pray you, have me excused." *¹⁹*And another said, "I have bought five yoke of oxen, and I go to examine them; I pray you, have me excused." *²⁰*And another said, "I have married a wife, and therefore I cannot*

come." ²¹So the servant came and reported this to his master. Then the householder in anger said to his servant, "Go out quickly to the streets and lanes of the city, and bring in the poor and maimed and blind and lame." ²²And the servant said, "Sir, what you commanded has been done, and still there is room." ²³And the master said to the servant, "Go out to the highways and hedges, and compel people to come in, that my house may be filled. ²⁴For I tell you, none of those men who were invited shall taste my banquet." '

The table talk in the Pharisee's house ends with a parable which is clearly directed against the Pharisees. It is called forth by a remark of conventional piety from one of Jesus' fellow guests: Blessed are those who are entitled to attend the great banquet of the kingdom of God. Such an exclamation could come only from one who is confident in the possession of his own invitation. The parable of Jesus shatters this complacency: the kingdom of God is not an other-worldly prospect to be contemplated with unctuous sentiment, but a present reality calling for immediate response; the banquet is now ready and, according to Jewish custom, the guests are being summoned by a servant to take their place at the table; and those who, having previously accepted the invitation, now discover other more pressing engagements, will lose their opportunity and find their place filled by others.

The original guests of the story represent the respectable, law-abiding Jews who, by turning a deaf ear to the preaching of Jesus, have shown that they care more for their own religious system than for the gracious calling of God. The beggars of the city streets and alleys are the spiritual waifs of the Jewish people, the tax gatherers and sinners whom the Pharisees regarded with contempt. The vagrants of the country roads, outside the city of Judaism, are the Gentiles. The parable clearly proclaims the universal inclusiveness of the kingdom, from which nobody is excluded but by his own choice. The one disqualifying sin is to find preoccupations more attractive than the friendship of God.

෴

23

Some scholars consider that this verse is a pro-Gentile elaboration of the original story, because it has no counterpart in Matt. 22²⁻¹⁰. The Matthean version is, however, seriously corrupt: the guests not only disregard but do violence to the servants sent to summon them, the preparations for dinner are interrupted by a punitive expedition to destroy the city in which they live, and after that the dinner is still ready.

25Now great multitudes accompanied him; and he turned and said to them, 26'If anyone comes to me and does not hate his own father and mother and wife and children and brothers and sisters, yes, and even his own life, he cannot be my disciple. 27Whoever does not bear his own cross and come after me, cannot be my disciple. 28For which of you, desiring to build a tower, does not first sit down and count the cost, whether he has enough to complete it? 29Otherwise, when he has laid a foundation, and is not able to finish, all who see it begin to mock him, 30saying, "This man began to build, and was not able to finish." 31Or what king, going to encounter another king in war, will not sit down first and take counsel whether he is able with ten thousand to meet him who comes against him with twenty thousand? 32And if not, while the other is yet a great way off, he sends an embassy and asks terms of peace. 33So, therefore, whoever of you does not renounce all that he has cannot be my disciple.

34'Salt is good; but if salt has lost its taste, how shall its saltness be restored? 35It is fit neither for the land nor for the dunghill; men throw it away. He who has ears to hear, let him hear.'

To the very end Jesus retained the enthusiastic support of the Galilean crowd, but theirs was an uncomprehending enthusiasm. They thought that his journey to Jerusalem was the victory march of the Messiah, and they wanted to be on hand when he claimed his throne to cheer and to enjoy a reflected glory. With relentless honesty Jesus disillusioned them; his business in Jerusalem was exacting and dangerous, calling not for spectators but for recruits, men with undivided loyalty and coldly calculated pertinacity.

To hate father and mother did not mean on the lips of Jesus what it conveys to the Western reader (cf. Mark 7^{9-13}). The semitic mind is comfortable only with extremes – light and darkness, truth and falsehood, love and hate – primary colours with no half-shades of compromise in between. The semitic way of saying 'I prefer this to that' is 'I like this and hate that' (cf. Gen. 29$^{30-31}$, Deut. 21$^{15-17}$). Thus for the followers of Jesus, to hate their families meant giving the family second place in their affections. Ties of kinship must not be allowed to interfere with their absolute commitment to the kingdom. As commonly happens with Q sayings, the conservative Luke has kept the stark, semitic form, while Matthew has substituted an accurate paraphrase which was more readily intelligible to his Gentile readers (Matt. 10^{37}). It is not quite so clear what is meant by bearing a cross. Crucifixion must have been appallingly familiar to all Galileans as a Roman method of executing political agitators. But did Jesus mean that discipleship was likely to bring men into fatal conflict with the Roman government? Or did he use the cross as a symbol for the extreme of torment and degradation which his followers must be prepared to accept as the price of their calling?

The twin parables of the tower-builder and the king were not meant to deter any serious candidates for discipleship, but only to warn them that becoming a disciple was the most important enterprise a man could undertake and deserved at least as much consideration as he would give to business or politics. Nobody can be swept into the kingdom on a flood-tide of emotion; he must walk in with clear-eyed deliberation. Jesus' disciples are called to be the salt of society – preservative, seasoning, fertilizer; and there is no room in their ranks for those who lack the distinctive qualities of discipleship, any more than there is room in the kitchen cupboard for savourless salt, which like other rubbish in the east is thrown out in the street.

15$^{1-10}$ RETRIEVING THE LOST:
(I) THE LOST SHEEP AND THE LOST COIN

I 5 *Now the tax collectors and sinners were all drawing near to hear him.* *²And the Pharisees and the scribes murmured, saying, 'This man receives sinners and eats with them.'*

³So he told them this parable: ⁴'What man of.you, having a hundred sheep, if he has lost one of them, does not leave the ninety-nine in the wilderness, and go after the one which is lost, until he finds it? ⁵And when he has found it, he lays it on his shoulders, rejoicing. ⁶And when he comes home, he calls together his friends and his neighbours, saying to them, "Rejoice with me, for I have found my sheep which was lost." ⁷Even so, I tell you, there will be more joy in heaven over one sinner who repents than over ninety-nine righteous persons who need no repentance.

⁸'Or what woman, having ten silver coins,ᵃ if she loses one coin, does not light a lamp and sweep the house and seek diligently until she finds it? ⁹And when she has found it, she calls together her friends and neighbours, saying, "Rejoice with me, for I have found the coin which I had lost." ¹⁰Even so, I tell you, there is joy before the angels of God over one sinner who repents.'

a The drachma, rendered here by *silver coin*, was about ninepence.

For the third time in Luke's Gospel Jesus is charged with encouraging loose morals by associating too freely with renegades. His critics believe that their whole duty is to avoid anything that could contaminate their sanctity, and they are bewildered at his disregard of their spiritual security policy. Jesus justifies his attitude to the outcast by claiming that it is also God's attitude, that God's merciful love does not wait for the penitence of the sinner, but takes the initiative to bring about his restoration.

The parables of the lost sheep and the lost coin belong together – Jesus made a habit of telling short parables in pairs (cf. 5³⁶⁻³⁷, 11³¹⁻³², 12²⁴⁻²⁷, 13¹⁸⁻²¹, 14²⁸⁻³²). The parables portray for us a man and a woman going to infinite trouble to recover their lost property. The sheep is a gregarious animal which does not wilfully separate itself from the flock, but in a mountainous district it can easily nibble its way to a place from which there is no return, and where, if it is not rescued, it will die of starvation. But the shepherd does not let that happen; for him the arduous search and the risks involved in bringing the exhausted but struggling animal to safety are all in a day's work. A coin is easily lost among the straw in a dark corner of a windowless oriental house, but the careful housewife will not rest until she finds it, even though it means turning the house upside down. In each case we are told that the friends and neighbours come to join the celebration for the recovery of that which had been lost. God, we are to understand, is not less persistent than men and women in seeking what he has lost nor less jubilant when his search is successful; and those who would be reckoned his friends will always share his jubilation and, wherever possible, will want to share his search as well. To call a man lost is to pay him a high compliment, for it means that he is precious in the sight of God. It is interesting to note with what confidence Jesus speaks of things that happen in heaven. He knows God well enough to know what will make him happy.

15^{11-32} RETRIEVING THE LOST:
(2) THE TWO SONS

¹¹And he said, 'There was a man who had two sons; ¹²and the younger of them said to his father, "Father, give me the share of property that falls to me." And he divided his living between them. ¹³Not many days later, the younger son gathered all he had and took his journey into a far country, and there he squandered his property in loose living. ¹⁴And when he had spent everything, a great famine arose in that country, and he began to be in want. ¹⁵So he went and joined himself to one of the citizens of that country, who sent him into his fields to feed swine. ¹⁶And he would gladly have fed on^a the pods that the swine ate; and no one gave him anything. ¹⁷But when he came to himself he said, "How many of my father's hired servants have bread enough and to spare, but I perish here with hunger! ¹⁸I will arise and go to my father, and I will say to him, 'Father, I have sinned against heaven and before you; ¹⁹I am no longer worthy to be called your son; treat me as one of your hired servants.'"

²⁰'And he arose and came to his father. But while he was yet at a distance, his father saw him and had compassion, and ran and embraced him and kissed him. ²¹And the son said to him, "Father, I have sinned against heaven and before you; I am no longer worthy to be called your son."^b ²²But the father said to his servants, "Bring quickly the best robe, and put it on him; and put a ring on his hand, and shoes on his feet; ²³and bring the fatted calf and kill it, and let us eat and make merry; ²⁴for this my son was dead, and is alive again; he was lost, and is found." And they began to make merry.

²⁵'Now his elder son was in the field; and as he came and drew near to the house, he heard music and dancing. ²⁶And he called one of the servants and asked what this meant. ²⁷And he said to him, "Your brother has come,

and your father has killed the fatted calf, because he has received him safe and sound." ²⁸But he was angry and refused to go in. His father came out and entreated him, ²⁹but he answered his father, "Lo, these many years I have served you, and I never disobeyed your command; yet you never gave me a kid, that I might make merry with my friends. ³⁰But when this son of yours came, who has devoured your living with harlots, you killed for him the fatted calf!" ³¹And he said to him, "Son, you are always with me, and all that is mine is yours.

³²*"It was fitting to make merry and be glad, for this your brother was dead, and is alive; he was lost, and is found." '*

a Other ancient authorities read *filled his belly with*
b Other ancient authorities add *treat me as one of your hired servants*

This story is the best known and best loved of all the parables of Jesus, justly treasured for its exquisite literary grace and penetrating delineation of character as well as for its assurance of a divine mercy surpassing all expectation. But the traditional title – 'The Prodigal Son' – does less than justice to the purpose of the parable, as the opening sentence makes clear. *'There was a man who had two sons'*, and he lost them both, one in a foreign country, the other behind a barricade of self-righteousness. The elder contrived, without leaving home, to be as far away from his father as ever his brother was in the heathen pigsty. Both brothers were selfish, though in totally different ways. The selfishness of the younger brother was a reckless love of life. He asked for his patrimony because he wanted to savour to the full the manifold delights the world could offer, not foreseeing that truant independence would lead to penury and ignoble serfdom. The selfishness of the older brother was less obvious and less vulnerable. He asked for nothing, desired nothing, enjoyed nothing. He devoted himself dutifully to his father's service, never disobeying a command of his father, and thought, no doubt, that he was the model of unselfishness; yet he himself was the centre of his every thought, so that he was incapable of entering sympathetically into his father's joys and sorrows.

It was common practice for a man, during his lifetime, to make over his property to his heirs by deed of gift, retaining the life rent for himself. The younger son persuaded his father to do this, but also to give him immediate control of the inheritance which, in the ordinary course of events, would have come to him at his father's death. This explains why, at a later stage in the story, the father could say to the other son, '*all that is mine is yours*', though he himself was still master of the family farm.

We are not told in detail how the younger son squandered his fortune. His brother, not trying to be just, let alone charitable, chose to believe that he had added profligacy to extravagance, but he had no more evidence for the harlots than his imagination and bad temper could supply. One way or another, however, the prodigal was reduced to extremity: to a Jew no fate could be more degrading than to feed pigs for a Gentile master.* Adversity brought him to his senses, calling up memories of comfort and security, once heedlessly enjoyed and now forfeited, compelling him to admit to himself that he had been a fool, steeling him to make a similar admission to his father. Yet even at this stage he knew too little of his father to think in terms of forgiveness and restoration. It took the impetuous munificence of his father's welcome, interrupting his carefully rehearsed confession and blotting out the recollection of disgrace, to make him realize, as he had never realized before, what it meant to be his father's son; '*they began to make merry*', and the prodigal began to discover at home what he had sought in vain among the counterfeit pleasures of the far country.

The elder son displays an unattractive facet of his personality with every word he speaks. When he hears the merriment, his impulse is not to join in but to ask for an explanation. The news of his scapegrace brother's return sets him thinking of his own rights and deserts, jealously supposing himself to be wronged because his brother is treated with more than justice. When his father pleads with him, he interrupts with a harsh protest, which contains perhaps more truth than he intended – 'Look how many years I have slaved for you'; working for his father has been an unrewarding servitude, and the obedience he is so proud of has been slavish and mercenary, never filial. He disowns his brother, calling him '*this son of yours*', and putting the worst possible construction on his conduct.

The father refuses to be forced into taking sides with the one brother against the other; with all their shortcomings he loves them both and has never ceased to regard them as sons, though each in his

* Compare the story in the Talmud (*Baba Kamma*, 82b).

own way has tried to contract out of his place in the family. He administers the gentlest of rebukes: his dear son who has remained with him all along should have understood him well enough to share his joy over *'this your brother'*.

The parable leaves us with an unanswered question: did the elder son persist in his jealous rage? or did he follow the lead of his brother, admit that he had made a fool of himself, and join the festivities? The question was left unanswered by Jesus because it was one which his listeners had to answer for themselves. The parable was told not to offer a generous pardon to the nation's prodigals, but to entreat the respectable Jews to rejoice with God over the restoration of sinners, and to warn them that, until they learnt to do this, they would remain estranged from their heavenly father and pitifully ignorant of his true character.

ॐ

21
The words *'treat me as one of your hired servants'* have impressive manuscript support, but are best regarded as an addition from v. 19 by a copyist who did not realize that the carefully rehearsed speech was interrupted by the impetuosity of the father.

16¹⁻¹⁵   THE USE OF OPPORTUNITIES:
(1) THE DISHONEST STEWARD

16 *He also said to the disciples, 'There was a rich man who had a steward, and charges were brought to him that this man was wasting his goods. ²And he called him and said to him, "What is this that I hear about you? Turn in the account of your stewardship, for you can no longer be steward." ³And the steward said to himself, "What shall I do, since my master is taking the stewardship away from me? I am not strong enough to dig, and I am ashamed to beg. ⁴I have decided what to do, so that people may receive me into their houses when I am put out of the stewardship." ⁵So, summoning his master's debtors one by one, he said to the first, "How much do you owe my master?" ⁶He said, "A hundred measures of oil." And he said to him, "Take your bill, and sit down quickly and write fifty." ⁷Then he said to* *another, "And how much do you owe?" He said, "A hundred measures of wheat." He said to him, "Take your bill, and write eighty." 8 The master commended the dishonest steward for his prudence; for the sons of this world^a are wiser in their own generation than the sons of light. 9And I tell you, make friends for yourselves by means of unrighteous mammon, so that when it fails they may receive you into the eternal habitations.*

10'He who is faithful in a very little is faithful also in much; and he who is dishonest in a very little is dishonest also in much.

11'If then you have not been faithful in the unrighteous mammon, who will entrust to you the true riches? 12And if you have not been faithful in that which is another's, who will give you that which is your own? 13No servant can serve two masters; for either he will hate the one and love the other, or he will be devoted to the one and despise the other. You cannot serve God and mammon.'

14 The Pharisees, who were lovers of money, heard all this, and they scoffed at him. 15But he said to them, 'You are those who justify yourselves before men, but God knows your hearts; for what is exalted among men is an abomination in the sight of God.'

a Greek *age*

The parable of the dishonest steward bristles with difficulties which have given rise to a great variety of conjectural explanations. Was the steward called dishonest because of the conduct which earned his dismissal or because of the transactions described in the parable? Is the lord (*kyrios*) who commended the steward the master who employed him (so R.S.V.) or Jesus? (i.e. is v. 8a part of the parable or a comment on it by the Evangelist?). If the verse is regarded as part of the parable, why did the master commend an action by which he himself lost a great deal of money? And what is the relation between the parable and the sayings which are appended to it? The choice appears to lie between two types of solution.

1. If we say that the transactions described in the parable were dishonest, we can hardly believe that they were praised by the landlord, the victim of the fraud. The *kyrios* in v. 8 must be Jesus, who commended the steward not for his dishonesty but for his realism and determination in dealing with a sudden emergency. In that case the parable must have been one of the parables of crisis, a warning from Jesus to his contemporaries to take resolute and immediate action

in the face of impending disaster.* When the crisis of the crucifixion
had passed and the story came to be used for homiletic purposes in
the early Church, it was taken to be a lesson on the right and wrong
use of money and attracted to itself a series of unrelated sayings
(already perhaps artificially connected by their use of the word mammon), which formed a more or less adequate commentary on it.
Stripped of its accretions, it is the story of an engaging rascal who,
faced with dismissal for incompetence, and being too soft for manual
labour and too proud to live on charity, made provision for the future
by a systematic falsification of his accounts, which put each of his
master's debtors under a lasting obligation to himself. Two examples
of his transactions are given, and the large amounts involved show
that the debtors were not tenants who had agreed to pay their rents
in kind, but merchants who had bought the produce of the estate on
the strength of a promissory note. The point is that worldlings like
this – the sons of this world – cope with an emergency in their
temporal affairs with a far-sighted realism and a resourceful acumen
which religious folk – the sons of light – would do well to emulate
in the pursuance of their spiritual calling.

2. Alternatively we can say that the steward is called dishonest
because of his previous mismanagement of the estate, that there was
nothing fraudulent about his negotiations with his master's debtors,
and that it was the landlord who commended him for the ingenuity
with which he extricated himself from his predicament. This solution
depends on the intricacies of the Jewish law of usury.† The Law of
Moses forbade the taking of interest from Jews on loans of any kind
(Exod. 22²⁵, Lev. 25³⁶, Deut. 23¹⁹⁻²⁰). The Pharisees, who had large
financial and commercial concerns,‡ had found ways of evading the
intention of the Law without transgressing its letter. They argued that
the purpose of the Law was to protect the destitute from exploitation,
not to prevent the lending of money for the mutual profit of lender
and borrower. There were some situations in which a loan could be
regarded as a business partnership and interest as a fair sharing of the

* See C. H. Dodd, *The Parables of the Kingdom*, p. 30; J. Jeremias, *The Parables of Jesus*, pp. 33–6.
† See J. Duncan M. Derrett, 'Fresh Light on St Luke xvi', *New Testament Studies*, vii (1961), pp. 198–219.
‡ See L. Finkelstein, *The Pharisees*.

profits of a joint enterprise, They had, therefore, laid down the rule that, if a man already possessed some of the commodity he wished to borrow, he was not destitute, and the taking of profit by his creditor was not usurious. However poor a man might be, he was likely to have a little wheat left in his bin and a little oil for his lamp. These were therefore the two commodities most commonly chosen for the working of this particular form of legal fiction. The two debtors mentioned in the parable had received large loans from the steward out of his master's estate. It matters not how their debts were incurred nor what form the loan took. What matters is that, for legal purposes, the loans were expressed in terms of wheat and oil, and were therefore free (by the law of man, though not by the law of God) from the taint of usury. There were no witnesses to the contract and as security the steward held simply a holograph note in which the debtor, without mentioning interest, undertook to pay to the estate a lump sum (principal + interest). After the steward had received notice of dismissal, but before he had surrendered his position by the final presentation of his accounts, he remained his master's agent, legally authorized to act in his master's name. What he did was to return to his master's debtors their promissory notes and to require them to write new ones, undertaking to repay the principal of their loans without interest. His action was legal, because he was still an accredited agent; it was also righteous, because, perhaps for the first time in his business career, he had done what the law of God required. In the absence of either witnesses or written evidence the landlord was in no position to repudiate his agent's action. Instead of complaining about his financial loss, he seized the opportunity presented to him, ratified his steward's transactions, and so acquired an entirely undeserved reputation for his pious observance of the Law against usury. He was, in fact, no less a son of this world than his steward, and, like many another rich man whose wealth has been amassed without too much scruple about business ethics, he was ready to make spiritual capital by a munificent gesture, especially when no other course was open to him.

Thus interpreted the parable is an attack on the niggling methods of scriptural interpretation by which the Pharisees managed to keep their religious principles from interfering with business, and an appeal for a whole-hearted service of God. If worldly men like the steward and the landlord can recognize in a crisis that their best interests will be served by keeping the good opinion of their neighbours, religious people ought to be equally astute in keeping the good opinion of God.

The collected sayings that follow provide a set of variations on the theme of the parable. If a dishonest man can use another's money to make friends so that there will be people to receive him into their houses when he is out of a job, how much more should honest men use their own money to make friends so that God will welcome them into the heavenly mansions. All the opportunities of this world are tests of character, and by his behaviour in small matters a man shows whether or not he is fit for larger responsibility. In particular, worldly wealth is given to men on trust; it does not belong to them, but by their use of it they can show whether or not they are fit to be entrusted with real wealth, the wealth of the heavenly kingdom. It will be noted that in two of these three sayings wealth is called '*unrighteous mammon*'. Jesus is not, of course, telling his friends how to dispose of ill-gotten gains, but warning them that where there is money there is menace. Indeed, the general import of these sayings is that money can be redeemed from its normally sinister character only if it is used as a means of promoting friendship; to invest money in benefaction is to exchange it for the currency of heaven. The reason why mammon is '*unrighteous*' is given in the fourth saying: it is the great rival of God for the devotion and service of men. All men must choose between the road of self-assertion that leads to the temple of mammon and the road of self-sacrifice that leads to the temple of God.

It was probably Luke himself who inserted at this point the criticism of the Pharisees. There is no evidence that they were addicted to avarice to the same extent as either the Sadducees or the tax gatherers, but they did tend, with ample justification from the Old Testament, to regard prosperity, or at least their own prosperity, as the reward of godliness. The word '*abomination*' always connotes idolatry: the pursuit of human recognition is idolatry in God's eyes.

ೞ

6-7
The liquid measure (*bath*) was approximately 8¾ gallons, and the dry measure (*cor*) was a little under 11 bushels. The value of 50 baths of oil and 20 cors of wheat would be the same – about 500 denarii, the de-

narius being a workman's daily wage (Matt. 20²) – so that the steward did not give his prospective benefactors any cause to complain that he had treated one more generously than another.

9

By '*unrighteous mammon*' the Pharisees meant money legally acquired but tainted in the sight of God. Jesus seems to have used the phrase with a slightly different emphasis. All money, however acquired, is tainted unless it is used in God's service. 'They' in this verse does not mean the friends: it is a reverential circumlocution for God (see Strack-Billerbeck, *Kommentar zum N.T. aus Talmud und Midrasch*, ad loc.).

16^{16–18}   THE USE OF OPPORTUNITIES:
         (2) COMING OF THE NEW ORDER

¹⁶'*The law and the prophets were until John; since then the good news of the kingdom of God is preached, and everyone enters it violently.* ¹⁷*But it is easier for heaven and earth to pass away, than for one dot of the law to become void.*

¹⁸'*Everyone who divorces his wife and marries another commits adultery, and he who marries a woman divorced from her husband commits adultery.*'

At this point Luke has inserted into his L material three sayings about the Law and the gospel which he found already linked in Q, and his reason for putting them here seems to be that the first of them contains a demand for strenuous action. The old order of the Law and the prophets is over, and the new order has arrived; the arrival of the kingdom is being proclaimed, and men of determination and energy are pressing into it.

It is not so clear what Luke believed to be the meaning of the second saying. It has usually been taken to mean that, although Jesus made the Law obsolete as a religious system and abrogated many of its ritual commandments, its great moral principles remained unchanged. But it is doubtful whether this sense can be got from the text. The word translated '*dot*' really means a serif or ornamental flourish added to a letter, and to say that not a serif of the Law can become void is to say that the whole Law, word for word and letter for letter, with all its minutiae and all its rabbinic embellishments, remains valid in perpetuity. Any rabbi might have said this, but we cannot imagine it on the lips of Jesus, especially in view of the fact that the very next verse contains an alteration of the Mosaic law of divorce. This being so, the simplest expedient is to regard the saying as an ironical attack on the pedantic conservatism of the scribes: it was easier for heaven and earth to pass away than for the scribes to surrender that scrupulosity which could not see the Law for the letters.

The third verse gives the most authentic form of a saying which is less accurately preserved in three other passages of the Gospels (Mark 10^{11-12}, Matt. 5^{31-32}, 19^9). Taken thus out of its context, however, this saying could be misleading: it could give the impression that for the Mosaic law which allowed divorce, Jesus was substituting another, stricter law which allowed no divorce; and this would be quite contrary to the assertion made above that with the coming of Jesus the régime of Law had come to an end. Mark 10^{1-12} enables us to see that Jesus was not legislating, but indicating the higher moral standards that become possible to those who live by the grace and power of the kingdom. Moses, said Jesus, allowed divorce for the hardness of your hearts: wherever there is hardness of heart, marriages break down, and society must be protected by divorce from a greater evil. Beyond that recognition civil law has no right to go. This does not alter the fact that, when God made mankind of two sexes, he intended man and woman to live in lifelong partnership, and that anything less than this perfection is a violation of God's intention. But it is only in the kingdom, where there is a cure for hardness of heart, that the ideal becomes practicable.

16^{19-31} THE USE OF OPPORTUNITIES:
(3) THE RICH MAN AND LAZARUS

19'*There was a rich man, who was clothed in purple and fine linen and who feasted sumptuously every day.* 20*And at his gate lay a poor man named Lazarus, full of sores,* 21*who desired to be fed with what fell from the rich* man's table; moreover the dogs came and licked his sores. ²²The poor man died and was carried by the angels to Abraham's bosom. The rich man also died and was buried; ²³and in Hades, being in torment, he lifted up his eyes, and saw Abraham far off and Lazarus in his bosom. ²⁴And he called out, "Father Abraham, have mercy on me, and send Lazarus to dip the end of his finger in water and cool my tongue; for I am in anguish in this flame." ²⁵But Abraham said, "Son, remember that you in your lifetime received your good things, and Lazarus in like manner evil things; but now he is comforted here, and you are in anguish. ²⁶And besides all this, between us and you a great chasm has been fixed, in order that those who would pass from here to you may not be able, and none may cross from there to us." ²⁷And he said, "Then I beg you, father, to send him to my father's house, ²⁸for I have five brothers, so that he may warn them, lest they also come into this place of torment."

²⁹'But Abraham said, "They have Moses and the prophets; let them hear them." ³⁰And he said, "No, father Abraham; but if someone goes to them from the dead, they will repent." ³¹He said to him, "If they do not hear Moses and the prophets, neither will they be convinced if someone should rise from the dead." '

In this parable Jesus was using a familiar folk-tale and adapting it to a new purpose by adding an unfamiliar twist to the end of it. The story of the wicked rich man and the pious poor man, whose fortunes were reversed in the afterlife, seems to have come originally from Egypt, and was popular among Jewish teachers. The picture of the fate in store for the good and the evil after death is also drawn from traditional Jewish sources (cf. 2 En. 9¹⁰). But it was not the intention of Jesus to propagate a strict doctrine of rewards and punishments (nothing is said about the piety of Lazarus), or to give a topographical guide to the afterworld. As he tells it, the point of the story is to be found in the character of the rich man and in the reasons for his failure to use the two kinds of opportunity granted to him, the first by his wealth, the second by his religion.

The rich man – Dives, as he is usually called – was clearly a Sadducee, not only because of his social standing, but because, as the sequel shows, he had no belief in an afterlife, in spite of the fact that he and his brothers professed obedience to the teachings of Moses and the prophets. He devoted himself to the enjoyment of luxurious pleasures, under the impression that this life was the only one he had to live and that it could not be better spent than in self-indulgence. He used his wealth irresponsibly because he did not believe in a judgement at which he would have to answer for his conduct. His wrong behaviour was born of a false creed. His fault was not merely that he used his money for selfish ends, but that he failed to use it for the relief of the beggar who lay at his gate, tormented by the pariahs that nosed about among his rags, tantalized by the sight of guests at the banquet table throwing to the ground the bread on which they had wiped their hands. Dives could have made of Lazarus a friend to welcome him into the eternal habitations, but he was too callous to care. Nor could he plead ignorance; for later, when he himself had become the suppliant, he showed that he recognized Lazarus and knew his name.

The scene changes and the roles are reversed: Lazarus is now at the banquet table, seated in the place of honour next to Abraham, and Dives is outside in torment. He had expected to go to Hades, believing it to be the universal repository of the dead, but he found that in fact it was a place of retribution. Yet even this discovery does not humble his arrogance; having ignored Lazarus during his lifetime, he now presumes to treat him as a lackey. He is even disposed to make excuses for himself: if only someone had warned him in advance, he would have taken the necessary steps to avoid coming to this place of torment. At this point the old story takes a novel turn. Dives asks Abraham to send Lazarus to his five brothers to give them the benefit of his first-hand knowledge of conditions after death, so that they may have the advantage he himself has missed. The answer is that no such precaution is necessary; in the scriptures the brothers already have all the warning they need that upon earthly conduct hang the issues of life and death. If they are not persuaded on moral grounds of the reality of the divine judgement, they are hardly likely to be convinced by apparitions. As formerly to the Pharisees who asked for a miracle to authenticate his teaching, so now to the Sadducees Jesus declares that there is no way of demonstrating spiritual truth to those whose minds are not open to conviction. The two failures of Dives belong together; because his mind was closed to the revelation of God, his heart was closed to the demands of compassion.

17 And he said to his disciples, 'Temptations to sin[a] are sure to come, but woe to him by whom they come! [2]It would be better for him if a millstone were hung round his neck and he were cast into the sea, than that he should cause one of these little ones to sin.[b] [3]Take heed to yourselves; if your brother sins, rebuke him, and if he repents, forgive him; [4]and if he sins against you seven times in the day, and turns to you seven times, and says, "I repent," you must forgive him.'

[5]The apostles said to the Lord, 'Increase our faith!' [6]And the Lord said, 'If you had faith as a grain of mustard seed, you could say to this sycamine tree, "Be rooted up, and be planted in the sea," and it would obey you.

[7]'Will any of you, who has a servant ploughing or keeping sheep, say to him when he has come in from the field, "Come at once and sit down at table"? [8]Will he not rather say to him, "Prepare supper for me, and gird yourself and serve me, till I eat and drink; and afterwards you shall eat and drink"? [9]Does he thank the servant because he did what was commanded? [10]So you also, when you have done all that is commanded you, say, "We are unworthy servants; we have only done what was our duty." '

[11]On the way to Jerusalem he was passing along between Samaria and Galilee. [12]And as he entered a village, he was met by ten lepers, who stood at a distance [13]and lifted up their voices and said, 'Jesus, Master, have mercy on us.' [14]When he saw them he said to them, 'Go and show yourselves to the priests.' And as they went they were cleansed. [15]Then one of them, when he saw that he was healed, turned back, praising God with a loud voice; [16]and he fell on his face at Jesus' feet, giving him thanks. Now he was a Samaritan. [17]Then said Jesus, 'Were not ten cleansed? Where are the nine? [18]Was no one found to return and give praise to God except this foreigner?' [19]And he said to him, 'Rise and go your way; your faith has made you well.'

a Greek stumbling blocks
b Greek stumble

We have here another group of assorted sayings, drawn partly from Q, partly from L. The first deals with the sin of causing others to sin. Matthew (18⁶⁻⁷) and Mark (9⁴²) have independent versions of this saying, in both of which 'little ones' is taken to mean disciples. But there was a tendency in the early Church to confuse what Jesus said about children with what he said about his disciples, and it is likely that this saying was originally spoken about children. Just as the smallest service to a child is certain to be rewarded (Mark 9⁴¹; Matt. 10⁴²), so the corruption of a child incurs a special condemnation.

Next we have some instruction on the settling of disputes. The injured person must be on his guard against the dangers of resentment, grudge-bearing, and spiteful talk; he must carry his grievance directly to the offender, and between them, with forgiveness on the one hand and repentance on the other, they must dispose of the matter once and for all. No matter how often offences occur, the same procedure must be followed with tireless goodwill. *'Seven times'* does not set a limit to forgiveness; in the Matthean parallel the figure is seventy-seven times, which is a deliberate reversal of Lamech's principle of multiple revenge (Matt. 18²¹⁻²²; cf. Gen. 4²³⁻²⁴).

Jesus' liking for hyperbole is well illustrated in the saying on faith (cf. Mark 10²⁵, 11²³, Matt. 17²⁰, 23²⁴). The sycamine is strictly a species of mulberry tree, but in the Septuagint the word is regularly used as the equivalent of sycamore, and this is no doubt the sense intended here. The sycamore was regarded as a particularly deep-rooted tree; thus to uproot a sycamore and transplant it in the sea was a double impossibility. But faith in God is a power that takes impossibilities in its stride.

The parable of the master and slave is a warning against the book-keeping mentality, which thinks that it can run up a credit balance with God. The slave's labour belongs to his master, and a full day's work is no more than his duty. There are no works of supererogation. Nothing he can do constitutes a claim on his master's gratitude or puts his master in his debt. The demands of God are equally exacting; his servants can neither earn his approval nor put him under an obligation. *'Unworthy servants'* does not mean useless servants; even the best service is no more than God is entitled to expect, since it gives him nothing that does not belong to him by right. The whole idea of merit is to be abandoned in our approach to God.

The story of the ten lepers contains some puzzling features. The lepers were directed by Jesus to go to Jerusalem and show themselves to the priest, who alone had the authority to certify their cure; why then were nine of them blamed for carrying out orders? Why did the Samaritan have to return to Jesus in order to express his thanks to God? Considering that all ten were cured, how could it be said especially of one of them that his faith had saved him? It may be that those critics are right who say that the story has been carelessly told. Yet it is possible to put forward an answer to all these questions. Cleansing came to the lepers from God, but through Jesus; and gratitude demanded that the agent, as well as the source, of healing be acknowledged. The cure was no random miracle, but part of the ministry of healing in which the kingdom of God had broken in upon the realm of disease and sin. Through Jesus, God was acting and through him God must be thanked. What Jesus actually said to the Samaritan was 'Your faith has saved you'; and salvation was more than cleansing, a new relationship with God and his kingdom of grace. For Luke the most attractive part of the story was that the Samaritan, by his eager appreciation, showed up his Jewish fellow-sufferers, and gave a foretaste of the opening of the kingdom to the Gentiles.

17$^{20-37}$ THE DAY OF THE SON OF MAN

^{20}*Being asked by the Pharisees when the kingdom of God was coming, he answered them, 'The kingdom of God is not coming with signs to be observed;* ^{21}*nor will they say, "Lo, here it is!" or "There!" for behold, the kingdom of God is in the midst of you.'ª*

^{22}*And he said to the disciples, 'The days are coming when you will desire to see one of the days of the Son of man, and you will not see it.* ^{23}*And they will say to you, "Lo, there!" or "Lo, here!" Do not go, do not follow them.* ^{24}*For as the lightning flashes and lights up the sky from one side to the other, so will the Son of man be in his day.ᵇ* ^{25}*But first he must suffer many things and be rejected by this generation.* ^{26}*As it was in the days of Noah, so will it be in the days of the Son of man.* ^{27}*They ate, they drank, they married, they were given in marriage, until the day when Noah entered the ark, and the flood came and destroyed them all.* ^{28}*Likewise as it was in the days of Lot – they ate, they drank, they bought, they sold, they planted, they built,* ^{29}*but on the day when Lot went out from Sodom, fire and brimstone rained from heaven and destroyed them all –* ^{30}*so will it be on the day when the Son of man is revealed.* ³¹*On that day, let him who is on the house-top, with his goods in the house, not come down to take them away; and likewise let him who is in the field not turn back.* ³²*Remember Lot's wife.* ³³*Whoever seeks to gain his life will lose it, but whoever loses his life will preserve it.*

³⁴'*I tell you, in that night there will be two men in one bed; one will be taken and the other left.* ³⁵*There will be two women grinding together; one will be taken and the other left.*'ᶜ ³⁷*And they said to him, 'Where, Lord?' He said to them, 'Where the body is, there the eaglesᵈ will be gathered together.'*

   a Or *within you*
   b Other ancient authorities omit *in his day*
   c Other ancient authorities add verse 36, '*Two men will be in the field; one will be taken and the other left.*'
   d Or *vultures*

The faith of the first Christians was eschatological: that is, they believed that they were living in the midst of the last event of history, the final act in God's drama of redemption. In Jewish theology the coming of the kingdom, the advent of the Messiah, the resurrection of the just and unjust, and the gift of the Spirit were all eschatological events, belonging to 'the latter end of the days'. Brought up on these beliefs, the disciples had heard Jesus proclaim the arrival of the king-dom, had hailed him as Messiah, had been witnesses of his resurrection, and had received from him the gift of the Spirit. Convinced that they were living in the last days, they expected these days to come to a close in the immediate future with the return of Christ in glory. A good example of this hope is to be found in the earliest of the New Testament writings (1 Thess. 4¹³–5¹¹): the Day of the Lord, arriving suddenly and unannounced, will be the occasion for the ingathering of the faithful, whether they have already died or are still alive, and for the last judgement, which, though it will come as sudden des-truction upon the unwary, will nevertheless hold no terrors for those who by faith are united with Christ. The primitive Church further believed that their expectations were founded on the teaching of Jesus, and accordingly made collections of those sayings which seemed to have a bearing on the subject. One such collection formed the final paragraph of the document Q, and Luke has here reproduced it with a few additions of his own (vv. 20–21, 25, 33).

The initial episode with the Pharisees, taken by itself, is capable of three very different interpretations. (i) The most natural meaning of the Greek word *entos* is 'within'. If this rendering is adopted, the reply of Jesus to his questioners is that the coming of the kingdom is not an outward and observable event but an inner experience. The most serious objection to this interpretation is that elsewhere Jesus speaks of the kingdom as a fact of history and not as a spiritual condition; thus, in the mission charge, the disciples are told to proclaim that whether men like it or not, whether they believe it or not, the kingdom has come upon them (10^{11}). (ii) Assuming that *entos* is an erratic translation of an Aramaic preposition, which could mean 'among' or 'in the midst of', we may paraphrase the words of Jesus as follows: there is no point in keeping watch for the future coming of the kingdom, since the kingdom is already present, waiting to be accepted and entered by those who have eyes to see it. This would bring the saying into line with the repeated assertion of the Gospel that the kingdom is a present reality (e.g. 10^{9,11}, 11^{20}). (iii) The third possibility is that Jesus was talking, not about the germinal presence of the kingdom in his ministry, but about its final consummation. The full realization of God's reign will come, not with premonitory signs nor by observable progress from one locality to another, but in an unheralded and universal manifestation. The world is going about its normal business and, in a moment, the kingdom of God is upon it.

By placing this saying in its present context, Luke has left us in no doubt that he took it to be a prophecy. It was to be understood in the light of the parallel saying about the Son of man. The kingdom and the Son of man alike will come with the unpredictable ubiquity of a lightning flash, defying all calculation, so that no sentries can be posted to give warning of their approach. Their coming will mean irrevocable disaster for a heedless and unprepared generation. Just as, in the time of Noah and Lot, a period of tranquillity, in which men were engrossed in daily pursuits and totally indifferent to the danger that threatened them, ended in a day of cataclysm from which those alone escaped who had taken resolute action; so the days of the Son of man will end in a day which will break in upon men's ordinary occupations, so that of the closest of companions one will be caught and the other survive.

We should have no difficulty in accepting this for what it purports to be, a consistent picture of the End, were it not for an apparently intrusive element in the middle of it (vv. 31–32). In time of an invasion by hostile armies it may be sound advice to the man who is taking his siesta on the flat roof of his house to make his escape by the outside staircase without taking time to go indoors to collect his belongings, or to the man working in the fields not to go home and risk having his retreat cut off; but such emergency evacuation would be meaningless in the face of a world-wide advent of the Son of man. It seems certain that, when Jesus spoke this warning, he had in mind the forthcoming siege and destruction of Jerusalem. Must we then conclude that the editor of Q has blundered by including this saying in a context dealing with the day of the Son of man? Or is it possible that in his mind, and also in the mind of Jesus, the judgement of God on Jerusalem and the last judgement were inseparably linked, that the historic crisis appeared as the embodiment of the eschatological crisis? Is it possible that Jesus used eschatological language, not because he thought that the world was shortly coming to an end, but because he believed that through his ministry Israel was being compelled to face a decision with eternal consequences, a decision between the fulfilment and the final negation of her national calling as the people of God?

This hypothesis gains powerful confirmation from a study of the Old Testament prophets. When the prophets looked forward to the future, they spoke about it in two ways which at first examination appear quite unconnected. Sometimes they predicted historical events which would happen because of observable causes and which would be followed by calculable results. Thus Jeremiah's prediction of the destruction of Jerusalem was based, in part at least, on an intelligent appraisal of the international situation. At other times the prophets spoke of 'the Day of the Lord', an event which would come upon the world with utter finality and by the direct intervention of God. On a closer scrutiny, however, we observe that these two types of prediction always tend to coalesce. Jeremiah's prophecy of the fall of Jerusalem merges into an eschatological vision of the return of primeval chaos (Jer. 4²³⁻²⁶). Joel has a vision of a locust plague, which he interprets partly as a temporal punishment for which Israel will receive compensation if she repents, partly as the onset of the Day of the Lord, with the locust horde playing the role of the eschatological army of God and inflicting God's final judgement on the nations in a grotesque Armageddon. Over and over again we read that the Day of the Lord is at hand (Isa. 13^6, Ezek. 30^3, Joel 1^{15}, 3^{14}, Obad. 15, Zeph. 1^7), not because the prophets lived under the incurable and morbid delusion that the end of the world was just round the corner, but because they saw in the historic crisis with which they were immediately concerned the point at which the circle of eternity touched the line of time, the moment when Israel was confronted with the ultimate issues of life and death. It is as though the prophets were endowed with stereoscopic second sight by which one picture of the imminent future and another of the ultimate future could be brought into a common focus in a single composite vision of divine judgement.

We have already in an earlier chapter had occasion to associate the day of the Son of man with the fall of Jerusalem (12^{40}), and it is conceivable that in the present passage the saying about Noah and Lot was meant to have the same double reference. It is to be noted that in neither of these cases of primeval catastrophe does Jesus say anything about the sin of the people concerned, although the generation of Noah was described in Genesis as morally corrupt, and the name of Sodom had become a byword for vice; it was their complacent disregard of coming calamity that brought about their downfall. Moreover, these stories have to do, not with God's judgement on individual men and women, but with a corporate judgement upon whole cities or a whole civilization. They thus provide a more obvious parallel with the sudden doom in store for Jerusalem than with the last judgement.

In the visions of Daniel, the Son of man is a symbol for Israel, and his coming with the clouds of heaven to receive royal dignity at the hands of the 'Ancient of Days' represented the overthrow of pagan empires and the establishment of the kingdom of God, in which 'the saints of the Most High' are to exercise world rule and world judgement (Dan. 7$^{13, 22}$). Jesus believed that he, with or without his followers, was called to fulfil this vision of Israel's destiny, but he introduced into it two modifications: for the Son of man the path to glory lay through rejection and suffering, and his ultimate vindication by God would mean judgement, not on the pagan nations, but on the Israel that repudiated him. Thus in the predictions of Jesus the destruction of Jerusalem is always an eschatological event, never clearly distinguishable from the final triumph of the Son of man and the establishment of God's kingdom. Luke has shown how well he understood the eschatology of Jesus by introducing into the Q passage about the day of the Son of man a reference to his rejection. The rejection of the Son of man by Israel was the beginning of a process which was to end only with the day of the Son of man; and once it had occurred, the judgement was bound to follow, as surely and as swiftly as vultures gather round a camel that dies in the desert.

꜍꜍

34–36
Matt. 24⁴⁰⁻⁴¹ has two men in the field and two women at the mill. The best text of Luke has two in one bed and two women at the mill. Some manuscripts of Luke add v. 36, a scribe's attempt to harmonize the text with that of Matthew. There is nothing in the Greek to justify the R.S.V. translation 'two *men* in one bed': if, as seems likely, man and wife are meant, Greek idiom requires that the words for 'the one' and 'the other' should be in the masculine.

18¹⁻⁸ PARABLES ON PRAYER: (I) THE UNJUST JUDGE

18 *And he told them a parable, to the effect that they ought always to pray and not lose heart.* ²*He said, 'In a certain city there was a judge who neither feared God nor regarded man;* ³*and there was a widow in that city who kept coming to him and saying, "Vindicate me against my adversary."* ⁴*For a while he refused; but afterwards he said to himself, "Though I neither fear God nor regard man,* ⁵*yet because this widow bothers me, I will vindicate her, or she will wear me out by her continual coming."'* ⁶*And the Lord said, 'Hear what the unrighteous judge says.* ⁷*And will not God vindicate his elect, who cry to him day and night? Will he delay long over them?* ⁸*I tell you, he will vindicate them speedily. Nevertheless, when the Son of man comes, will he find faith on earth?'*

Our interpretation of the eschatological passage in the last chapter is borne out by the parables that follow it. Luke was deeply interested in prayer and mentions it more often than the other synoptists, and it is natural that he should bring together two parables that had a bearing on one of his favourite themes; but he has placed them at this point in his narrative because they contribute to the understanding of the final paragraph of Q. The closing comment of the first parable identifies the coming of the Son of man with the vindication of God's elect, and the second parable deals incisively with the conditions of man's vindication by God.

The perversion of justice is mentioned so often in the Old Testament that it can have been by no means uncommon (e.g. Exod. 23⁶, Deut. 16¹⁹, Eccles. 5⁸, Isa. 10²). It was the function of the judge to be not only an impartial arbiter but also the champion of the helpless and down-trodden – the widow, the orphan, the poor, and the foreigner; whatever other cases he heard, he must be sure that these at least received their rights (Exod. 22²², Deut. 10¹⁸, Ps. 68⁵, Isa. 1¹⁷, Jer. 22³). The judge in the story was swayed neither by religious principle nor by public opinion, so that the widow, too poor to resort to bribery and lacking influential friends, had no weapon but her persistence. God, on the other hand, is the righteous Judge, the champion of the needy and the oppressed, who listens patiently to their plea when they call upon him; he can therefore be relied on to intervene on their behalf with swift and sudden vindication. If persistence prevails with one who cares only for his own peace and comfort, how much more will it prevail with One who has compassion on his elect.

Election might seem to be a sign of God's favouritism towards his own people, but this is true only in a rather paradoxical fashion. Israel came to be known as 'God's elect' only in the days of her national humiliation. The elect are those who are specially called to serve God through suffering for their faith at the hands of an ungodly world. It is their loyalty to God that makes them pray day and night to him for that deliverance which only he can bring. If, then, election means favouritism, it is because God has a bias in favour of the innocent victims of persecution.

PARABLES ON PRAYER:
(2) THE PHARISEE AND THE TAX COLLECTOR

⁹*He also told this parable to some who trusted in themselves that they were righteous and despised others:* ¹⁰*'Two men went up into the temple to pray, one a Pharisee and the other a tax collector.* ¹¹*The Pharisee stood and prayed thus with himself.* *"God, I thank thee that I am not like other men, extortioners, unjust, adulterers, or even like this tax collector.* ¹²*I fast twice a week, I give tithes of all that I get."* ¹³*But the tax collector, standing far off, would not even lift up his eyes to heaven, but beat his breast, saying, "God, be merciful to me a sinner!"* ¹⁴*I tell you, this man went down to his house justified rather than the other; for everyone who exalts himself will be humbled, but he who humbles himself will be exalted.'*

Two men went into the temple to pray, but only one of them prayed. Prayer must be addressed to God, and the Pharisee was not really interested in God, but only in himself. All his verbs are in the first person. His prayer is a catalogue of negative virtues and minor pieties. Where a humble man is content to put his trust in God, this man's trust is in his own righteousness and religious achievement; and the inevitable result is that he despises those who fail to reach his own standard. Not all Pharisees were like this, but the Pharisaic emphasis on merit and legal observance must always have carried with it the danger of spiritual pride. Rabbinic literature provides enough parallels to show that Jesus' portrait was no caricature. An old prayer from the Jewish Prayer Book runs: 'Blessed art Thou, O Lord our God, King of the Universe, who hast not made me a Gentile. Blessed art Thou ... who hast not made me a slave. Blessed art Thou ... who hast not made me a woman' (cf. Gal. 3²⁸). It is reported also in the Talmud (*Berakoth*, 28b) that Rabbi Nehunia ben Hakaneh used to pray daily on leaving the rabbinical school: 'I give thanks to thee, O Lord my God, that thou hast set my portion with those who sit in the house of instruction, and thou hast not set my portion with those who sit in street corners, for I rise early and they rise early, but I rise early for words of Torah and they rise early for frivolous talk; I labour and they labour, but I labour and receive a reward and they labour and do not receive a reward; I run and they run, but I run to the life of the world to come and they run to the pit of destruction.' No man can genuinely place himself in the presence of the holy God and still congratulate himself on his own piety; and this means that piety can become a barrier between man and God.

The tax collector, with all his faults and follies, has thought only for God; and because his mind is on God, he knows himself to be a sinner. He has lived a disreputable life, and can find no help for his condition but in God; and he finds also that such honest humility is the one sure way into the divine presence. He rather than the Pharisee is justified, declared righteous; not that he is good and the other bad – this is not the case – but because he has done the one thing that God requires of those who seek access to him: he has faced the truth about himself and cast himself on God's compassion. Whether his repentance was deep or shallow we are not told; God can use even the first traces of a nascent faith.

18$^{15-34}$ ENTERING THE KINGDOM

^{15}Now they were bringing even infants to him that he might touch them; and when the disciples saw it, they rebuked them. ^{16}But Jesus called them to him, saying, 'Let the children come to me, and do not hinder them; for to such belongs the kingdom of God. ^{17}Truly, I say to you, whoever does not receive the kingdom of God like a child shall not enter it.'

^{18}And a ruler asked him, 'Good Teacher, what shall I do to inherit eternal life?' ^{19}And Jesus said to him, 'Why do you call me good? No one is good but God alone. ^{20}You know the commandments: "Do not commit adultery, Do not kill, Do not steal, Do not bear false witness, Honour your father and mother."' ^{21}And he said, 'All these I have observed from my youth.' ^{22}And when Jesus heard it, he said to him, 'One thing you still lack. Sell all that you have and distribute to the poor, and you will have treasure in heaven; and come, follow me.' ^{23}But when he heard this he became sad, for he was very rich. ^{24}Jesus looking at him said, 'How hard it is for those who have riches to enter the kingdom of God! ^{25}For it is easier for a camel to go through the eye of a needle than for a rich man to enter the kingdom of

God.' ²⁶ Those who heard it said, 'Then who can be saved?' ²⁷But he said, 'What is impossible with men is possible with God.' ²⁸And Peter said, 'Lo, we have left our homes and followed you.' ²⁹And he said to them, 'Truly, I say to you, there is no man who has left house or wife or brothers or parents or children, for the sake of the kingdom of God, ³⁰who will not receive manifold more in this time, and in the age to come eternal life.'

³¹And taking the twelve, he said to them, 'Behold, we are going up to Jerusalem, and everything that is written of the Son of man by the prophets will be accomplished. ³²For he will be delivered to the Gentiles, and will be mocked and shamefully treated and spit upon; ³³they will scourge him and kill him, and on the third day he will rise.'

³⁴But they understood none of these things; this saying was hid from them, and they did not grasp what was said.

At this point Luke begins again to make excerpts from Mark's Gospel, which he has not used since 9⁵⁰. He takes over with little alteration the two stories of the children and the rich man, which Mark has placed side by side, because together they describe the conditions of entry into the kingdom of God.

The story of the blessing of the children is a rebuke to that adult complacency which regards children as incomplete adults, as yet beneath the notice of God or his Messiah, and assumes that the world exists for those who have reached 'years of discretion'. It assures us that children (even infants, according to Luke) whose parents bring them to God in faith belong already to God's family and therefore to God's kingdom. For God the King is also God the Father, and we grossly misunderstand the nature of his kingdom unless we see it as the rule of a Father over his children. Children are the natural models of discipleship, for who is in a better position than a child to under-stand what it means to be a child of God? Jesus does not ask his dis-ciples to become childish: he commends to them only one of the characteristics of childhood – its receptivity, its ability to accept what is given without embarrassment, its delight in receiving presents. Without this quality nobody, whether child or adult, can enter the kingdom.

By contrast with the children the rich man (Luke tells us he was a ruler, Matthew that he was young) wished for nothing he could not earn. He supposed that entry into the kingdom was by competitive

examination: he had passed Elementary Religion to his own satisfaction and, as he believed, to the satisfaction of the Examiner; now
he wished to attempt Advanced Religion. It is not to be thought that
Jesus acceded to his request and prescribed the syllabus whereby he
could graduate with distinction into life eternal. In bidding him dispose of his fortune, he was trying to bring him to the point where
he could put his trust in God, and not in his own wealth and achievements. In this connexion the opening question of Jesus – '*Why do you
call me good?*' – is of supreme importance. Jesus is not casting doubt
on his own sanctity; he is pointing out to the inquirer the true nature
of the blessing he sought. Eternal life is not a graduation certificate;
it is life in the company of God, and that means in the company of
the Eternal Goodness. What the ruler should have asked was, 'How
can I become fit to dwell in the presence of utter goodness?' But he
went away, sorrowful, not having glimpsed the question, let alone
the answer.

The answer is given in Jesus' conversation with his disciples.

> *The sons of ignorance and night*
> *May dwell in the eternal Light*
> *Through the eternal Love.*

The entry of any man into eternal life or into the kingdom is a
miracle of God's grace, which cannot be earned but only accepted
with humility and faith. The peril of possessions is that they stand in
the way of this receptive faith. The rich man trusts in his riches; and
this tends to be true, not only of material wealth, but of intellectual,
moral, and spiritual wealth also. The ruler could not face parting with
his possessions, but he would have found it equally difficult to lay
aside his education, righteousness, and piety, and to cast himself
simply on the divine compassion. '*It depends not upon man's will or
exertion, but upon God's mercy*' (Rom. 9^{16}). Even Peter does not
really understand; he thinks that he and his fellows deserve better
than the rich ruler because they have made the sacrifice at which he
baulked. Whimsically Jesus promises that those who have left home
and family for the service of the kingdom will find themselves caring
for a far bigger family than the one they left, before ever they reach
the eternal life of the age to come.

The passage ends with the third prediction of the Passion, which

Luke has amplified by introducing his favourite theme of the fulfilment of prophecy. He has also added an almost Johannine comment that the real significance of the saying was not revealed to the disciples until later (cf. John 12¹⁶). The crucifixion was the miracle of grace by which God made it possible for men to enter the kingdom, breaking through their self-sufficiency with a demonstration of his all-sufficient love; but the event itself had to happen before they could understand the predictions of it.

18³⁵⁻⁴³   PASSING THROUGH JERICHO:
(I) THE BLIND BEGGAR

³⁵*As he drew near to Jericho, a blind man was sitting by the roadside begging,* ³⁶*and hearing a multitude going by, he inquired what this meant.* ³⁷*They told him, 'Jesus of Nazareth is passing by.'*

³⁸*And he cried, 'Jesus, Son of David, have mercy on me!'* ³⁹*And those who were in front rebuked him, telling him to be silent; but he cried out all the more, 'Son of David, have mercy on me!'* ⁴⁰*And Jesus stopped, and commanded him to be brought to him; and when he came near, he asked him,* ⁴¹*'What do you want me to do for you?' He said, 'Lord, let me receive my sight.'* ⁴²*And Jesus said to him, 'Receive your sight; your faith has made you well.'* ⁴³*And immediately he received his sight and followed him, glorifying God; and all the people, when they saw it, gave praise to God.*

The long period of journeying towards Jerusalem, which began at 9⁵¹, now draws to its close. Somewhere on the pilgrim route from Galilee to Jerusalem, which passed through Jericho, Jesus and his disciples join a large company of pilgrims on their way up to Jerusalem for the feast of the Passover. Almost a year has passed since, at Caesarea Philippi, Peter declared Jesus to be Messiah. Now a blind beggar (Mark calls him Bartimaeus) addresses him as Son of David. This is the only occasion in the Gospels when Jesus is addressed by this title, but it can hardly represent the beggar's own private conviction. Behind it there must have lain a widespread popular belief that Jesus was the promised king from the house of David – a belief

which found vociferous utterance a few days later when Jesus rode into Jerusalem. It is even possible that the beggar's cry and the response which Jesus made to it helped to stimulate the messianic outburst of the triumphal entry.

The man's persistence was to Jesus an indication of his faith. But Jesus insists on bringing that faith to articulate expression; he will not bestow healing on a beggar who in reality was interested only in alms. The beggar, it seems, had not always been blind, for what he asks is that his sight be restored.

19$^{1-10}$ PASSING THROUGH JERICHO:
(2) ZACCHAEUS

19 *He entered Jericho and was passing through.* ²*And there was a man named Zacchaeus; he was a chief tax collector, and rich.* ³*And he sought to see who Jesus was, but could not, on account of the crowd, because he was small of stature.* ⁴*So he ran on ahead and climbed up into a sycamore tree to see him, for he was to pass that way.* ⁵*And when Jesus came to the place, he looked up and said to him, 'Zacchaeus, make haste and come down; for I must stay at your house today.'* ⁶*So he made haste and came down, and received him joyfully.*

⁷*And when they saw it they all murmured, 'He has gone in to be the guest of a man who is a sinner.'* ⁸*And Zacchaeus stood and said to the Lord, 'Behold, Lord, the half of my goods I give to the poor; and if I have defrauded anyone of anything, I restore it fourfold.'*

⁹*And Jesus said to him, 'Today salvation has come to this house, since he also is a son of Abraham.* ¹⁰*For the Son of man came to seek and to save the lost.'*

Zacchaeus is called a chief tax collector, but the title occurs nowhere else in extant Greek literature, so that its precise meaning is in doubt. He may have been a contractor who bought the local taxation rights from the Roman government. Whatever his rank, he belonged to a calling which automatically carried with it popular detestation and social ostracism. No sightseeing curiosity would have induced such a man to risk either ridicule or violence by mixing with a large mob in the city street. He must have been prompted by some powerful urge, whether it was a desire to escape from his self-imposed loneliness with the help of one who had the name of being friendly to the outcast, or the half-formed determination to have done with a profession that had become burdensome to his conscience. He had heard reports of Jesus which had begun a good work in his soul, but he was to discover that the half had not been told him. By bursting through the barrier of religious prejudice that isolated him, Jesus awakened to vibrant life impulses that had long lain dormant, and revealed to him the man he was capable of becoming. In a dramatic and comprehensive demonstration of gratitude, he broke with the past, admitting his fraudulent practices, undertaking restitution far beyond what the Law required (Lev. 6⁵, Num. 5⁷; cf. Exod. 22¹, ⁴, ⁷), and forsaking even the legitimate profits of his profession – a 'sinner' treading without hesitation the path of renunciation from which the respectable ruler had been too easily deterred. In his former degradation his family had been involved; but now, in the person of Jesus, the messianic salvation had come to him and to his household, and by his enthusiastic response to it he had shown himself a true son of Abraham and an heir to the promises of God.

19¹¹⁻²⁸   PASSING THROUGH JERICHO:
              (?) MONEY IN TRUST

¹¹*As they heard these things, he proceeded to tell a parable, because he was near to Jerusalem, and because they supposed that the kingdom of God was to appear immediately.* ¹²*He said therefore, 'A nobleman went into a far country to receive kingly power*ᵃ *and then return.* ¹³*Calling ten of his servants, he gave them ten pounds,*ᵇ *and said to them, "Trade with these till I come."* ¹⁴*But his citizens hated him and sent an embassy after him, saying, "We do not want this man to reign over us."* ¹⁵*When he returned, having received the kingly power,*ᵃ *he commanded these servants, to whom he had given the money, to be called to him, that he might know what they had gained by trading.* ¹⁶*The first came before him, saying, "Lord, your pound has made ten pounds more."* ¹⁷*And he said to him, "Well done, good servant!*

208

Because you have been faithful in a very little, you shall have authority over ten cities." [18] *And the second came, saying, "Lord, your pound has made five pounds."* [19] *And he said to him, "And you are to be over five cities."* [20] *Then another came, saying, "Lord, here is your pound, which I kept laid away in a napkin;* [21] *for I was afraid of you, because you are a severe man; you take up what you did not lay down, and reap what you did not sow."* [22] *He said to him, "I will condemn you out of your own mouth, you wicked servant! You knew that I was a severe man, taking up what I did not lay down and reaping what I did not sow?* [23] *Why then did you not put my money into the bank, and at my coming I should have collected it with interest?"*

[24] *And he said to those who stood by, "Take the pound from him, and give it to him who has the ten pounds."* [25] *(And they said to him, "Lord, he has ten pounds!")* [26] *"I tell you, that to everyone who has will more be given; but from him who has not, even what he has will be taken away.* [27] *But as for these enemies of mine, who did not want me to reign over them, bring them here and slay them before me."* '

[28] *And when he had said this, he went on ahead, going up to Jerusalem.*

a Greek *a kingdom*
b The mina, rendered here by *pound*, was equal to about £6

The introductory verse is so full of Lucan characteristics of style and vocabulary that it must be regarded as his editorial contribution, in which he has given his own interpretation of the parable. The parable was told as a warning to those who expected an imminent return of Christ to bring in the final consummation of the kingdom. Throughout the early Church there was a general expectation that Christ would return in glory within a generation; and, when the first generation had passed, it was natural that there should be some reappraisal of the eschatological hope. Matthew constantly emphasizes the future coming of the kingdom, but Luke adopted the opposite course. He gives prominence to sayings in which the kingdom is a present reality, and tones down the futuristic note in others (9^{27}, 22^{69}; cf. Mark 9^1, 14^{62}). In his view, as we have seen, the imminent crisis predicted by Jesus was the crisis of his own death, involving persecution for his followers and judgement for Jerusalem; the final crisis of history would be sudden, but might be indefinitely delayed.

As we read the parable, however, we cannot help wondering whether the meaning Luke found in it was the right one, and whether he received the parable in anything like its original form. The main point of the parable is not the prolonged absence of the master, but the conduct of the servants; and the fault of the third servant would have been the same, whether his master's absence was long or short. There is also a double plot to the story: the merchant who distributes his capital to his servants, so that they can carry on his business in his absence, is also the nobleman being elevated to royal dignity in the teeth of strenuous opposition from his prospective subjects. It looks as though, during the period of oral transmission, two stories have somehow been amalgamated.

These impressions are confirmed when we turn to Matt. 25$^{14-30}$, which is obviously a variant version of the same parable. A comparison of the two versions shows that in each case the story underwent some elaboration before it reached the Evangelist. In Matthew's account the huge sums of money, the division of the money according to the ability of the servants (which it was the object of the test to discover), and the consigning of the untrustworthy servant to the outer darkness are secondary elaborations. In Luke's source the parable of the money in trust was already conflated with the independent story of the nobleman. Eliminating these accretions, we are left with a simple and striking parable. A man entrusted each of his servants with a sum of money with which they were to engage in trade on his behalf during his absence. When he returned and called them to account, two of them had made a handsome profit and were promoted. A third, who had timidly hidden his share for safe keeping, expected to be praised for having preserved it intact, but in fact was charged with breach of trust, because he had defrauded his master of his legitimate gain. The parable must, in the first instance, have been directed against the Pharisees, who believed that their whole duty was to preserve intact what God had entrusted to them, not realizing that God expected his capital to be invested in a world mission for the redemption of the outcast and the sinful.

The sub-plot of Luke's story has its counterpart in actual history. When Herod the Great died in 4 B.C., his son Archelaus went to Rome to ask Augustus to appoint him King of Judea, and a deputation of fifty Jews also went to Rome to oppose the appointment

(Josephus, *Antiquities*, XVII, 9, 1; 11, 1–2). Josephus does not mention any reprisals after Archelaus returned to Palestine. To the Christian reader the sub-plot would readily convey an allegorical reference to the return of Jesus after having received his kingly power.

Luke 19²⁹-24⁵³

Death and Victory

²⁹*When he drew near to Bethphage and Bethany, at the mount that is called Olivet, he sent two of the disciples,* ³⁰*saying, 'Go into the village opposite, where on entering you will find a colt tied, on which no one has ever yet sat; untie it and bring it here.* ³¹*If any one asks you, "Why are you untying it?" you shall say this, "The Lord has need of it."'* ³²*So those who were sent went away and found it as he had told them.* ³³*And as they were untying the colt, its owners said to them, 'Why are you untying the colt?'* ³⁴*And they said, 'The Lord has need of it.'* ³⁵*And they brought it to Jesus, and throwing their garments on the colt they set Jesus upon it.* ³⁶*And as he rode along, they spread their garments on the road.* ³⁷*As he was now drawing near, at the descent of the Mount of Olives, the whole multitude of the disciples began to rejoice and praise God with a loud voice for all the mighty works that they had seen,* ³⁸*saying, 'Blessed be the King who comes in the name of the Lord! Peace in heaven and glory in the highest!'* ³⁹*And some of the Pharisees in the multitude said to him, 'Teacher, rebuke your disciples.'* ⁴⁰*He answered, 'I tell you, if these were silent, the very stones would cry out.'*

⁴¹*And when he drew near and saw the city he wept over it,* ⁴²*saying, 'Would that even today you knew the things that make for peace! But now they are hid from your eyes.* ⁴³*For the days shall come upon you, when your enemies will cast up a bank about you and surround you, and hem you in on every side,* ⁴⁴*and dash you to the ground, you and your children within you, and they will not leave one stone upon another in you; because you did not know the time of your visitation.'*

⁴⁵*And he entered the temple and began to drive out those who sold,* ⁴⁶*saying to them, 'It is written, "My house shall be a house of prayer"; but you have made it a den of robbers.'*

The final act of the divine drama of redemption opens with the entry of Jesus into Jerusalem. The modern reader is apt to assume that Jesus had made previous arrangements about the colt with friends who lived in Bethphage, and that he had agreed with them on a password to be used for the sake of security by his emissaries. But Luke probably thought that the precise instructions given by Jesus on this occasion and before the Last Supper (22^{7-13}) were evidence of his prophetic power of clairvoyance (cf. 1 Sam. 10^{2-9}). Whichever view we take, we can be sure that Jesus intended a demonstration. This is particularly clear in Mark's original narrative, where we are told that Jesus, having entered the city amid popular acclaim, immediately left it again to spend the night at Bethany where his triumphal progress had begun. Probably he had in mind the prophecy (Zech. 9^{9-10}) that one day a king would come to Zion, riding on a donkey to show that his authority rested not on military force but on his ability to establish a reign of universal peace. The enthusiastic disciples hail Jesus as the inaugurator of the messianic kingdom; and Luke has actually taken the words of Ps. 118^{26} – originally the priest's blessing pronounced on pilgrims coming up to the temple for a festival – and has inserted the word 'King', so as to leave no doubt that the crowd believed themselves to be taking part in the coronation procession of the Messiah.

If we are right in thinking that Jesus intended to act out the Old Testament prophecy, his purpose must have been not to excite nationalist fervour, but to allay it. Patriotic feeling was always at its highest at the Passover season, which was the time when the Messiah was expected to appear in Jerusalem. Jesus wanted to proclaim that God was now asserting his sovereignty over Jerusalem, but he wanted to encourage no misapprehensions about the nature of this long-promised reign; it was not to be confused with the Zealot plans for a national uprising against Rome.

The prophecy had foretold the advent of peace on earth; Luke goes a step further and has the crowd sing of peace in heaven. By this he means either that God has the gift of peace prepared in heaven, ready to be bestowed upon men; or, more likely, that God has now achieved, on the heavenly plane, the victory over the forces of evil (cf. 10^{17}), so that all that now remains is for the implications of the heavenly triumph to be worked out among men.

The Pharisees who protested apparently thought that this outburst of enthusiasm would be regarded by the Romans as a seditious action, and would bring reprisals not on Jesus only, but on the whole nation. Jesus replies that his coming is the event for which the whole of

Israel's history has been a preparation, so that the very stones of the pilgrim road would cry out in protest if he did not receive his proper welcome (cf. Hab. 2^{11}).

The lament which follows shows how little Jesus had counted on the success of his final appeal. He came to Jerusalem ready for tragedy, and the heart of the tragedy lay in the word '*visitation*'. Luke began his Gospel by declaring that God had visited and redeemed his people, and the long central section of his work was designed to lead up to the day when Jerusalem would receive the royal visit. Now, he tells us, the day has come and Jerusalem is not ready for it. Yet the fact remains that God has visited his people either for salvation or for judgement; and, if Jerusalem will not have him as her Saviour, she must have him as her Judge. Some scholars have thought that this passage must have been compiled by Luke after A.D. 70, when he had knowledge of the actual course of the siege of Jerusalem, but in fact the military terminology used here is quite general, having more in common with similar prophetic passages in the Old Testament (cf. Isa. 29^3, Ezek. 4^2, Ps. 137^9) than with the distinctive horrors of the destruction of Jerusalem by Titus as it is described by Josephus. Nor is there any reason to doubt that Jesus foresaw in grim detail the ruin of the city he had tried to save.

In Mark's Gospel the cleansing of the temple occurred the day after the triumphal entry and was an independent act of prophetic symbolism. The temple authorities had allowed the establishment of a market in which worshippers could exchange their everyday money for the temple coinage in which the annual half-shekel tax had to be paid, and could buy for sacrifice animals which were guaranteed '*without blemish*' (Lev. 1^3). Jesus made his dramatic protest – he can hardly have expected to achieve lasting reform – partly because of the commercialism which threatened to obscure the purpose of the temple and its worship, which existed in order to bring men near to God, partly because the market was held in the Court of the Gentiles, and was therefore a denial of Israel's missionary calling to be 'a light to the Gentiles'. Luke, however, has so abbreviated Mark's account that in his Gospel it has become simply an illustration of Jerusalem's unreadiness for the day of God's visit. It is strange that he should have made so little of the incident which apparently provoked the Jewish authorities to decisive action. It is stranger that he, the universalist,

should have curtailed the quotation from Isaiah, omitting the words
'for all the nations'.

ﭏﭏﭏ

30

The prophecy of Zechariah about the colt is quoted in two different
versions by Matthew and John in their accounts of the entry into Jerusalem, though John comments that the disciples did not recognize the
connexion between the event and the prophecy until afterwards. Mark
and Luke do not openly allude to the prophecy, but their versions seem
also to be based on it. To an ordinary Greek the word colt (*pōlŏs*) would
probably mean a young horse, but to a reader of the Septuagint it
would certainly mean a young donkey; and this donkey was unbroken,
'virgin', and so fit to be used for a sacred purpose (Num. 19^2, Deut.
21^3, 1 Sam. 6^7).

$19^{47}-20^8$ THE BATTLE OF ARGUMENTS:
            (1) THE AUTHORITY OF JESUS

⁴⁷*And he was teaching daily in the temple. The chief priests and the scribes
and the principal men of the people sought to destroy him;* ⁴⁸*but they did not
find anything they could do, for all the people hung upon his words.*

20 *One day, as he was teaching the people in the temple and preaching the
gospel, the chief priests and the scribes with the elders came up* ²*and said to
him, 'Tell us by what authority you do these things, or who it is that gave
you this authority.'* ³*He answered them, 'I also will ask you a question; now
tell me,* ⁴*Was the baptism of John from heaven or from men?'* ⁵*And they
discussed it with one another, saying, 'If we say, "From heaven,"* he will
say, "Why did you not believe him?"* ⁶*But if we say, "From men," all
the people will stone us; for they are convinced that John was a prophet.'*
⁷*So they answered that they did not know whence it was.* ⁸*And Jesus said
to them, 'Neither will I tell you by what authority I do these things.'*

Jesus had seen to it that the religious leaders could not ignore his
arrival. He had entered the city in triumph, he had shown outstanding
moral courage and authority in clearing the temple court, and now he

was dominating the whole temple area with daily teaching which commanded a huge audience. His popularity was such that, without endangering their own position, the leaders could neither overlook his presence nor take effective action against him; it did not occur to them to give him their support. The only course open to them was to try and trap him into making some statement which would either incriminate him with the Roman government or discredit him with his supporters. If, in answer to the question about his authority, Jesus asserted his Messiahship, a charge of sedition could be laid before Pilate (as ultimately happened); if, on the other hand, he declined to make such a claim, he would soon forfeit the approval of the crowd. But Jesus deftly caught his questioners in their own cleft stick, inviting them to answer their own question; for whatever answer they gave to his question would apply *a fortiori* to their own. It must have been exceedingly embarrassing for members of the Sanhedrin to admit that they had formed no opinion about John's great movement of national reawakening, especially since, by their admission, they forfeited the right to form an opinion about Jesus. It is interesting to note that, in framing their catch question, they assumed, as other ecclesiastical bureaucrats have commonly done, that no man is entitled to exercise authority unless he has received authorization through the proper channels.

20$^{9-19}$ THE BATTLE OF ARGUMENTS:
              (2) THE WICKED TENANTS

9*And he began to tell the people this parable: 'A man planted a vineyard, and let it out to tenants, and went into another country for a long while.* 10*When the time came, he sent a servant to the tenants, that they should give him some of the fruit of the vineyard; but the tenants beat him, and sent him away empty-handed.* 11*And he sent another servant; him also they beat and treated shamefully, and sent him away empty-handed.* 12*And he sent yet a third; this one they wounded and cast out.* 13*Then the owner of the vineyard said, "What shall I do? I will send my beloved son; it may be they will respect him."* 14*But when the tenants saw him, they said to themselves, "This is the heir; let us kill him, that the inheritance may be ours."*

^{15}'*And they cast him out of the vineyard and killed him. What then will the owner of the vineyard do to them?* ^{16}*He will come and destroy those tenants, and give the vineyard to others.' When they heard this, they said, 'God forbid!'* ^{17}*But he looked at them and said, 'What then is this that is written:*

"*The very stone which the builders rejected*
has become the head of the corner"?

^{18}'*Everyone who falls on that stone will be broken to pieces; but when it falls on anyone it will crush him.*'

^{19}*The scribes and the chief priests tried to lay hands on him at that very hour, but they feared the people; for they perceived that he had told this parable against them.*

In occupied territory like Palestine there were many large estates owned by foreigners, who leased them out to tenants for a proportion of the annual produce. Economic depression combined with nationalist unrest may well have tempted farmers to withhold rent from an absentee landlord, even if they had to resort to violence and, in the end, to murder. If through the death of the heir the estate should be declared 'ownerless property', the actual occupants would have first claim to the possession of it. Jesus was drawing, as usual, from life when he told this story and invited his listeners to find in it an illustration of their own attitude to the claims of God. Any Jew, hearing this story, would be reminded of Isaiah's parable of the vineyard (Isa. 5$^{1-7}$), in which the vineyard represented Israel. It was, therefore, inevitable that the Jewish authorities should recognize *that he had told this parable against them*. It was inevitable also that, when the parable was expounded as part of the teaching tradition of the early Church, it should be treated as an allegory. The landlord was identified with God, the servants with the prophets, the son with Jesus, the tenants with the Jewish leaders, the 'others' with the Gentile Church. Some traces of this allegorical interpretation have found their way into Luke's version of the parable. According to Mark, the son was killed inside the vineyard and his body thrown unceremoniously over the wall. Luke, like Matthew, has altered this to make the death occur outside the vineyard, and so to assimilate it to the death of Jesus, who *suffered outside the gate* (Heb. 13^{12}). The comment of the bystanders, '*God forbid!*', is a Lucan addition which makes sense only if we suppose that they were treating the end of the story as an allegorical forecast of the fall of Jerusalem.

৩৫৩

17
The quotation from Ps. 118²², which stands in all three Synoptic Gospels, looks like an early Christian attempt to work the resurrection into a parable which originally ended with a murder and its punishment.

18
This saying has no connexion with the parable, but was inserted by Luke at this point, following the accepted practice of grouping isolated sayings with only a common keyword to link them together (cf. 11³³⁻³⁶, Mark 9⁴⁹⁻⁵⁰). The stone which becomes the head of the corner was hardly likely to fall on anyone or to be fallen on. As we do not know the original context, it is not easy to determine what Jesus intended by this saying.

20²⁰⁻²⁶   THE BATTLE OF ARGUMENTS:
            (3) TRIBUTE TO CAESAR

²⁰*So they watched him, and sent spies, who pretended to be sincere, that they might take hold of what he said, so as to deliver him up to the authority and jurisdiction of the governor.* ²¹*They asked him, 'Teacher, we know that you speak and teach rightly, and show no partiality, but truly teach the way of God.* ²²*Is it lawful for us to give tribute to Caesar, or not?'* ²³*But he perceived their craftiness, and said to them,* ²⁴*'Show me a coin.ᵃ Whose likeness and inscription has it?' They said, 'Caesar's.'* ²⁵*He said to them, 'Then render to Caesar the things that are Caesar's, and to God the things that are God's.'* ²⁶*And they were not able in the presence of the people to catch him by what he said; but marvelling at his answer they were silent.*

a Greek *denarius*

The authorities next put to Jesus a second double-edged question concerning the poll-tax which the Romans levied annually upon every adult male. A negative answer to the question would lay Jesus open to a charge of treason; an affirmative answer would alienate his followers. For this tax was deeply resented by most Jews, both as a sign of national subjection, and because it had to be paid in silver coinage, stamped with the emperor's laurelled head, which violated the Jewish law against images. (In deference to Jewish scruples the Romans minted for circulation inside Palestine copper coins without the imperial image.) The fulsome flattery that preceded the question defeated its own purpose by betraying to Jesus the insincerity of the questioners. According to Mark they were Pharisees and Herodians, according to Luke suborned men making a pretence of an honest perplexity of conscience.

By asking to be shown a silver denarius Jesus exposed the dishonesty of his adversaries. He knew that the denarius was freely circulating in Judea, he had undoubtedly seen it in piles on the tables of the money-changers, he rightly suspected that his interrogators had one in their possession. By accepting the Roman coinage and with it the benefits conferred by Rome in the way of economic stability and political order, they had committed themselves to an answer to their own question. But Jesus was not content to score a debating point over his opponents. If they did not take the question seriously, he insisted on doing so, and nothing in the Gospels speaks more eloquently of the robust quality of his mind than his ability, in the momentary exchange of controversy, to enunciate a principle which has proved to be the basis of all future discussion of the problem of Church and State (cf. Rom. 13^{1-7}, I Pet. 2^{13-17}).

Jesus' answer does not, of course, mean that the secular and the sacred belong to two independent and unrelated compartments of life. It means that man, by the very nature of his historical existence, is a subject of two kingdoms, an earthly and a heavenly, to both of which he owes a debt of loyalty, the one conditional and the other absolute. For God deals with man partly through the impersonal and fallible institutions of society and civil government, partly through the direct and personal impact of his own sovereign love. As long as Caesar performs his God-given function of providing a framework of order for the common life of men, he has the right to claim his due; taxes are not an imposition extorted by the victor from the vanquished, to be paid under duress, but a debt to be acknowledged as a

moral obligation. It is of course another matter if Caesar should lay
claim to that which belongs by right only to God – the unconditional
and absolute obedience of men. This is totalitarianism, the ascription
of absolute worth to that which is essentially human and transient.
But it is to be noted that the same result ensues if religion attempts to
absorb the functions of the State. The Zealots believed that allegiance
to Caesar was disloyalty to God, and that the only course open to the
people of God was to regain their independence by force in order to
establish a theocracy. But all theocracy is by nature totalitarian,
involving the confusion of human institutions with divine ordinances.

Jesus' answer, then, was no mere evasion of a verbal trap. It was a
messianic manifesto, in which he disavowed all connexion with the
Jewish nationalist movement and affirmed his own conviction that it
was feasible for Israel to discharge her total commitment to God even
as loyal subjects of a pagan empire.

20²⁷⁻⁴⁰   THE BATTLE OF ARGUMENTS:
            (4) THE GOD OF THE LIVING

²⁷There came to him some Sadducees, those who say that there is no resurrection, ²⁸and they asked him a question, saying, 'Teacher, Moses wrote for
us that if a man's brother dies, having a wife but no children, the manª must
take the wife and raise up children for his brother. ²⁹Now there were seven
brothers; the first took a wife, and died without children; ³⁰and the second
³¹and the third took her, and likewise all seven left no children and died.
³²'Afterward the woman also died. ³³In the resurrection, therefore, whose
wife will the woman be? For the seven had her as wife.'

³⁴And Jesus said to them, 'The sons of this age marry and are given in
marriage; ³⁵but those who are accounted worthy to attain to that age and to
the resurrection from the dead neither marry nor are given in marriage, ³⁶for
they cannot die any more, because they are equal to angels and are sons of
God, being sons of the resurrection. ³⁷But that the dead are raised, even
Moses showed, in the passage about the bush, where he calls the Lord the
God of Abraham and the God of Isaac and the God of Jacob. ³⁸Now he is
not God of the dead, but of the living; for all live to him.' ³⁹And some of the

*scribes answered, 'Teacher, you have spoken well.' 40For they no longer
dared to ask him any question.*

  a Greek *his brother*

The question with which the Sadducees thought to ridicule Jesus was
based on the law of levirate marriage (Deut. 25$^{5-6}$), the object of
which was to provide a legal heir for a man who died childless. In the
time of Jesus the law had fallen into abeyance, so that the question was
a somewhat academic one. The Sadducees, no doubt, would have
argued that, since the commandment was in the Torah, and since
it made belief in resurrection absurd, therefore the Torah excluded
belief in an afterlife. Jesus, however, did not hold the naïve view of
resurrection they attributed to him. He had simply to state, therefore,
that in an existence which has no place for death, marriage as a means
of propagating the species or assuring a legal succession becomes
irrelevant.

  Once again, however, Jesus takes the question more seriously than
the questioner, and turns to the important assumptions that underlie
it. By a quotation from Exod. 3^6 he argues that the Torah does imply
a belief in eternal life, so that even on their own premises the Sadducees are wrong. The argument runs as follows: inanimate things may
have a Creator, but only the living can have a God. When God says
to Moses, 'I am the God of Abraham . . .', this implies that Abraham
is still alive. In form the argument is typically rabbinic, relying as it
does on the precise wording of the sacred text; and, as Luke tells us,
the scribes were impressed by it. But the substance of the argument
has a deeper validity, and is capable of being expressed in a form more
congenial to the modern mind. Jesus is saying, in effect: all life, here
and hereafter, consists in friendship with God, and nothing less is
worthy of the name of life. Abraham was the friend of God, and it is
incredible that such friendship should be severed by death. Death may
put an end to physical existence, but not to a relationship that is by
nature eternal. Men may lose their friends by death, but not God.

ඞ

27
The Sadducees were the conservative party of Judaism, religiously as
well as politically. They accepted as scripture only the Torah – the five

books of Moses – and refused to entertain any doctrine not contained in this narrowly circumscribed canon. They repudiated, for example, the popular belief in angels and demons, which had grown up after the Exile under Persian influence, and which played so large a part in the apocalyptic writings of the period between the Testaments. They rejected also the belief in an afterlife, which developed so late in Israel's history that it scarcely finds mention in the Old Testament, let alone in the Torah (Dan. 12^2, Isa. 26^{19}). This was one of the themes of continuing controversy between Sadducee and Pharisee (Acts 23$^{6-10}$). In this debate, it must be granted, the Sadducean objection had a good deal of point, for the Pharisees tended to identify resurrection with resuscitation to a carnal life on a grander scale, and many of their pictures of the afterlife are gross in their materialism (e.g. *Shab.* 30b: 'the women will bear children daily'; and see *Sohar. Gen, f.* 24.96 for a discussion of the status of the remarried widow).

20$^{41-44}$ THE BATTLE OF ARGUMENTS:
             (5) THE SON OF DAVID

^{41}*But he said to them, 'How can they say that the Christ is David's son?*
^{42}*For David himself says in the Book of Psalms,*
  "The Lord said to my Lord,
   Sit at my right hand,
 ^{43}*till I make thy enemies a stool for thy feet."*
 ^{44}*David thus calls him Lord; so how is he his son?'*

It is now the turn of Jesus to ask the questions. This passage is important in the first instance because of what it tells us about Jesus himself.
Christian piety has always tended to be so preoccupied with his
divinity as to forget that he was a real man with human limitations
and, in particular, sharing the limited knowledge and outlook of his
contemporaries. The Jews of the first century believed that David
wrote the Psalms and Moses the Torah, and Jesus apparently shared
both these beliefs, though neither of them would receive any support
from modern critical scholarship. Jesus had an unparalleled knowledge of God and a marvellous insight into the workings of the human

heart; but there were things he did not know (cf. Mark 13³²). This does not, however, seriously affect the validity of the present argument.

We need not suppose that Jesus was denying his own descent from David, which the New Testament elsewhere abundantly affirms (Matt. 1²⁰, Luke 1²⁷, 2⁴, Rom. 1³, Rev. 5⁵, 22¹⁶). Nor is it likely that he regarded Davidic descent as totally irrelevant to the status of the Messiah, for the whole messianic hope had its origin in God's promise to David that there would never be lacking a son to sit upon his throne – a promise which was projected into the eschatological future when the dynasty of David was dethroned in 586 B.C. (2 Sam. 7⁸⁻¹⁶, Ps. 89³⁻⁴, Isa. 9²⁻⁷, 11¹⁻¹⁰, Jer. 23⁵⁻⁶, Ezek. 34²³⁻²⁴, 37²⁴⁻²⁵, Amos 9¹¹, Mic. 5², Zech. 12⁶⁻13¹). He means that the Son of David is, by itself, an inadequate and misleading description of the Messiah, and that the Old Testament contains intimations that the Coming One will be a far more exalted figure who, instead of merely occupying the throne of David, will share the throne of God.

What the title Son of David meant to the ordinary Jew can be seen in the *Psalms of Solomon*, written less than a century before the ministry of Jesus, probably by a Pharisee.

> Behold, O Lord, and raise up for them their king, the Son of David,
> At the time which thou, O God, dost decree for his reign to begin over Israel thy servant;
> And gird him with strength to crush unjust rulers,
> And to purge Jerusalem from Gentiles that trample her down to destruction;
> With wisdom and righteousness to expel sinners from the inheritance;
> To break the pride of sinners like a potter's vessel;
> With a rod of iron to break down all their confidence;
> To destroy the lawless Gentiles with the word of his mouth,
> So that, at his threatening, Gentiles shall flee before him;
> And to convict sinners for the thoughts of their hearts.
>
> (*Ps. Sol.* 17²³⁻²⁷)

Jesus was making a last attempt at persuading Jerusalem that Messiahship did not have to be identified with this kind of nationalist frenzy.

20⁴⁵–21⁴   THE BATTLE OF ARGUMENTS:
     (5) RELIGION, FALSE AND TRUE

⁴⁵*And in the hearing of all the people he said to his disciples,*
    ⁴⁶*'Beware of the scribes, who like to go about in long robes, and love salutations in the market places and the best seats in the synagogues and the places of honour at feasts, ⁴⁷who devour widow's houses and for a pretence make long prayers. They will receive the greater condemnation.'*

2 1 *He looked up and saw the rich putting their gifts into the treasury; ²and he saw a poor widow put in two copper coins. ³And he said, 'Truly, I tell you, this poor widow has put in more than all of them; ⁴for they all contributed out of their abundance, but she out of her poverty put in all the living that she had.'*

Throughout the whole of the present section Luke has been following Mark closely, and he here takes over from Mark almost verbatim a final controversial saying, a doublet of which he has already included earlier in a Q context (11⁴³). The story of the widow's offering follows at this point probably because, during the period of oral transmission, the two units of tradition were artificially linked together by the keyword widow. The link may be artificial, but the self-forgetful widow forms a striking contrast to the self-important scribes. They gave out of their surplus, she out of her deficit.

21$^{5\text{-}38}$ *The Fall of Jerusalem*

For the first seven verses of this passage Luke is obviously following Mark, and there are other equally clear echoes of Mark throughout the rest of the chapter. It was once assumed by scholars that the whole discourse was nothing more than a free rewriting of Mark 13. In recent years, however, there has been a growing support for the theory that, where the discourse strikingly diverges from Mark, Luke is drawing on his source L, and that this is one of the rare occasions when he has combined Marcan and non-Marcan material. To Mark belong vv. 5-11, 16-17, 21a, 23a, 26b-27, 29-31, and to L vv. 12-15, 18-20, 21b-22, 23b-26a, 28, 34-36. The dovetailing of the sources has been done carefully, but not so carefully that we cannot here and there see the seams showing. Verse 21a, for instance, is clearly intrusive in the context in which it stands: a literal translation of v. 21b is 'let those who are inside her depart and let not those who are in the country enter her' – the 'her' in each case referring to Jerusalem, mentioned in v. 20, and not to the Judea of the intervening half-verse.

The two independent prophecies which Luke has fused into one were of a very different character. Mark 13 begins with a prediction of the destruction of the temple and a question from the disciples as to when this may be expected, which is followed, not by an answer to the question, but by a closely knit series of premonitory signs that will lead up to the final climax of history, the coming of the Son of man; and in the opinion of many scholars this series of warnings existed as a separate fly-sheet before it came to be incorporated in the Gospel. The L material, read by itself, forms a continuous and homogeneous prophecy of a succession of historic events: the persecution of the Church by the Jewish people, the punishment of Jerusalem by God for her refusal of the gospel – a punishment executed unwittingly by Gentile armies – the subsequent overthrow of Gentile imperial power, and finally the vindication of those who by loyalty and endurance have proved themselves worthy to stand before the Son of man. The pattern for this composition is to be found in a number of Old Testament passages concerning a coming Day of the Lord, which is to be a day both of vengeance and of redemption, vengeance on the pagan oppressors of Israel and redemption for the oppressed people of God (Deut. 32³⁵⁻³⁶, Isa. 34⁸, 35⁴, 61², 63⁴). In the Christian adaptation of this theme, however, the picture is radically altered: the true Israel is the Church, and Jerusalem, instead of being able to look forward to ultimate vindication, finds herself classed with the enemies of God; the Gentiles must first inflict God's vengeance on Jerusalem before themselves undergoing the divine judgement, and only with the removal of both these threats to her existence can the Church expect to see her redemption. The whole complex of events was apparently regarded as the fulfilment of the Daniel prophecy that, with the erection of God's throne of judgement, world dominion would pass out of the hands of godless nations into the hands of the Son of man (see notes on 12³⁵⁻⁴⁸ and 17²⁰⁻³⁷).

In combining these two prophecies Luke made his own peculiar contribution to New Testament eschatology, by distinguishing those parts of the Church's expectation which had already been fulfilled in his day from those that remained outstanding. The crisis which Jesus had predicted would happen within a generation, bringing death to himself, persecution to his disciples, and destruction to Jerusalem, was now accomplished; Luke and his contemporaries were living in a period of indeterminate length, the times of the Gentiles, during which God's judgement on Jerusalem must run its course, and only after that would the End come and with it the consummation of the kingdom.

5And as some spoke of the temple, how it was adorned with noble stones and offerings, he said, 6'As for these things which you see, the days will come when there shall not be left here one stone upon another that will not be thrown down.' 7And they asked him, 'Teacher, when will this be, and what will be the sign when this is about to take place?' 8And he said, 'Take heed that you are not led astray; for many will come in my name, saying, "I am he!" and, "The time is at hand!" Do not go after them. 9And when you hear of wars and tumults, do not be terrified; for this must first take place, but the end will not be at once.'

10Then he said to them, 'Nation will rise against nation, and kingdom against kingdom; 11there will be great earthquakes, and in various places famines and pestilences; and there will be terrors and great signs from heaven. 12But before all this they will lay their hands on you and persecute you, delivering you up to the synagogues and prisons, and you will be brought before kings and governors for my name's sake. 13This will be a time for you to bear testimony. 14Settle it therefore in your minds, not to meditate beforehand how to answer; 15for I will give you a mouth and wisdom, which none of your adversaries will be able to withstand or contradict. 16You will be delivered up even by parents and brothers and kinsmen and friends, and some of you they will put to death; ¹⁷*you will be hated by all for my name's sake.* ¹⁸*But not a hair of your head will perish.* ¹⁹*By your endurance you will gain your lives.'*

Jesus' prediction of the destruction of the temple calls forth from the disciples a question which, in all three Synoptic Gospels, leads to a long prophetic discourse. Mark's discourse, however, is no answer to the question; it relates to the end of the present age and the signs that will foreshadow it, and one of those signs is, not the destruction, but the desecration of the temple. Matthew has removed the inconsistency by making the question fit the answer, Luke by making the answer fit the question.

The false Messiahs, who in Mark's scheme of things were simply the first of many signs of the approaching End, are made by Luke to serve a different purpose; by attributing to them the words '*The time is at hand*', and denouncing this as a false prophecy, he has established the first main point of his own thesis: that the final crisis of history is not to be confused with the historic crisis which Jesus said would happen within a generation, and that anyone who declares the End to be imminent is a fraud. The wars, earthquakes, famines, pestilences, terrors, and other portents are regular features of Jewish apocalyptic writing. The apocalyptists looked forward to a great deliverance, which they believed had been foreshadowed and typified by the deliverance of Israel from bondage in Egypt, and which would therefore be heralded by messianic woes similar to the plagues that preceded the Exodus. To people who interpreted history in this fashion the battles of A.D. 69, when four claimants contended for the imperial throne vacated by the suicide of Nero, and the eruption of Vesuvius in A.D. 79 must have produced a considerable heightening of expectation.

In the description of the persecution Luke follows, in the main, his L source; yet even so it is strange that he, of all people, should have omitted Mark's prediction that the gospel must first be preached to all nations (cf. the similar omission at 19⁴⁶).

²⁰*'But when you see Jerusalem surrounded by armies, then know that its desolation has come near.* ²¹*Then let those who are in Judea flee to the mountains, and let those who are inside the city depart, and let not those who are out in the country enter it;* ²²*for these are days of vengeance, to fulfil all that is written.* ²³*Alas for those who are with child and for those who give suck in those days! For great distress shall be upon the earth and wrath upon this people;*

²⁴*they will fall by the edge of the sword, and be led captive among all nations; and Jerusalem will be trodden down by the Gentiles, until the times of the Gentiles are fulfilled.*

²⁵*'And there will be signs in sun and moon and stars, and upon the earth distress of nations in perplexity at the roaring of the sea and the waves,* ²⁶*men fainting with fear and with foreboding of what is coming on the world; for the powers of the heavens will be shaken.*

²⁷*'And then they will see the Son of man coming in a cloud with power and great glory.* ²⁸*Now when these things begin to take place, look up and raise your heads, because your redemption is drawing near.'*

Some have thought that this description of the siege of Jerusalem is too detailed to be a genuine prophecy, and that it must have been written after A.D. 70 by someone who had a knowledge of the actual course of events; and this is the obvious explanation for those who believe that at this point Luke was rewriting Mark's obscure reference to the desecration of the temple by the *'desolating sacrilege'* (Mark 13¹⁴). But none of the distinctive features of the siege as it is described by Josephus are found here; the language of this passage (as of 19⁴¹⁻⁴⁴) is drawn from Old Testament prophecies and descriptions of the fall of Jerusalem in 586 B.C. Luke was certainly writing after A.D. 70, but there is no reason why the source he was using should not have antedated the siege. Whether this L prophecy was a precise transcript of the words of Jesus is another matter, but there can be no doubt that Jesus repeatedly foretold the violent end to which Jerusalem was hastening. 'The times of the Gentiles' is an echo of the Book of Daniel, which asserts that God has given to a Gentile kingdom the authority to devastate Israel for a time, two times, and half a time (Dan. 12⁷). This period is also described as days of vengeance – a phrase which is apt to conjure up a misleading picture of a vengeful deity. What is meant is a time when sin, long unchecked and unpunished, is at last confronted inexorably with God's retributive justice.

The retribution visited on Jerusalem is to be followed by the distress of the Gentiles. This upheaval too is described in traditional terms. The sea which threatens to engulf the world is the turbulent ocean upon which God imposed his will at Creation, the reservoir of evil things (Rev. 13¹) over which he has still to secure his final conquest. The powers of heaven are the heavenly bodies, identified with the gods of oriental and Greco-Roman religion, and regarded by the Jews as angelic beings created by God and allowed by him to preside over the destinies of pagan nations (Deut. 32⁸, Isa. 24²¹, 34¹⁻⁴). Thus the shaking of the powers of heaven denotes not so much the ruin of the physical universe as the overthrow of pagan imperial supremacy.

ᗄᘏᗄ

27
By introducing into his L source this verse from Mark, Luke has considerably altered the tenor of the L prophecy. The redemption of the people of God, which in the L source was their vindication in the course of history through the removal of their Jewish and Gentile persecutors, is now identified with the eschatological coming of the Son of man, and also with the final establishment of the kingdom (v. 31). It is worth noting that in place of 'the clouds of heaven', which Mark derived from Dan. 7¹³, Luke has simply *a cloud* – an alteration which establishes a link between the glorious advent of Christ and other events in the gospel story in which the same cloud of the divine presence is menioned (9³⁴, Acts 1⁹⁻¹¹).

²⁹*And he told them a parable: 'Look at the fig tree, and all the trees;* ³⁰*as soon as they come out in leaf, you see for yourselves and know that the*

summer is already near. ³¹*So also, when you see these things taking place, you know that the kingdom of God is near.*

³²*'Truly, I say to you, this generation will not pass away till all has taken place.* ³³*Heaven and earth will pass away, but my words will not pass away.*

³⁴*'But take heed to yourselves lest your hearts be weighed down with dissipation and drunkenness and cares of this life, and that day come upon you suddenly like a snare;* ³⁵*for it will come upon all who dwell upon the face of the whole earth.* ³⁶*But watch at all times, praying that you may have strength to escape all these things that will take place, and to stand before the Son of man.'*

³⁷*And every day he was teaching in the temple, but at night he went out and lodged on the mount called Olivet.* ³⁸*And early in the morning all the people came to him in the temple to hear him.*

By placing the parable of the fig tree after the description of the coming of the Son of man, Mark has shown that he understood it to be a warning to be ready for the imminent parousia. By itself, however, the parable suggests quite a different application: for it could easily have been spoken by Jesus as a warning to be ready for the disaster which was overhanging Jerusalem and which would one day be, quite literally, *'at the very gates'* (Mark 13²⁹). Luke has followed Mark's interpretation and has eliminated any possible ambiguity by introducing the words *'the kingdom of God'*.

As in Mark's Gospel, this parable is followed by a declaration that all things will be accomplished within a generation. Mark undoubtedly understood this prediction to include the parousia, and he was writing at a date near enough to the time of Jesus to feel no embarrassment about such a prophecy. But Luke, writing fifteen to twenty years later, was in a different case; we should expect him to interpret the saying otherwise, and there is every indication that he did so. For his discourse ends with instructions to the disciples to pray that they may have strength to escape *'all these things'*, and it is a reasonable assumption that for him *'all things'* in v. 32 covered the same set of events as *'all these things'* in v. 36. But from the parousia and the final consummation of the kingdom there could be no escape, nor can we imagine the disciples of Jesus being taught to pray for any. The disciples were taught to pray that they might survive the preliminary crises of persecution and the siege of Jerusalem; and these, according to Luke, were the events which Jesus declared would happen before a generation has passed away.

THE UPPER ROOM:
(1) PREPARING THE PASSOVER

22 *Now the feast of Unleavened Bread drew near, which is called the Passover.* ²*And the chief priests and the scribes were seeking how to put him to death; for they feared the people.*

³*Then Satan entered into Judas called Iscariot, who was of the number of the twelve;* ⁴*he went away and conferred with the chief priests and captains how he might betray him to them.* ⁵*And they were glad, and engaged to give him money.* ⁶*So he agreed, and sought an opportunity to betray him to them in the absence of the multitude.*

⁷*Then came the day of Unleavened Bread, on which the passover lamb had to be sacrificed.* ⁸*So Jesus*ᵃ *sent Peter and John, saying, 'Go and prepare the passover for us, that we may eat it.'* ⁹*They said to him, 'Where will you have us prepare it?'* ¹⁰*He said to them, 'Behold, when you have entered the city, a man carrying a jar of water will meet you; follow him into the house which he enters,* ¹¹*and tell the householder, "The Teacher says to you, Where is the guest room, where I am to eat the passover with my disciples?"* ¹²*And he will show you a large upper room furnished; there make ready.'* ¹³*And they went, and found it as he had told them; and they prepared the passover.*

a Greek *he*

The instructions given by Jesus on this occasion resemble those given before the entry into Jerusalem, and in both cases we must assume either that Jesus had made careful prearrangements to ensure secrecy (perhaps in view of the expected defection of Judas), or that he was manifesting his prophetic powers of supernatural vision. A man with a waterpot would be a conspicuous sign in a land where all water-carrying was done by women. The preparations for the Passover would include the purchase, sacrifice, and roasting of the lamb and the purchase of unleavened bread, bitter herbs, and wine.

While these preparations were in train, Judas was busy elsewhere. The character of Judas is one of the unsolved conundrums of the gospel story. He must at one time have been an enthusiastic disciple who had won his way into Jesus' confidence. Why should such a man in the end turn traitor? Was it 'just for a handful of silver', because he had embezzled the common purse of the disciples, of which he was treasurer? (John 12⁶). Or because, in the débâcle of Jesus' cause which he foresaw, he hoped to save his skin by turning 'king's evidence'? Or because he was a disillusioned Zealot, who had followed Jesus under the misapprehension that he would lead the Jewish revolt against Rome?* Or because he was a disillusioned idealist who wanted to force Jesus' hand by putting him in a situation where only a display of supernatural power could save him? Luke has his own answer to this question: Judas betrayed Jesus because Satan entered him, because he became the catspaw of the Enemy in the final stages of the campaign which Jesus had been waging against Satan's kingdom ever since the day of his baptism. This is an answer which reminds us that the early Church saw the crucifixion as the decisive battle in a cosmic struggle, but one which still leaves the modern reader asking by what error of judgement or flaw of character Judas gave Satan the latch-key to his soul. We should be better able to assess the character of Judas if we knew his fate. Matthew tells us that he returned the blood money to the treasury and committed suicide; and this suggests that he had not intended, or at least had not envisaged, the actual outcome of his treachery. But Luke in Acts has preserved a different tradition that he kept the money to buy a farm and died by some sort of punitive miracle, presumably without contrition. On the other hand we may without hesitation endorse Luke's answer to the other question, What did Judas betray? The Jewish authorities were afraid to take open action against Jesus because of his popularity with the crowd of Galilean pilgrims, and Judas undertook to lead the temple guards to the place where Jesus bivouacked every night on the Mount of Olives, so that they could arrest him in the absence of the multitudes.

༄

---

* It has even been suggested that Iscariot was a corrupted form of *sicarius*, the Latin name for a nationalist partisan.

I

Luke's information about the Jewish festivals is not strictly accurate. The Passover was a meal, commemorating the Exodus, eaten on the evening of Nisan 15th, the day of the spring full moon. The hours when it could legitimately be eaten happened to coincide with the beginning of the first day of the feast of Unleavened Bread, a seven-day agricultural festival in the course of which the first sheaf of the harvest was offered in the temple.

7

It is not strictly true to say that the paschal lambs were sacrificed on the (first) day of Unleavened Bread. The Jewish day began at sunset, so that by Jewish reckoning the sacrificing of the lambs in the afternoon fell on Nisan 14th, and the Passover meal a few hours later fell on Nisan 15th, the first day of Unleavened Bread. The mistake, which Luke copied from Mark, is probably due to the fact that both Evangelists, for the benefit of their Gentile readers, were using Greco-Roman reckoning, according to which the day ran from midnight to midnight, so that both events occurred on the same day.

22¹⁴⁻²³ THE UPPER ROOM: (2) THE LAST SUPPER

¹⁴And when the hour came, he sat at table, and the apostles with him. ¹⁵And he said to them, 'I have earnestly desired to eat this passover with you before I suffer; ¹⁶for I tell you I shall not eat it*a* until it is fulfilled in the kingdom of God.' ¹⁷And he took a cup, and when he had given thanks he said, 'Take this, and divide it among yourselves; ¹⁸for I tell you that from now on I shall not drink of the fruit of the vine until the kingdom of God comes.'

¹⁹And he took bread, and when he had given thanks he broke it and gave it to them, saying, 'This is my body.*b* ²¹But behold the hand of him who betrays me is with me on the table. ²²For the Son of man goes as it has been determined; but woe to that man by whom he is betrayed!' ²³And they began to question one another, which of them it was that would do this.

a Other ancient authorities read *never eat it again*
b Other ancient authorities add 'which is given for you. Do this in remembrance of me.' ²⁰And likewise the cup after supper, saying, 'This cup which is poured out for you is the new covenant in my blood.'

236

The Lucan account of the Last Supper is a scholar's paradise and a beginner's nightmare; for it raises problems in almost every department of New Testament study and has provided a basis for a welter of conflicting theories. Firstly, there is a textual problem: the vast majority of manuscripts have what is known as the longer text, including vv. 19b–20; the Western text (Codex D, some Old Latin manuscripts, and probably the old Syriac version), here followed by the R.S.V., omits these verses. In spite of the preponderance of manuscript evidence, Westcott and Hort believed that this was one of the places where the Western text must be regarded as original. The disputed verses appear to have been drawn partly from 1 Cor. 11$^{24-25}$, partly from Mark 14^{24}, and could have been inserted in the text at an early date by a scribe who considered Luke's account to be defective. But the longer text still has its champions. Secondly, there is the question of sources: supposing the shorter text to be what Luke wrote, is it the product of Luke's editorial freedom in rewriting Mark, or was he using in the main a non-Marcan source? Our answer to this question will depend on our general theory of the composition of the Gospel, but the modern tendency is to ascribe the whole passage to L, except for two Marcan additions (vv. 19a, 22). Thirdly, there is a question of eucharistic origins: was the L source at this point simply a historical tradition of an event in the life of Jesus, or was it related to the eucharistic practice of some part of the early Church? Two theories may be mentioned under this heading. Some scholars have pointed out that in the shorter text the usual order – the breaking of bread followed by the blessing of the cup – is reversed, and have argued that, since a similar order is found in 1 Cor. 10$^{16, 21}$ and in an early second-century manual of Church rules (*Didache*, ix. 1–3), this is evidence for the existence of a eucharistic form different from that which underlies Mark 14$^{22-25}$ and 1 Cor. 11$^{23-27}$. But it is more likely that the reversal of order here is due to the editorial hand of Luke, who wanted to include v. 19a from Mark without interrupting the rhythmic structure of his main source L. The second theory is that in the early Church there were two distinct forms of eucharistic observance: the Pauline Lord's Supper, which was primarily a commemoration of the death of Christ, and 'the breaking of the bread', a fellowship meal held in joyful anticipation of the messianic banquet and without any reference to the Cross as an atoning sacrifice. This is, however, an unreal distinction; for the accounts of Mark and Paul have both the backward and the forward look, and it is likely that from the start the eucharist included both commemoration and anticipation. Fourthly, there is the theological question, why Luke, with Mark's Gospel before him, omitted the saying over the cup, which gave a sacrificial interpretation to the Cross. It has been suggested that Luke acted out of reverence, lest the sacred formula should be profaned by pagan lips, knowing that Christians could readily supply the missing words from memory. But the explanation is rather to be sought in Luke's theology: for believing, as he did, that God's saving act was the whole of Jesus' life of service and self-giving, and that the Cross was simply the preordained price of friendship with the outcast, he naturally felt little interest in sayings which appeared to concentrate the whole of God's redemption in the Cross. Finally, there is the historical question, whether the Last Supper was a passover or not. Both Luke's sources (Mark and L) asserted that it was. John (18²⁸, 19¹⁴) tells us that the passover was not eaten until the evening after the crucifixion. And on this subject all that can be said is that the debate continues.

Where there is so much room for differences of opinion, dogmatism is out of the question, but this much may be said by way of simplification and summary. The shorter text is probably what Luke wrote. He used as his main source the L tradition, which had preserved a collection of sayings, spoken by Jesus in the upper room, but never incorporated in any form of eucharistic liturgy. These sayings treated the supper as a passover, celebrated by Jesus and his disciples as an anticipation of the great feast of the kingdom, in which the Passover theme of redemption from bondage would receive its final fulfilment.

22²⁴⁻³⁸   THE UPPER ROOM:
          (3) THE FAREWELL DISCOURSE

²⁴*A dispute also arose among them, which of them was to be regarded as the greatest. ²⁵And he said to them, 'The kings of the Gentiles exercise lordship over them; and those in authority over them are called benefactors. ²⁶But*

not so with you; rather let the greatest among you become as the youngest, and the leader as one who serves.

²⁷'*For which is the greater, one who sits at table, or one who serves? Is it not the one who sits at table? But I am among you as one who serves.*

²⁸'*You are those who have continued with me in my trials;* ²⁹*as my Father appointed a kingdom for me, so do I appoint for you* ³⁰*that you may eat and drink at my table in my kingdom, and sit on thrones judging the twelve tribes of Israel.*

³¹'*Simon, Simon, behold, Satan demanded to have you,ᵃ that he might sift youᵃ like wheat,* ³²*but I have prayed for you that your faith may not fail; and when you have turned again, strengthen your brethren.'*

³³*And he said to him, 'Lord, I am ready to go with you to prison and to death.'* ³⁴*He said, 'I tell you, Peter, the cock will not crow this day, until you three times deny that you know me.'*

³⁵*And he said to them, 'When I sent you out with no purse or bag or sandals, did you lack anything?' They said, 'Nothing.'* ³⁶*He said to them, 'But now, let him who has a purse take it, and likewise a bag. And let him who has no sword sell his mantle and buy one.*

³⁷'*For I tell you that this scripture must be fulfilled in me, "And he was reckoned with transgressors"; for what is written about me has its fulfilment.'* ³⁸*And they said, 'Look, Lord, here are two swords.' And he said to them, 'It is enough.'*

ᵃ The Greek word for *you* here is plural; in verse 32 it is singular.

The words of Jesus have directed the thoughts of the twelve to the coming of God's kingdom, and they begin to discuss the positions they are to occupy when that kingdom comes. Jesus silences their ambition by instructing them that it is pagan and worldly to confuse greatness with power and dignity with recognition. The only greatness which is acknowledged in the kingdom is humble service, and this greatness Jesus has displayed throughout his ministry and will display to the end.

Once again we are reminded of the loneliness of Jesus. His life has been marked out from the common life of men, not merely by what he taught and achieved, but by what he experienced. Looking back now on his ministry he sees it as a series of trials, tests of his spiritual stamina. His call has been to drink the cup of experience to the dregs, to walk a path of obedience never before explored by man; and from

the first wrestling with Satan in the wilderness to the last grim agony
that now awaits him on the Mount of Olives he has had to face this
destiny alone. His faithful friends have been with him throughout,
unable to share his burden, but supporting him with their companionship; and their loyalty is not to go without its reward.

Luke, as we have seen, omitted the Marcan saying which described
the cup of the last supper as the blood-sacrifice by which the new
covenant was to be sealed, but the idea of covenant is not absent from
his account. The word translated 'appoint' is really a verbal form of
the word for covenant. As God has made a covenant with Jesus,
entrusting the kingdom to his keeping, that he might make it real to
men in his life of redemptive service, so Jesus in turn makes a covenant
with the twelve and through them with the Church that is to be. For
this saying proves beyond doubt that, in choosing the twelve, Jesus
had intended them to be the symbol and nucleus of the new Israel.
Over the Israel of God they will exercise authority (judging has here
its Old Testament sense of ruling) in the heavenly kingdom, but only
such authority as belongs to those who on earth have learnt the
meaning of service.

With the utmost pathos Jesus now predicts that those who have
remained with him in his trials will desert him in the greatest trial of
all. For them the road to the celestial city lies through the valley of
humiliation. They must wrestle with the demons of disillusionment,
self-contempt, and despair. For Satan, the Great Accuser, who as
prosecutor in the heavenly lawcourt demands the death penalty
without recommendation to mercy, has asked to have them, as once
he asked to have Job, confident that they too, in the midst of catastrophe, will learn to curse the God who called them into the service
of a lost cause. Peter by his threefold denial will sink lower than the
rest; yet he is singled out as the rock to which, in the midst of their
ordeal, others will turn and find a strength derived not from his own
character but from the prayers of his Master.

The story of the upper room ends with a conversation which shows
how deep was the gulf of misunderstanding which still separated the
disciples from Jesus. He begins by reminding them (in words drawn
from the mission charge to the seventy) of the halcyon days of the
Galilean mission, when they were able to go out on their missionary
tours relying wholly on hospitality for their maintenance. Now times

have changed: Jesus is about to be executed as a criminal, and they, as the criminal's accomplices, will find every man's hand against them. The instruction to sell their coats and buy swords is an example of Jesus' fondness for violent metaphor (cf. Matt. 23²⁴, Mark 10²⁵), but the disciples take it literally, as pedants have continued to do ever since. The words '*It is enough*' indicate, not satisfaction with the disciples' military preparedness, but a sad dismissal of the subject (cf. 1 Kings 19⁴, Mark 14⁴¹).

ಐಐ

38
It was on this verse that Boniface VIII in A.D. 1302, in his Bull *Unam Sanctam*, based the doctrine that God has entrusted to the Church the two swords of civil and spiritual authority.

22³⁹⁻⁵³   THE LAST NIGHT:
(1) THE MOUNT OF OLIVES

³⁹*And he came out, and went, as was his custom, to the Mount of Olives; and the disciples followed him.* ⁴⁰*And when he came to the place he said to them, 'Pray that you may not enter into temptation.'*

⁴¹*And he withdrew from them about a stone's throw, and knelt down and prayed,* ⁴²'*Father, if thou art willing, remove this cup from me; nevertheless not my will, but thine, be done.'* ⁴³*And there appeared to him an angel from heaven, strengthening him.* ⁴⁴*And being in an agony he prayed more earnestly; and his sweat became like great drops of blood falling down upon the ground.ᵃ* ⁴⁵*And when he rose from prayer, he came to the disciples and found them sleeping for sorrow,* ⁴⁶*and he said to them, 'Why do you sleep? Rise and pray that you may not enter into temptation.'*

⁴⁷*While he was still speaking, there came a crowd, and the man called Judas, one of the twelve, was leading them. He drew near to Jesus to kiss him;* ⁴⁸*but Jesus said to him, 'Judas, would you betray the Son of man with a kiss?'* ⁴⁹*And when those who were about him saw what would follow, they said, 'Lord, shall we strike with the sword?'*

⁵⁰*And one of them struck the slave of the high priest and cut off his right ear.* ⁵¹*But Jesus said, 'No more of this!' And he touched his ear and healed*

him. 52 *Then Jesus said to the chief priests and captains of the temple and elders, who had come out against him, 'Have you come out as against a robber, with swords and clubs?*

53 *'When I was with you day after day in the temple, you did not lay hands on me. But this is your hour, and the power of darkness.'*

a Other ancient authorities omit verses 43 and 44

Under the paschal moon Jesus and his disciples leave the city and cross the ravine of the Kidron. According to Mark, Jesus now began to be overwhelmed with bewilderment and horror, and spoke to his disciples of a sorrow by which his very life was being drained away; and, unable to bear the company of his dearest friends, he spent the night in successive spasms of anguished prayer. Luke's briefer account gives us, if possible, an even stronger impression of turbulence: for it is he who tells us that Jesus tore himself away from his companions, that he was in an agony, and that his sweat became like great drops of blood. When we remember the calm courage with which other brave men have faced death in all its barbarous and excruciating forms, we cannot but ask what were the ingredients of the cup which Jesus prayed God to remove from him.

The prayer of Jesus shows us that among the elements of his complex woe was an agony of doubt. He has long since foretold his Passion; but now, on the eve of it, he hangs back, not simply with a natural shrinking from physical torture, but with an apprehension lest this be not after all the will of God. Is it really God's purpose that he should so soon bequeath the cause of the kingdom to men whom he knew to be ill-prepared for such responsibility? Is it really God's decision to foreclose now upon the spiritual bankruptcy of his people? The horrors he has foreseen need not happen, if he were to slip quietly into obscurity: Judas need not offer the traitor's kiss, nor Peter hear the accusing cock, the conspiracy of priest and Pharisee need not bear its grim fruit, nor need Jerusalem commit her crowning iniquity. But all these ideas he puts from him; it is not thus that he must save his people from their sins. The warning to the disciples about the danger of temptation shows that Jesus felt himself and them to be surrounded by the same spiritual powers of darkness with which he had wrestled at the outset of his ministry, and part of his agony was his sense of appalling exposure to their final assault upon his integrity.

We can be sure, too, that into his cup was poured an agony of love. A Stoic may face the prospect of falling victim to betrayal and desertion, to religious bigotry, political corruption, and nationalistic frenzy and remain unmoved, securely wrapped in the mantle of his own rectitude. But Jesus was facing rejection by his own people, to whom he was bound by ties of kinship, loyalty, and affection. Always the champion of sinners, he could not now dissociate himself from the national sin that was to deprive him of life: the shame and guilt of it descended upon him like a dense fog, blotting out the light of his Father's presence. He had already wept over Jerusalem in passionate regret, and now that the hour of her judgement had come, the weight of her doom threatened to break his heart.

Meanwhile the disciples had fallen asleep through nervous exhaustion. Jesus roused them with a rebuke, but his words were cut short by the arrival of Judas. According to Mark the arrest was carried out by a hired mob, armed with knives and cudgels. Luke has deduced from the words of Jesus (*I was with you day after day in the temple*) that some of the temple dignitaries and officials must have been present, no doubt well in the background. The crowd had clearly been warned to expect resistance, and not without reason, for the disciples were quite prepared to defend Jesus, if he had not ordered them to allow events to take their course. As Jesus points out, this is no legal arrest of a common criminal. The forces of law and order do their work publicly and in the light of day. The darkness is Satan's realm, and those who do Satan's business keep Satan's hours.

ॐ

43-44

These verses are missing from Codex Vaticanus and a few other manuscripts, and some scholars regard them as a scribal 'improvement'. But the passage was known to Justin Martyr, Irenaeus, Tatian, and Hippolytus in the second century, and is found in the majority of manuscripts, including Codex Sinaiticus and Codex Bezae. Its omission is best explained as the work of a scribe who felt that this picture of Jesus overwhelmed with human weakness was incompatible with his own belief in the Divine Son who shared the omnipotence of his Father.

⁵⁴*Then they seized him and led him away, bringing him into the high priest's house. Peter followed at a distance;* ⁵⁵*and when they had kindled a fire in the middle of the courtyard and sat down together, Peter sat among them.* ⁵⁶*Then a maid, seeing him as he sat in the light and gazing at him, said, 'This man also was with him.'* ⁵⁷*But he denied it, saying, 'Woman, I do not know him.'* ⁵⁸*And a little later someone else saw him and said, 'You also are one of them.' But Peter said, 'Man, I am not.'* ⁵⁹*And after an interval of about an hour still another insisted, saying, 'Certainly this man also was with him; for he is a Galilean.'* ⁶⁰*But Peter said, 'Man, I do not know what you are saying.' And immediately, while he was still speaking, the cock crowed.* ⁶¹*And the Lord turned and looked at Peter. And Peter remembered the word of the Lord, how he had said to him, 'Before the cock crows today, you will deny me three times.'* ⁶²*And he went out and wept bitterly.*

⁶³*Now the men who were holding Jesus mocked him and beat him;* ⁶⁴*they also blindfolded him and asked him, 'Prophesy! Who is it that struck you?* ⁶⁵*And they spoke many other words against him, reviling him.*

From this point on Luke's story runs parallel to Mark's, but with considerable divergence both in order and in content. According to Mark Jesus was taken straight before a midnight session of the Sanhedrin, the mocking took place in the court after the hearing, Peter's denial occurred in an outer courtyard during the trial, and at a second session held at daybreak the decision was made to send Jesus to Pilate. According to Luke Jesus was kept under guard in the high priest's house until the Sanhedrin could be called, and it was during the long night of waiting that the guards amused themselves at the expense of the prisoner and Peter denied his Master. The Lucan order is by far the more probable.

ƒ

63–64

The story of the mocking, as it stands in the three Synoptic Gospels, presents an interesting puzzle. Only Luke's account is self-explanatory. He tells us that the guards blindfolded Jesus, struck him on the face, and said, 'Now use your prophetic powers to put a name to the man who struck you.' Mark mentions the blindfold, but omits the question which explains the purpose of it. Matthew has the question, but it is a pointless one in his version, since he does not mention the blindfold. Any explanation is bound to be conjectural, but the simplest one is that the question in Matthew and the blindfold in Mark were early scribal harmonizations drawn from Luke. In that case Mark's original narrative told only of spitting and buffeting, and Luke's story of the blindfold came from a tradition independent of Mark.

22⁶⁶⁻⁷¹ THE TRIAL: (I) BEFORE THE SANHEDRIN

66When day came, the assembly of the elders of the people gathered together, both chief priests and scribes; and they led him away to their council, and they said, 67'If you are the Christ, tell us.' But he said to them, 'If I tell you, you will not believe; 68and if I ask you, you will not answer. 69But from now on the Son of man shall be seated at the right hand of the power of God.' 70And they all said, 'Are you the Son of God, then?' And he said to them, 'You say that I am.' 71And they said, 'What further testimony do we need? We have heard it ourselves from his own lips.'

The examination of Jesus before the Sanhedrin was not a regular trial according to the legal rules of procedure. The fate of Jesus had been decided at an earlier meeting. The purpose of the present session was to build up a case which could be submitted to Pilate. Scholars have argued inconclusively whether at this time the Sanhedrin had the right to execute the death sentence without the consent of the procurator. But even if they had the right, they had in the present instance no intention of using it. Better that the Romans should bear whatever odium attached to the removal of Jesus.

Luke omits the preliminary investigation described by Mark and comes straight to the crucial question, Are you the Messiah? At first Jesus declines to answer; 'Messiah' is an ambiguous term, and he recognizes that the court is in no mood to discuss definitions. He still prefers the title Son of man; and he reminds the court that this Son of man is destined to receive from God the authority both to rule and to judge (Dan. 7¹³). The Sanhedrin think that they are sitting in judgement on him, but in fact the roles are reversed: he is the judge and from this moment they and their nation are on trial before the heavenly tribunal. Finally, however, Jesus replies to the question with a veiled answer, which the interrogators take as assent. It is all they need for the framing of their charge.

23^{1-5} THE TRIAL: (2) BEFORE PILATE

23 *Then the whole company of them arose, and brought him before Pilate.* ²*And they began to accuse him, saying, 'We found this man perverting our nation, and forbidding us to give tribute to Caesar, and saying that he himself is Christ a king.'* ³*And Pilate asked him, 'Are you the King of the Jews?' And he answered him, 'You have said so.'* ⁴*And Pilate said to the chief priests and the multitudes, 'I find no crime in this man.'* ⁵*But they were urgent, saying, 'He stirs up the people, teaching throughout all Judea, from Galilee even to this place.'*

No Roman court would take cognizance of a charge of blasphemy. Jesus' hesitant admission must be translated into political terms. But there is a savage irony in the threefold accusation that he is an insurgent leader who has been inciting the people to disaffection against Rome and laying claim to royal status. His accusers know very well that it is precisely because he has refused to be this kind of Messiah that his own nation has rejected him. The charge is a deliberate and malicious inversion of the truth. Pilate has enough sagacity to see through their duplicity, but not enough character to abide by his own judgement. Three times he declares Jesus innocent, but three times is twice too many; what should have been a single, authoritative, and final verdict becomes first an argument, then a losing argument. The decline and fall of Pilate begins when he hears that Jesus comes from Galilee and tries to shift the responsibility on to Herod Antipas. From then on he has lost control of the case.

⁶When Pilate heard this, he asked whether the man was a Galilean. ⁷And when he learned that he belonged to Herod's jurisdiction, he sent him over to Herod, who was himself in Jerusalem at that time.

⁸When Herod saw Jesus, he was very glad, for he had long desired to see him, because he had heard about him, and he was hoping to see some sign done by him. ⁹So he questioned him at some length; but he made no answer. ¹⁰The chief priests and the scribes stood by, vehemently accusing him. ¹¹And Herod with his soldiers treated him with contempt and mocked him; then, arraying him in gorgeous apparel, he sent him back to Pilate. ¹²And Herod and Pilate became friends with each other that very day, for before this they had been at enmity with each other.

The trial before Herod is not mentioned in any of the other Gospels, and some scholars have wondered whether, between daybreak and 9 a.m. (Mark 15²⁵), there could have been time for so much coming and going. On the other hand Luke probably had contacts with the household of Herod from which he drew his information (8³). Moreover, one of the traditions on which he depended for the early chapters of Acts preserved a prayer in which the complicity of Herod and Pilate in the death of Jesus was treated as a fulfilment of Psalm 2² – 'the kings of the earth set themselves in array . . . against the Lord and against his Anointed' (Acts 4²⁶). In the same passage Jesus is called 'thy holy servant' – a reference to Isaiah 53 – and it is in the guise of the Servant of the Lord, who in the face of injustice 'opened not his mouth', that Jesus is portrayed in the present passage.

According to Luke, it was Herod's soldiers, not Pilate's, who dressed Jesus in royal robes. His curiosity thwarted by Jesus' silence, Herod determined to treat the whole episode as a joke. Nothing is known of any quarrel between Herod and Pilate.

13Pilate then called together the chief priests and the rulers and the people, 14and said to them, 'You brought me this man as one who was perverting the people; and after examining him before you, behold, I did not find this man guilty of any of your charges against him; 15neither did Herod, for he sent him back to us. Behold, nothing deserving death has been done by him; 16I will therefore chastise him and release him.'a

18But they all cried out together, 'Away with this man, and release to us Barabbas' – 19a man who had been thrown into prison for an insurrection started in the city, and for murder. 20Pilate addressed them once more, desiring to release Jesus; 21but they shouted out, 'Crucify, crucify him!' 22A third time he said to them, 'Why, what evil has he done? I have found in him no crime deserving death; I will therefore chastise him and release him.'

23But they were urgent, demanding with loud cries that he should be crucified. And their voices prevailed. 24So Pilate gave sentence that their demand should be granted. 25He released the man who had been thrown into prison for insurrection and murder, whom they asked for; but Jesus he delivered up to their will.

    a Here, or after verse 19, other ancient authorities add verse 17, *Now he was obliged to release one man to them at the festival*

The Barabbas incident serves to emphasize the irony of the accusation against Jesus. Here was a member of the Jewish resistance movement, who was guilty of sedition against Rome. On one and the same charge the crowd are demanding the acquittal of the guilty in order to secure the condemnation of the innocent. Pilate does everything in his power to secure the discharge of Jesus, short of discharging him.

ॐ

17

This verse is no part of the original text of Luke, but its excision leaves the Barabbas episode very clumsily connected to the main narrative. Verses 18–25 are certainly the work of Luke and not a later addition; but one constantly has the impression that Luke's Marcan insertions were made with less artistic efficiency than he displays in the non-Marcan sections (cf. 21^{21a}; 22^{19a}). The awkwardness of the join is accentuated by v. 16, which is repeated verbatim in v. 22. Without vv. 16, 18–20, 25 the story reads much more smoothly.

CALVARY:
          (I) THE DAUGHTERS OF JERUSALEM

²⁶*And as they led him away, they seized one Simon of Cyrene, who was coming in from the country, and laid on him the cross, to carry it behind Jesus.* ²⁷*And there followed him a great multitude of the people, and of women who bewailed and lamented him.* ²⁸*But Jesus turning to them said, 'Daughters of Jerusalem, do not weep for me, but weep for yourselves and for your children.* ²⁹*For behold, the days are coming when they will say, "Blessed are the barren, and the wombs that never bore, and the breasts that never gave suck!"* ³⁰*Then they will begin to say to the mountains, "Fall on us"; and to the hills, "Cover us."* ³¹*For if they do this when the wood is green, what will happen when it is dry?'*

The Roman army had the power to requisition assistance from civilians (Matt. 5⁴¹). Simon was pressed into service to carry, not the whole cross, which would have been too much for any one man, but the *patibulum* or cross-bar, to which the condemned man was fastened either by ropes or by nails before it was hoisted into position on the upright post.

A touch of the macabre is given to the grim procession by the women who anticipate the end by beginning the conventional funeral rites and raising the death wail. Jesus, ever ready to believe the best, credits them with genuine sympathy and sorrow, but warns them, in a last terrifying beatitude, to keep their pity for themselves, who need it most. To a Jewish woman barrenness was the great disgrace, but in the horrors coming upon Jerusalem it will be the crowning blessing; the childless woman may pray for catastrophic death to release her from her own anguish, but at least she will not suffer in her children.

The metaphor of the final saying is an echo of those passages in the Old Testament where a nation's manpower is compared to a great forest, about to be consumed by the forest fire of the divine judgement (Isa. 10¹⁶⁻¹⁹, Ezek. 20⁴⁷). Israel's intransigence has already kindled the flames of Roman impatience, and if the fire is now hot enough to destroy one whom Roman justice has pronounced innocent, what must the guilty expect? Simon may carry the patibulum; but Jesus is already carrying on his heart the cross of Israel's condemnation.

ৡ

26

Simon came from Cyrene, where the Jewish population was large enough to have one of the four administrative districts of the city allotted to it. He may have been a pilgrim who had come to Jerusalem for the Passover and, finding the city overcrowded, had spent the night in the country. But he may also have been a local resident, a repatriated, Greek-speaking Jew of the Dispersion; for we know that there were synagogues in Jerusalem where the services were conducted in Greek for the benefit of such returned exiles (Acts 6⁹).

23^{32-38} CALVARY: (2) THE CRUCIFIXION

³²*Two others also, who were criminals, were led away to be put to death with him.* ³³*And when they came to the place which is called The Skull, there they crucified him, and the criminals, one on the right and one on the left.* ³⁴*And Jesus said, 'Father, forgive them; for they know not what they do.'ᵃ And they cast lots to divide his garments.* ³⁵*And the people stood by, watching; but the rulers scoffed at him, saying, 'He saved others; let him save himself, if he is the Christ of God, his Chosen One!'* ³⁶*The soldiers also mocked him, coming up and offering him vinegar,* ³⁷*and saying, 'If you are the King of the Jews, save yourself!'* ³⁸*There was also an inscription over him,ᵇ 'This is the King of the Jews.'*

   a Other ancient authorities omit the sentence *And Jesus . . . what they do*

   b Other ancient authorities add *in letters of Greek and Latin and Hebrew*

In the preaching of the early Church the crucifixion was declared to be the fulfilment of the Old Testament prophecies about the sufferings of the righteous Servant of the Lord, and this belief has been allowed to colour the traditional form and language of the Passion narrative. All the Gospels at this point have allusions to Psalms 22 and

69. The parting of the clothes and the scoffing are described in words drawn from Ps. 22⁷, ¹⁸ and the gift of the vinegar in words drawn from Ps. 69²¹. Luke treats the offer of vinegar, not as an act of compassion, but as part of the mockery. With restraint and economy he portrays the different attitudes of the spectators: the vulgar curiosity of the crowd, the contemptuous derisions of the rulers, the callous frivolity of the guard, the bitter invective of the criminal.

roa

34
The prayer of Jesus is omitted by Codex Vaticanus, Codex Bezae, and other important manuscripts, but it is well attested in other manuscripts, and most modern textual critics accept it as a genuine part of the text. It could be taken to refer either to the Roman soldiers or to all those responsible for the crucifixion. In the light of Acts 3¹⁷, ¹⁹, 7⁵⁹f. it is probable that the sentence stood in the original text of Luke and that Luke himself took it to refer to the Jews. It has been suggested that the prayer may have been excised from an early copy of the Gospel by a second-century scribe who thought it incredible that God should pardon the Jews and, in view of the double destruction of Jerusalem in A.D. 70 and 135, certain that he had not in fact done so.

23 39-43   CALVARY: (3) THE TWO CRIMINALS

39One of the criminals who were hanged railed at him, saying, 'Are you not the Christ? Save yourself and us!' 40But the other rebuked him, saying, 'Do you not fear God, since you are under the same sentence of condemnation? 41And we indeed justly; for we are receiving the due reward of our deeds; but this man has done nothing wrong.' 42And he said, 'Jesus, remember me when you come in your kingly power.'a 43And he said to him, 'Truly, I say to you, today you will be with me in Paradise.'

a Greek kingdom

The one criminal, lacking any sense of guilt, was ready to blame anyone for what he regarded as a vindictive twist of fate. The other, whatever else may be said of him, at least knew that he was guilty and Jesus innocent. But did he really believe that, beyond the present travesty of justice, the future held for Jesus the royal triumph of the Messiah? If so, then the approach of death must have given him an acuteness of vision denied as yet to Jesus' closest friends. Perhaps he simply wanted to be kind to this innocent enthusiast who had fallen victim to passion and intrigue, and seized upon the words of the placard over his head as a means of saying something to offset the taunts of his companion. In this case, his was the cup of cold water that did not go without its reward. Whatever he expected, the promise of Jesus was out of all proportion to his request. Not in some far-off assize but now he is acquitted before the divine tribunal, and his reward is not in some age to come but today and in Paradise.

 юси

43
Paradise is a Persian word, meaning park or garden, which was taken over, first into Greek, then into Hebrew. In the Septuagint it was used to translate 'the garden of Eden'. Then, because of the belief that the day of God would bring a restoration of primeval bliss, Paradise became the name of the future home of the righteous. Finally, this earthly Paradise was distinguished from the heavenly one, of which the garden of Eden was only an earthly copy. Jewish beliefs about the afterlife were too multifarious to be reduced to a single consistent pattern. At first it was held that the dead waited in the sleep of death in Sheol, the universal graveyard, until the general resurrection and judgement. But later, alongside of this earlier hope, and never quite replacing it, there grew up another belief that the souls of the righteous went at death immediately to heaven. It is this assumption that lies behind the promise of Jesus.

23⁴⁴⁻⁵⁶   CALVARY: (4) DEATH AND BURIAL

⁴⁴*It was now about the sixth hour, and there was darkness over the whole land^a until the ninth hour, ⁴⁵while the sun's light failed;^b and the curtain of the temple was torn in two. ⁴⁶Then Jesus, crying with a loud voice, said, 'Father, into thy hands I commit my spirit!' And having said this he breathed his last. ⁴⁷Now when the centurion saw what had taken place, he praised*

God, and said, 'Certainly this man was innocent!' 48And all the multitudes who assembled to see the sight, when they saw what had taken place, returned home beating their breasts. 49And all his acquaintances and the women who had followed him from Galilee stood at a distance and saw these things.

50Now there was a man named Joseph from the Jewish town of Arimathea. He was a member of the council, a good and righteous man, 51who had not consented to their purpose and deed, and he was looking for the kingdom of God. 52This man went to Pilate and asked for the body of Jesus. 53Then he took it down and wrapped it in a linen shroud, and laid him in a rock-hewn tomb, where no one had ever yet been laid. 54It was the day of Preparation, and the sabbath was beginning.c 55The women who had come with him from Galilee followed, and saw the tomb, and how his body was laid; 56then they returned, and prepared spices and ointments.

On the sabbath they rested according to the commandment.

a Or earth
b Or the sun was eclipsed. Other ancient authorities read the sun was darkened
c Greek was dawning

An eclipse of the sun while the moon is full is an astronomical impossibility, but this would only enhance the value of the story for its earliest readers. It was a widespread belief in antiquity that events of great and tragic moment were accompanied by portents, nature showing its sympathy with the distress of man. Among the Jews this belief was especially associated with the Day of the Lord (Amos 8⁹, Joel 2¹⁰, ³¹, 3¹⁵), perhaps on the analogy of the plagues of Egypt (see notes on 21⁵⁻¹⁹). It is quite possible, therefore, that what is here recorded as miracle had its origin in symbolic descriptions of the significance of the Cross. The rending of the curtain symbolized the opening of access to the inner presence of God (Heb. 10¹⁹f.).

Pilate and the penitent criminal have declared Jesus innocent; now the centurion adds his testimony. According to Mark he said, 'Truly this man was a son of God'; but the version given here better fitted Luke's apologetic purpose.

Joseph is described in terms which remind us of the godly company in the infancy narrative (2²⁵, ³⁸). Matthew and John describe him as a disciple of Jesus, but on this point Mark and Luke are silent. They give the impression that he was sympathetic towards the mission of Jesus and wanted to make a practical gesture to dissociate himself from the decision of the Sanhedrin. No doubt his action was prompted also by the Law which required that an executed criminal should be buried before nightfall, lest the land be defiled by the curse under which he died (Deut. 21²²⁻²³). This law certainly made a deep impression on the mind of the early Church (Acts 5³⁰, 10³⁹, John 19³¹, Gal. 3¹³, 1 Pet. 2²⁴).

৹৹

45
The curtain of the temple divided the *heykal* or holy place, where the daily worship was conducted, from the *debir* or holy of holies, the shrine of the invisible God, into which only the high priest went, and that only on the Day of Atonement.

53
The description of the tomb contains an echo of the description of the donkey in 19³⁰. Both were unsullied and so fit for sacred use.

54
Preparation is still the Greek word for Friday. The sabbath began at sundown.

55
The women did not have time to carry out the embalming of the body, but they did have time to prepare the spices and ointments for use as soon as the sabbath was over.

24^{I-II} THE RESURRECTION: (I) THE EMPTY TOMB

24 *But on the first day of the week, at early dawn, they went to the tomb, taking the spices which they had prepared. ²And they found the stone rolled away from the tomb, ³but when they went in they did not find the body.ᵃ ⁴While they were perplexed about this, behold, two men stood by them in dazzling apparel; ⁵and as they were frightened and bowed their faces to the ground, the men said to them, 'Why do you seek the living among the dead?ᵇ ⁶Remember how he told you, while he was still in Galilee, ⁷that the*

Son of man must be delivered into the hands of sinful men, and be crucified, and on the third day rise.' [8]*And they remembered his words,* [9]*and returning from the tomb they told all this to the eleven and to all the rest.* [10]*Now it was Mary Magdalene and Joanna and Mary the mother of James and the other women with them who told this to the apostles;* [11]*but these words seemed to them an idle tale, and they did not believe them.*[c]

    a Other ancient authorities add *of the Lord Jesus*
    b Other ancient authorities add *He is not here, but has risen*
    c Other ancient authorities add verse 12, *But Peter rose and ran to the tomb; stooping and looking in, he saw the linen cloths by themselves; and he went home wondering at what had happened*

The earliest evidence for the resurrection is provided, not by the Gospels, but by the Epistles of Paul, and particularly by 1 Cor. 15, written at least ten years before the earliest Gospel. In this chapter Paul quotes a tradition which he had received from those who were Christians before him, perhaps at the time of his conversion, twenty years or more earlier, which contained a list of the eyewitnesses to the resurrection. It has sometimes been thought that the evidence of Paul makes it difficult for us to accept the story of the empty tomb, and that for three reasons: Paul bases the resurrection faith of the Church wholly on the recorded appearances of Jesus, among which he includes the appearance to himself; he nowhere shows any knowledge of the empty tomb tradition; and he emphasizes that the resurrection body is not a body of flesh but a spiritual body or a body of glory (1 Cor. 15[44], Phil. 3[21]). But a closer reading of Paul's argument shows that the empty tomb, though not mentioned, is assumed throughout. Having drawn a careful distinction between the physical body of this life and the spiritual body of the life to come, and having declared explicitly that flesh and blood cannot inherit the kingdom of God, he goes on to explain that the spiritual body must be produced out of the physical body by a process of transformation. 'We must all be changed.' It is this perishable and mortal nature (not a disembodied and immortal soul) that must put on immortality; and it is essential to the argument that the body of Jesus should already have undergone such a metamorphosis. To this we may add one further piece of evidence that the empty tomb belonged to the very earliest deposit of Christian belief – the word 'resurrection'. No Jew would have dreamed of using this word to describe an afterlife in which the physical body was abandoned to the grave. Yet the word was certainly in use from the beginnings of Christianity.

ﬨ

Luke's story of the empty tomb runs parallel to Mark's, but differs from it at four points. Where Mark mentions one young man at the tomb, Luke has two; and the identical phrase (*behold, two men*) is found in the stories of the transfiguration and the ascension (9³⁰, Acts 1¹⁰), perhaps as a form of cross-reference linking the three events. According to Mark 16⁷, the women were told: '*go, tell his disciples and Peter that he is going before you to Galilee; there you will see him, as he told you.*' In place of this Luke has a reference to teaching given formerly in Galilee; for according to Luke's special source the resurrection appearances occurred not in Galilee but only in and around Jerusalem. Again, according to Mark, the women, having been entrusted with a message, failed to deliver it because they were afraid; but Luke tells us that they made a full report to the other disciples of what they had seen and heard. Finally, the list of names is different, Luke giving Joanna in the place of Mark's Salome.

24^{13-35}   THE RESURRECTION:
             (2) THE ROAD TO EMMAUS

¹³ *That very day two of them were going to a village named Emmaus, about seven miles^a from Jerusalem,* ¹⁴*and talking with each other about all these things that had happened.* ¹⁵*While they were talking and discussing together, Jesus himself drew near and went with them.*

¹⁶*But their eyes were kept from recognizing him.* ¹⁷*And he said to them, 'What is this conversation which you are holding with each other as you walk?' And they stood still, looking sad.* ¹⁸*Then one of them, named Cleopas, answered him, 'Are you the only visitor to Jerusalem who does not know the things that have happened there in these days?'* ¹⁹*And he said to them, 'What things?' And they said to him, 'Concerning Jesus of Nazareth, who was a prophet mighty in deed and word before God and all the people,* ²⁰*and how our chief priests and rulers delivered him up to be condemned to death, and crucified him.* ²¹*But we had hoped that he was the one*

to redeem Israel. Yes, and besides all this, it is now the third day since this happened.

22'*Moreover, some women of our company amazed us. They were at the tomb early in the morning* 23*and did not find his body; and they came back saying that they had even seen a vision of angels, who said that he was alive.* 24*Some of those who were with us went to the tomb, and found it just as the women had said; but him they did not see.*'

25*And he said to them, 'O foolish men, and slow of heart to believe all that the prophets have spoken!* 26*Was it not necessary that the Christ should suffer these things and enter into his glory?'* 27*And beginning with Moses and all the prophets, he interpreted to them in all the scriptures the things concerning himself.*

28*So they drew near to the village to which they were going. He appeared to be going further,* 29*but they constrained him, saying, 'Stay with us, for it is toward evening and the day is now far spent.' So he went in to stay with them.* 30*When he was at table with them, he took the bread and blessed, and broke it, and gave it to them.* 31*And their eyes were opened and they recognized him; and he vanished out of their sight.* 32*They said to each other, 'Did not our hearts burn within us while he talked to us on the road, while he opened to us the scriptures?'* 33*And they rose that same hour and returned to Jerusalem; and they found the eleven gathered together and those who were with them,* 34*who said, 'The Lord has risen indeed, and has appeared to Simon!'* 35*Then they told what had happened on the road, and how he was known to them in the breaking of the bread.*

a Greek *sixty stadia*

From the experience of this couple we can learn much about the resurrection appearance of Jesus. As they walked along the road, Jesus suddenly appeared at their side, and they assumed that he was a fellow traveller who had overtaken them; but later, when he disappeared just as suddenly from their supper table, they realized the truth, that he was no longer subject to limitations of time and place. The remarkable fact was that, all the time he was with them, the idea never crossed their minds that he was other than a being of flesh and blood, a foreigner on a visit to Jerusalem. In retrospect their failure to recognize him seemed so odd that they could only suppose a supernatural restraint had been imposed on their vision and not removed until their minds were prepared for the staggering revelation which came to them as they watched Jesus perform the familiar action of breaking bread.

Humanly speaking, they failed to recognize Jesus because, like many a modern sceptic, they were convinced that miracles of that sort could not happen. Jesus was dead, and no amount of hearsay evidence about visions of angels and an empty tomb could persuade them otherwise. They had thought that he would be the Messiah of Jewish nationalist expectation who would redeem Israel from Gentile domination, and that hope had proved illusory.

Jesus dispelled their disillusionment by expounding the scriptures, not a handful of proof texts drawn at random from the Old Testament, but all the scriptures. We look in vain for Old Testament predictions that the Messiah must reach his appointed glory through suffering, unless we realize that the Old Testament is concerned from start to finish with the call and destiny of Israel, and that the Messiah, as King of Israel, must embody in his own person the character and vocation of the people of which he is leader and representative. What Luke is here claiming is that, underlying all the Old Testament writings, Jesus detected a common pattern of God's dealings with his people, which was meant to foreshadow his own ministry. God's purpose in creation was the emergence of a holy people, dedicated to his service; and, in a world organized to resist his will, this purpose could be achieved only if the people themselves were prepared first to undergo humiliation and suffering. In some parts of the Old Testament the suffering is imposed by the tyranny of pagan empires from which Israel is shortly to be liberated (e.g. Dan. 7). In other parts the suffering is the divinely inflicted punishment for Israel's own sins, which is to be followed by reinstatement to favour (e.g. Hos. 5⁸–6³, Isa. 6¹–9⁷). In others again Israel is called upon, as the righteous Servant of the Lord, to suffer vicariously for the sins of the Gentiles in order that God's salvation may reach to the ends of the earth (e.g. Isa. 40–55). In each case the common pattern is the Exodus pattern; for at the outset of her history Israel had been constituted a nation when God brought her from the humiliation of Egyptian bondage into the glory of a new day, so that the Exodus, annually celebrated at the Passover, had become the prototype of the messianic deliverance. Thus Moses and all the prophets could be said to bear witness to the one divine method of dealing with the problem of evil. But if Israel was called to suffer in order to break the power of pagan despotism, to atone for her national sin, and to bear vicariously the transgressions of the many, then this must be *par excellence* the vocation of the Messiah, Israel's symbolic head and leader. Thus the Cross, so far from being a cause for dejection, was a necessary element in the divine purpose of redemption.

The disciples recognized Jesus by the way in which he broke the bread. Luke and his friends would no doubt find in the solemn scene at the supper table an anticipation of their own eucharistic observances. Yet these two disciples had not been present at the last supper. The memories which Jesus' action evoked must have been of other meals which he had held with his friends, perhaps, like the last supper, as anticipations of the messianic banquet of the kingdom.

On returning to Jerusalem, the disciples discovered that Peter had also seen the risen Lord, an interesting confirmation of the tradition preserved by Paul (1 Cor. 15⁵).

ונא

25
'O foolish men' goes beyond the limits of strict translation; for there is no noun in the Greek, and a man and woman would necessarily be addressed in the masculine (cf. 17³⁴). The two disciples lived in the same house and were therefore presumably man and wife. If Cleopas is the Clopas of John 19²⁵, then his wife Mary had been one of the group of women at the cross.

24^{36-53} THE RESURRECTION:
(3) THE FINAL PARTING

³⁶*As they were saying this, Jesus himself stood among them.*ᵃ ³⁷*But they were startled and frightened, and supposed that they saw a spirit.* ³⁸*And he said to them, 'Why are you troubled, and why do questionings rise in your hearts?* ³⁹*See my hands and my feet, that it is I myself; handle me, and see; for a spirit has not flesh and bones as you see that I have.'*ᵇ ⁴¹*And while they still disbelieved for joy, and wondered, he said to them, 'Have you anything here to eat?'*

⁴²*Then they gave him a piece of broiled fish,* ⁴³*and he took it and ate before them.*

⁴⁴*Then he said to them, 'These are my words which I spoke to you, while I was still with you, that everything written about me in the law of Moses and the prophets and the psalms must be fulfilled.'*

⁴⁵*Then he opened their minds to understand the scriptures,* ⁴⁶*and said to them, 'Thus it is written, that the Christ should suffer and on the third day rise from the dead,* ⁴⁷*and that repentance and forgiveness of sins should be preached in his name to all nations,ᶜ beginning from Jerusalem.* ⁴⁸*You are witnesses of these things.* ⁴⁹*And behold, I send the promise of my Father upon you; but stay in the city, until you are clothed with power from on high.'*

⁵⁰*Then he led them out as far as Bethany, and lifting up his hands he blessed them.* ⁵¹*While he blessed them, he parted from them.ᵈ*

⁵²*And theyᵉ returned to Jerusalem with great joy,* ⁵³*and were continually in the temple blessing God.*

a Other ancient authorities add *and said to them, 'Peace to you!'*
b Other ancient authorities add verse 40, *And when he had said this, he showed them his hands and his feet*
c Or *nations. Beginning from Jerusalem you are witnesses*
d Other ancient authorities add *and was carried up into heaven*
e Other ancient authorities add *worshipped him, and*

The last episode of Luke's Gospel has a close resemblance to John 20¹⁹⁻²⁹ (see Introduction), and in some manuscripts Luke's account has been amplified by interpolation from John. Both narratives agree that Jesus appeared in a bodily form not subject to ordinary, physical restrictions, but both are at pains to emphasize its solidly corporeal nature. There are four possible motives for this emphasis. For Luke the foremost reason was fidelity to his sources, for he had inherited from the Aramaic-speaking Church a tradition which spoke of Jesus eating and drinking with his disciples after he had risen (Acts 10³⁶⁻⁴³). Underlying this tradition was the characteristic cast of the semitic mind. Whereas the Greeks tended to think of reality in terms of abstractions and universal truths, to the Jews reality was always particular and concrete, and it was inevitable that this concreteness should find expression in materialistic imagery. Thus the highly material splendours of the heavenly city in the Revelation are a symbolic assurance that heaven is utterly real, a place not of rarefied spirituality but of 'solid joys'. This means that to a Jew a disembodied spirit could only seem a ghost, not a living being, but a thin, unsubstantial carbon-copy which had somehow escaped from the filing system of death; and since the authorities would certainly attempt to explain away the claims of the disciples by arguing that they had seen a ghost, an apologetic motive may be discerned behind Luke's story. Finally, we know that towards the end of the first century there grew up in the Church a heresy called Docetism, which denied the reality of Christ's human life and asserted that the divine Christ descended upon the human Jesus at his baptism and withdrew again before his crucifixion. The Epistles and Gospel of John certainly contain polemical references to this heresy (1 John 2²², 4²f·, John 1¹⁴, 6⁵³, 20²⁴⁻²⁹), and it is possible that Luke too wanted, for this reason, to indicate the identity of the risen Christ with the flesh-and-blood Jesus.

The Old Testament instruction given on the road to Emmaus is now carried a stage further. Not only were the suffering and subsequent vindication of the Messiah integral to the divine purpose which was foretold or foreshadowed throughout the whole corpus of scripture; they were the divinely ordained means of dispensing forgiveness to the Gentile peoples. Accordingly the disciples are formally commissioned to undertake the missionary work of the Church. The stress on witness, the command to remain in Jerusalem (as against the tradition of Galilean appearances recorded by Matthew and implied by Mark), the description of the Holy Spirit as power from on high promised by God through the prophets (Joel 2²⁸ff·), and the leave-taking on the Mount of Olives are themes that are taken up and expanded in the early chapters of Acts. It was typical of the earliest Christianity that the Spirit was not regarded as a doctrine to be believed but as an access of power to be received (Acts 19², 1 Thess. 1⁵, Heb. 2⁴).

The Gospel ends as it began, in the courts of the temple.

Index of References

OLD TESTAMENT

GENESIS

1^{26}	121
3^{15}	143
4^{23-24}	194
10^{24}	19
11^{12}	19
17^5	58
22^{11}	51
29^{30-31}	179
32^{28}	58

EXODUS

3^6	224
4^{22}	52
8^{19}	154
13^{12}	64
20^2	47
$22^{1, 4, 7}$	208
22^{22}	201
23^6	201
23^{20}	51, 113

LEVITICUS

1^3	217
6^5	208
11^{7-8}	122
12	64
13^{45-46}	92
15^{19-30}	124
19^{18}	148
24^9	99

NUMBERS

5^7	208
6^{1-8}	51
18^{16}	64

19^2	218
19^{11}	109

DEUTERONOMY

6^{4-9}	87
6^5	148
$6^{13, 16}$	81
8^3	81
10^{18}	201
12	140
16^{19}	201
18^{15}	133
18^{15-19}	113
21^3	218
21^{15-17}	179
21^{22-23}	254
25^{5-6}	31, 224
32^8	232
32^{11}	174
32^{35-36}	228

JOSHUA

10^{12-13}	31

JUDGES

15^1	58

RUTH

2^{12}	174

I SAMUEL

2^{1-10}	55
6^7	218
10^{2-9}	216
12^3	37
16^6	37
17^{18}	58
21^{1-6}	99

2 SAMUEL

7^{8-16}	226
7^{14}	38, 53

I KINGS

17^{23}	109
19^4	241

2 KINGS

1^2	154
19^{-16}	140
29^{-11}	140

I CHRONICLES

1^{18}	19

2 CHRONICLES

24^{22}	159

JOB

1	143
38^7	61

PSALMS

2^2	247
2^{8-9}	80
8	121
18^2	58
$22^{7, 18}$	251
33^9	70
39^5	164
46^3	121
57^1	174
61^4	174
65^7	121
66^{12}	167
68^5	201

NEW TESTAMENT

Index of Authors

Index of Subjects

271